Fostering Innovation in the Public Sector

OECD

BETTER POLICIES FOR BETTER LIVES

This work is published under the responsibility of the Secretary-General of the OECD. The opinions expressed and arguments employed herein do not necessarily reflect the official views of OECD member countries.

This document and any map included herein are without prejudice to the status of or sovereignty over any territory, to the delimitation of international frontiers and boundaries and to the name of any territory, city or area.

Please cite this publication as:
OECD (2017), *Fostering Innovation in the Public Sector*, OECD Publishing, Paris.
http://dx.doi.org/10.1787/9789264270879-en

ISBN 978-92-64-27086-2 (print)
ISBN 978-92-64-27087-9 (PDF)

The statistical data for Israel are supplied by and under the responsibility of the relevant Israeli authorities. The use of such data by the OECD is without prejudice to the status of the Golan Heights, East Jerusalem and Israeli settlements in the West Bank under the terms of international law.

Photo credits: Cover © Sergey Furtaev/Shutterstock.com, Introwiz1/Shutterstock.com, umanuma/Shutterstock.com.

Foreword

Three years after the launch of the OECD Observatory of Public Sector Innovation, public administrations are pursuing innovation more actively than ever, and embedding it in government budgets and programmes. Yet, innovation is, necessarily, an unfinished business. Governments must continually adapt to address new and ever more complex challenges facing societies. Simply improving existing solutions is not always possible nor desirable. Today, governments are starting to look at transforming systems to put individual and social outcomes at the heart of policy approaches.

To achieve this, governments must not only be innovative; they must also create the right conditions for innovation within and across systems. This means being able to identify problems and translate ideas into projects that can be piloted on a small scale and then implemented and diffused to effect system-wide change. It also means recognising the processes and structures that can support and accelerate innovation.

This report looks at how governments can create an environment that supports rather than hinders innovation. It examines the role that government management processes, such as public sector regulations (chapter 2), human resources management (chapter 3) and budgeting (chapter 4) play in inhibiting or enabling innovation. It also considers the specific support that dedicated organisations for innovation can provide (chapter 5), the strategies governments can adopt to manage risk (chapter 6) and how information, data and knowledge can be effectively managed to support innovation (chapter 7). Drawing from the observation and analysis of country innovation approaches developed by the OECD Observatory of Public Sector Innovation, the report concludes with a framework for collecting and examining data on how well adapted central government functions are supporting more public sector innovation.

To meet the innovation challenge, the report suggests that governments need to address four areas:

- People matter: invest in civil servants as the catalysts of innovation. This involves building the culture, incentives and norms to facilitate new ways of working.

- Knowledge is power: facilitate the free flow of information, data and knowledge across the public sector and use it to respond creatively to new challenges and opportunities

- Working together: promote new organisational structures and partnerships to improve approaches and tools, share risks, and harness the information and resources available for innovation.

- Rules and processes to support not hinder: ensure that internal rules and processes balance their capacity to mitigate risks with protecting resources and enabling innovation.

The report builds on the initial framework developed by the observatory in the report *The Innovation Imperative in the Public Sector – Setting an Agenda for Action*. It contributes to the Public Governance and Territorial Development Directorate's exploratory work on new ways to approach policy and service design and implementation in support of stronger, fairer and more inclusive growth. It combines theoretical perspectives and direct experiences of governments in enabling change, providing examples of good practices in fostering the ability, motivation and opportunity to innovate in the civil service. It draws from the case studies and examples collected from OECD countries through the OPSI online platform and the work of the network of the OPSI National Points of Contact. Draft chapters of the report were presented and discussed at Public Employment and Management Working Party (PEM), Senior Budget Official Working Party (SBO) and OPSI National Points of Contact. The report is part of the Public Governance and Territorial Development Directorate's exploratory work on new ways to approach policy and service design and implementation in support of stronger, fairer and more inclusive growth. Another forthcoming report, Working with Change, explores how systems can be made more adaptive and fit for purpose in a context of external threats and internal pressures.

ACKNOWLEDGEMENTS

This report was prepared by the Public Governance and Territorial Development Directorate of the OECD. The mission of the Public Governance and Territorial Development Directorate is to help governments at all levels design and implement strategic, evidence-based and innovative policies to strengthen public governance, respond effectively to diverse and disruptive economic, social and environmental challenges and deliver on government's commitments to citizens.

The report was prepared by Marco Daglio in the OECD Public Governance and Territorial Development Directorate. Strategic directions were provided by Edwin Lau. The work has been conducted under the leadership of Rolf Alter and Luiz de Mello. The report resulted from the contributions of many authors. Chapter 1 was drafted by Marco Daglio and Hannah Kitchen (OECD Directorate for Education and Skills). Chapter 2 is based on a paper prepared by Jorrit de Jong (Harvard University, United States). Chapter 3 was drafted by Daniel Gerson (OECD Directorate of Public Governance and Territorial Development). Chapter 4 was drafted by Paul Posner and Tim Higashi (George Mason University, United States). Chapter 5 is based on a paper authored by Jo Casebourne and Ruth Puttick (Nesta, United Kingdom). Chapter 6 was drafted by Marco Steinberg (Snowcone & Haystack, Finland). Chapter 7 was drafted by Jamie Berryhill (OECD Directorate of Public Governance and Territorial Development).

The full report benefited from contributions and revisions provided by Edwin Lau, Stephane Jacobzone, Daniel Gerson, Daniel Trnka, Faisal Naru, Filippo Cavassini, Hannah Kitchen, Ronnie Downes, Alex Roberts, Matt Kerlogue and Piret Tonurist. Special thanks to Geoff Mulgan for commenting the report. Marie-Claude Gohier helped with the preparation of the final publication. Bettina Huggard and Susan Rantalainen provided administrative support.

Table of contents

Figures

Tables

Executive summary

Public sector innovation is about finding new and better means to achieve public ends. Innovation, especially breakthrough innovation, is complex and challenging for governments. Yet, the scale and nature of the challenges that governments face today require responses that go beyond incremental improvements. The public sector context has also changed with low level of productivity calling for a re-thinking and re-scoping of public sector processes, structures and systems.

This report looks at how the different aspects of public sector governance can support such innovation at all stages of its lifecycle, from identifying problems to generating ideas, developing proposals, implementing and evaluating projects, and diffusing them more widely throughout the organisation.

Many innovators feel held up by bureaucracy and red tape; however, it is often not the laws and regulations themselves that are the barrier, but the way in which they are used. Bureaucracy reflects a society's underlying values, and in most democratic countries these include stability, efficiency, effectiveness, accountability and transparency – none of which are inherently hostile to innovation. Some tensions do arise, however, between the nature of public sector organisations and the attitudes underlying innovation. In some organisations, risk aversion, "silos", hierarchical structures and a lack of diversity may have become embodied in rules and regulations, or they may have become part of the wider culture. Either way, they act as a barrier to innovation. Some countries have attempted to overcome these barriers through red tape reduction programmes or targeted rule exemptions, while others have used cross-organisational innovation delivery teams or behavioural insight approaches. Governments should assess the extent to which their employees feel inhibited in innovating and then diagnose the causes. If rules and procedures are indeed the barrier, these can be rewritten; but, if the problem stems from the underlying culture and behaviour of the organisation, building capacity to solve problems through innovation will be a more effective approach.

People are at the heart of public sector innovation, so one of the goals of public human resource management should be to support employees in innovating – that is, ensuring they have the ability, motivation and opportunity to come up with new approaches. Ability requires not just technical skills but also creativity and associative thinking, as well as the behavioural and social skills needed to bring about change. Motivation can be intrinsic, but is also strongly determined by the work environment, such as task design, organisational culture and management. Opportunity means giving people the autonomy, resources and connections they need to innovate. Four main approaches to promoting innovation emerge from case studies across OECD countries: awards and recognition programmes encouraging ideas from all levels of government, innovation-oriented networks and mobility programmes to bring people together across organisational boundaries, and holistic approaches to managing staff that create a framework supporting innovation. One key element is the organisational culture: how organisations treat risk, and whether employees feel empowered to experiment and to learn from their experiments.

Traditionally, budget offices might be the last place to expect support for innovation. However, in recent years budgeting has evolved away from only allocating resources towards also creating the conditions for innovation to flourish. Financial incentives, including dedicated funds, can play an important role in promoting innovation in government. However, in a fiscally constrained environment fiscal frameworks and targets are needed to keep a cap on overall expenditures. Greater budget flexibility within the caps, coupled with outcomes goals, can support innovation. The use of performance management and evidence to promote the widespread adoption of innovative approaches help link budgetary and policy objectives. Fiscal austerity in recent years has challenged budget processes, with mixed consequences for innovation. While cuts, especially targeted ones, can serve as a driver of change, across-the-board cuts can diminish the capacity of some organisations to create innovative solutions. Budget agencies need to strike a balance between giving line ministries the flexibility and capacity they need to pursue innovation, while retaining a focus on achieving the government's central strategic goals.

Dedicated innovation units can overcome some of the barriers to public sector innovation, providing "room" to develop new ways of doing things. They are a structural response to the cross-cutting and interdisciplinary nature of innovation projects, and to the tension between continuing business-as-usual while introducing new approaches. Innovation teams serve five broad functions: supporting and co-ordinating the implementation of innovative solutions, experimenting with different approaches to problems, supporting the delivery of a cross-cutting initiative or agenda such as digitisation, providing the investment needed to give emerging ides the space to grow, and capacity building and networking support. An organisation setting up an innovation team should consider what it wants the team to achieve and choose its functions and structure accordingly. The closer teams are to the centre of government, the more authority they will have to implement changes; on the other hand, a team located more on the periphery will tend to be more open to radical innovation.

A risk management strategy can help ensure the success of an innovation. An effective strategy starts by understanding the context of the innovation: what it is trying to achieve, whether it is changing an established practice or introducing something new, where its mandate lies, and whether it is a solution in itself or is creating the conditions for one. The preconditions for success include proper resourcing, both financial and human. New processes - such as prototyping (quick iterations of solutions to test feasibility) and co-creation (engaging all stakeholders in the development of solutions) - offer ways to translate uncertainty into known risks faster than traditional approaches and to better control the use of public resources.

Innovation that harnesses the power of data, information and knowledge has the potential to transform all sectors, and the public sector is one of the most data-intensive parts of the economy. There are four phases to improving public sector information management for innovation: sourcing it, making it available and discoverable, and combining it with data from other sources; exploiting it, transforming it into knowledge and using it for decision making; sharing it as freely as possible inside and outside the public sector; and creating feedback loops and encouraging collaboration to create a rapidly evolving information system.

Chapter 1.

Overview: The role of government management in fostering public sector innovation

The nature and scale of public sector challenges require governments to develop a response that goes beyond incremental process improvements, but rather introduces new ways to frame problems and develop solutions. Because public sector innovation does not happen by itself, governments have a key role to play to promote innovative behaviours and create conducive environments for innovation. This chapter starts by discussing the change of trajectory of public sector innovation, from "green-field" to "disruptive" and what this entails in terms of governments' capacity to respond to a changing context and the citizens' needs. It discusses the key policy tools governments can use to support public sector organisations to accelerate their innovation activity. It introduces the innovation lifecycle as a useful framework to map the use of different policy tools for overcoming innovation barriers and strengthening organisations' capacity to innovate. The chapter concludes with the key factors that explain the innovativeness of public sector organisations: capability, motivation and opportunity to innovate.

Introduction

Public sector innovation uses new approaches to create public value for individuals and for society. It is changing how the public sector operates to deliver better outcomes:[1] in Finland, socially excluded people are getting free medical checks in bars or on the street through a new mobile health check system. It is developing effective collaborations with other actors to target public resources where they are needed: in Mexico, people living in rural areas do not need to travel long distances to get public services and can get social transfer and other payment services at the nearest gas station or village store. It is helping to build more inclusive, open and caring societies, enhancing trust among citizens: in France, families are helping old people with no family connections to live autonomously in a caring environment by sharing housing facilities and common space.

Public sector innovation is about finding new means to achieve public ends. By using open policy design approaches that draw on the input from citizens and businesses from all walks of life, innovation can help governments create public policies which are more broadly based, inclusive and better targeted on citizens' needs. This creates new spaces to challenge the architecture of problems, overcome old administrative legacies and channel public resources to where they are most needed. Participatory budgeting schemes, regarded as a powerful innovation, are being used across the world, distributing opportunity more equally across society.

Generating public value through innovation is complex and challenging for governments. Innovation runs contrary to the perceived role of bureaucratic organisations. Innovation is new, unknown and risky; by contrast governments have a statutory duty, democratic responsibility and political mandate to deliver public services in consistent and equal ways. Managing these tensions can be complicated for governments, where the risk of innovating appears far greater than the risk of maintaining the status quo. Nor does innovation sit well with the control function of hierarchies which, while they ensure stewardship and accountability over the use of resources, they tend to discourage risk-taking.

Yet the context in which most governments find themselves today alters the risk equation. Growing fiscal austerity, social inequality and changing demographics are just some of the forces putting extraordinary pressures on the public sector to transform itself. The nature and scale of these challenges require responses that are not geared around incremental process improvements, but rather strategic improvements to how governments frame problems and develop solutions. This requires governments to be able to generate new solutions underpinned by new principles, rather than on improving and refining existing ones. While innovation has always played a part in the development of the public sector, this is arguably the first time that the sector has been under such radical pressure to fundamentally transform the focus of innovation itself thereby creating new opportunities to embed innovative processes.

Low levels of productivity within the public sector also undermine the growth potential and put the provision of public services at risk. The adoption of common procurement, changing employment terms, shifting users to online channels, and the use of shared services, can be seen as delivering a "transactional" improvement to public sector productivity by improving one-time efficiency. However more radical improvements in productivity can only be delivered by re-thinking, re-scoping, re-designing and re-engineering the processes/procedures, services or systems of the public sector.

The evolutionary path that innovation has taken in the public sector can be characterised by a move from "green-field" (where the innovation creates a new system) to "sustaining" (where innovation improves an existing system) to "disruptive" innovation (where the system need to be reinvented). In the early days, when the first models of modern government were being formed, there were whole areas of activities that had to be literally invented. The 1913 UK Ancient Monuments Act and the invention of the heritage system, as well as the 1958 establishment of NASA and the first man on the moon are good examples of innovative government in the green-field era. There were no real precedents, no established ways of performing these new tasks. This era of innovation was characterised by a high degree of freedom and little existing legacy to deal with.

As the public sector began to establish approaches to policy making and delivery, innovation itself began to shift away from green-field invention towards sustaining or incrementally improving existing models. Today, it could be argued that this sustaining phase is coming to an end as it is clearly providing diminishing returns. The current emphasis on co-production as a tool to transform public services is partly the result of the levelling-out of the impact of other models (OECD, 2011). This does not mean that the quest for efficiency-based solutions has been exhausted, but that breakthrough innovation - creating new and more effective solutions that better respond to a changing context and the citizenry's needs – is required to respond to the current set of demands and constraints faced by the public sector.

This evolution from green-field to sustaining to breakthrough innovation poses some important challenges for governments:

- First, it is easier to create new solutions in a green-field context, as there are fewer biases, entrenched interests and established expectations. It may be hard to overcome public sector rigidities when it comes to challenging established values and vested interests, such as common wisdom about what works. The cost of changing conventional methods may also be difficult especially when building on previous well-established generations of innovations.

- Second, the public sector is built to sustain existing solutions, not to challenge them. This means that there is a growing need to build the capacity for breakthrough innovation where there is currently little to none. Political foresight is arguably becoming less strategic as the sense of crisis deepens. As a consequence, it is harder to get political support for investing in innovation.

- Third, while the public sector has a growing need to redesign how it delivers, it also has an obligation to ensure continuity of service. Governments can't shut down existing hospitals while they work on the future; they need to change a tyre while driving the car. In other words, governments need to maintain sustaining innovation practices while investing in breakthrough innovation.

- Fourth, as a consequence of the point above, maintaining two distinct types of innovation requires maintaining two separate modes of operation, incentives and human resourcing. And because sustaining innovation is the incumbent mode, breakthrough innovation must be well resourced and the practice itself professionalised if it is to stand a chance.

Why does innovation need to be supported?

Public sector innovation does not happen by itself: problems need to be identified and ideas translated into projects which can be piloted on a small scale and then implemented and diffused. This requires public sector organisations to identify the processes and structures which can support and accelerate the innovation activity at each stage of its lifecycle. While there is a growing body of evidence on innovative practices in the public sector, there is still limited knowledge of what policy tools governments can use to overcome innovation barriers and strengthen organisations' capacity to innovate (Figure 1.1).

Figure 1.1. Barriers to innovation across its lifecycle and related policy tools

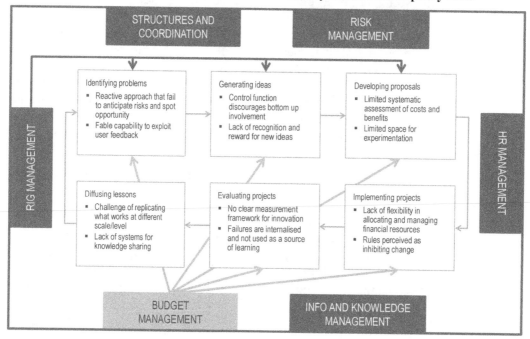

Source: OECD elaboration.

The phases of the innovation lifecycle and the associated challenges for government that are considered critical are summarised here:

- **Identifying problems**: understanding the nature and characteristics of a problem is a first step towards triggering innovative ideas to respond to it. Public sector organisations often lack the capacity to identify risks and opportunities coming from their environment and to effectively capture and interpret demand from the users. There is scope to investigate how public sector organisations can be supported to become better at scanning the horizon and make effective use of data to capture and analyse relevant trends and demands and transform them into information which can drive decision making.

- **Generating ideas**: ideas that fuel innovation can either be generated from the bottom up by civil servants in the frontline or be initiated by executive leadership. Supporting the creation of ideas often involves providing the right level of incentives and rewards, creating opportunities to share experiences, and ensuring public servants' mobility to support a broad understanding of issues and the tools to respond to them. For many public sector leaders, the rewards on offer from successful innovation are low, even if the innovation could create huge gains for the public sector and citizens as a whole, while the impact of failure can be significantly higher. This can be a major burden to innovation, given the central importance of senior-level champions for many innovation projects.

- **Developing proposals**: proof of concepts, idea testing and trials are important steps towards translating ideas into workable projects with potential for implementation. This means creating space for public sector organisations to experiment and try new things. Innovation, by definition, entails novelty and therefore requires organisations to accept a certain level of uncertainty and transform it into manageable risk. However, the very nature of the public sector's role, with its statutory and moral responsibilities to ensure the basic safety and welfare of its citizens and be accountable for the use of public funds, means that any practice that can pose risks to meeting these responsibilities must be viewed with caution. Supporting this phase involves developing tools to better navigate uncertainty and creating the conditions for experimentation.

- **Implementing projects**: detailed financial rules and controls may impede the investments needed to bring a project to scale. Budgeting can stimulate innovation through financial incentives, promoting greater flexibility, aligning budgeting and investment frameworks to scale up innovation and diffuse its benefits through the system, and promoting methodologies to ensure return on investment. Innovation is also likely to emerge from interactions between different bodies, so appropriate frameworks are needed to allow these interactions to happen. Government organisations need opportunities to think about how their interventions interact with those of other bodies, and how they can collaborate more effectively to solve common challenges.

- **Evaluating projects**: innovative projects need to be monitored and evaluated to determine whether or not they are resolving the problems they are trying to address. Evaluating innovative projects can be a non-linear process – for example fast iteration allows assessments to be conducted early on, during development phases. Yet few countries have developed systematic approaches to evaluating the success of innovative projects. Countries' experiences suggest that information from project data and social media could be used to evaluate the effectiveness of a project and assess whether it should be iterated, scaled more broadly or cancelled. Innovation requires evidence, but often at a faster and more agile pace than through the traditional policy cycle.

- **Diffusing lessons:** sharing ideas and experiences are a constituent part of the innovation process and allow successful approaches to be replicated in different contexts. Understanding what went wrong is a powerful source of learning, given the level of risk inherent in innovative projects. At the same time, political and media scrutiny can reduce tolerance for failure, making the uncertainty and risk that innovation may carry seem unduly expensive for the public sector. Cumulatively these factors may create the perception that the public sector is adverse to risk, but internal learning can reduce risk and uncertainty by pooling experience and results.

Creating government architectures for innovation

In this context, what role does government have to ensure that public sector organisations continue to generate and implement ideas to address the most pressing societal issues? Drawing on analysis of innovation cases from the Observatory of Public Sector Innovation (OPSI), research and country cases and dialogue with policy makers and innovation practitioners during the OECD Innovation Conference "From Ideas to Impact", the OECD has identified four actions that governments need to address to meet the innovation challenge (Box 1.1).

Box 1.1. The innovation imperative: A call for action

Action 1: people matter – Governments must invest in the capacity and capability of civil servants as the catalysts of innovation. This includes building the culture, incentives and norms to facilitate new ways of working.

Action 2: knowledge is power – Governments must facilitate the free flow of information, data and knowledge across the public sector and use it to respond creatively to new challenges and opportunities.

Action 3: working together solves problems – Governance must advance new organisational structures and leverage partnerships to enhance approaches and tools, share risks and harness available information and resources for innovation.

Action 4: rules and process to support not hinder – Government must ensure that internal rules and processes are balanced in their capacity to mitigate risks while protecting resources and enabling innovation.

Source: OECD (2015), *The Innovation Imperative in the Public Sector: Setting an Agenda for Action*, http://dx.doi.org/10.1787/9789264236561-en.

This report looks at how governments can use the state architecture at their disposal to create an environment that supports innovation. Chapter 2 looks at the role that the processes of government management, such as public sector regulations, play in inhibiting or enabling innovation. The report then considers how specific functions in government, such as human resources management (Chapter 3) and budgeting (Chapter 4) can play roles in innovation. Chapter 5 examines the specific support dedicated organisations for innovation can provide and Chapter 6 covers the strategies governments can adopt to manage risk. Finally, Chapter 7 looks at how information, data and knowledge can be effectively managed to support innovation. Drawing from the observations it has gathered and analysis of country innovation approaches developed by the OECD Observatory of Public Sector Innovation, the report concludes with an analytical framework to analyse a country's central enablers of innovation which can be used to collect and examine data on how central government functions are geared to support more public sector innovation.

Creating innovative government is by no means an exact science and to that end, this report aims to add evidence and analysis in support of government actions. It fleshes out some of the relevant considerations for governments who are seeking to promote innovation and, drawing on practices from across OECD countries, provides suggestions as to how governments may wish to organise their operations to optimise the opportunities for innovation.

Rules, procedures and regulations

Public servants often perceive rules, procedures and regulations to be constraining their capacity to innovate. Yet there is relatively limited evidence that rules and procedures are actually blocking innovation. Few governments have taken any specific action in this area, in contrast to the widespread practice of "red tape reduction" to simplify practices and stimulate economic activity in the practice sector. However those governments which have explored this area, for example the Australian government, found that it was not necessarily the internal regulations themselves that were blocking innovation but rather a poor understanding of those rules by public servants, leading to a perception that they did not allow innovation (Australian Government, 2010).

This highlights the importance of understanding what dynamics are at play between public sector rules, processes and regulations, civil servants' perceptions, and innovation. The central question is whether it is actually the rules, processes and procedures which are constraining innovation, or their interpretation in the public sector. Organisational culture, human resources, risk management and behavioural science may provide insights into how to improve a shared understanding of what behaviour is permissible and desirable.

Human resources management

People are at the centre of innovation, and their commitment and determination drives every stage of the innovation process. Research shows that innovations are born from ideas that come from staff at all levels of an organisation. Frontline staff and middle managers who interact with clients and put policies into practice often have the best understanding of the need to innovate. This is reflected in various case studies collected by OPSI, where employee involvement has been cited as key.

A good example is Belgium's Out of Agency innovation, which established a network of satellite agencies closer to employees' homes, reducing the use of expensive agency space in the capital, whilst improving work/life balance within the federal public service. The project was developed as the result of a contest in which all public employees could submit efficiency ideas.

Recognising that human factors are core to innovation raises questions about human resources (HR) policies and practices and their role in supporting innovation. For example, training and development programmes can develop creative thinking as a professional competency, and performance evaluation and management could either encourage or discourage innovative thinking and actions by focusing on desired outcomes rather than compliance with processes

Individual employees do not innovate in a vacuum, but instead within an organisational culture which may support or hinder innovation. Factors that might shape this include leadership practices, diversity (cultural, age, gender, backgrounds and educational levels, etc.) in the workplace, alignment of organisational and individual values, and active management to strengthen employee engagement.

Budgeting

Given the inherent uncertainty involved in innovating, investments may need to be more flexible than funding for day-to-day activities. Several cases in the OPSI database highlighted resource flexibility as an enabling factor. Some organisations have also experimented with dedicated innovation financing. For example, Canada's National Anti-

Drug Strategy intends to spawn innovation by providing seed funding to new projects that foster systemic change. This programme also funds pilot projects to test and validate new treatment services and system enhancements.

Other aspects of budget processes and financial management procedures may serve to either encourage or discourage innovation. The recent financial crisis has forced governments around the world to implement a variety of budget cuts. During such difficult financial times, efficiency-focused innovation becomes even more important but incentives to innovate or to put innovation into practice may change drastically depending on whether the savings are reinvested within the organisation or are harvested for deficit reduction.

Partnerships are another area where budget policies may support or hinder innovation. Breaking down departmental silos has been shown to be instrumental in supporting innovation, but public sector financial accountability structures are often departmentally focused, which can make it challenging to fund collaborative innovation networks.

Innovation organisations

The capacity of the public sector to innovate also depends on the quality and effectiveness of the institutional arrangements supporting innovation. These arrangements may include institutionalising innovation in governments' mandate (such as a specific public sector innovation portfolio) and the articulation of formal responsibilities (such as dedicated organisations tasked with the promotion of innovation or "shared" responsibility models).

These arrangements are expected to vary across OECD countries depending on culture and tradition, as well as the degree of autonomy organisations and individuals have. A trend of creating public agencies either as new bodies or split off from existing ministries sought to strengthen innovation by giving agencies the flexibility to set their working methods and rules to respond to their given mandate. After over 30 years of experience, this trend, known as agencification, has shown that the level and type of autonomy needs to reflect the nature of the mandate and outputs of an organisation: individual autonomy may encourage staff to think more creatively, but can also lead to fragmentation and "stove-pipe" thinking in response to complex societal problems

Collaboration and co-ordination frameworks might be needed to regulate interactions with actors outside government. As the sample of innovations collected by the OPSI indicates, innovations are often spurred by partnerships that extend beyond traditional organisational boundaries, either with other public sector organisations, other sectors or citizens.

Such partnerships can lead to the development of innovative institutional arrangements, entities and governance approaches. For example, Denmark's MindLab is a cross-ministerial entity that works with services users, public sector organisations and companies to co-design and prototype innovative solutions for public services. Such arrangements can help pool both competencies and risk.

Managing risk and uncertainty

Given all of the challenges described in this document, public sector innovation may benefit from specific approaches to risk management to ensure that innovative projects are able to monitor risks and correct course early, avoid unnecessary failure and minimise potential negative impacts.

The OPSI examples highlighted risk-management tools such as the use of prototypes and pilots. In both cases, limited testing of an innovation enable countries to identify potential problems with their innovations and develop appropriate solutions. For example, piloting the initial concept of the Canadian Open Policy Development highlighted barriers such as cultural discomfort with change and lack of technological skills. Identifying these barriers enabled the development of solutions, such as voluntary training in ministries on new technologies, and the emergence of staff "champions" to guide change.

Knowledge

The availability of accurate, timely performance information is important to support the innovative capacity of organisations so that they can identify areas that require innovation, and learn from their successes and failures. "Learning organisations" are capable of collecting the right information and using it to innovate in response to changes in their environments. This is a key element of the public sector innovation cycle.

Academic research and a variety of cases in the OPSI database highlight the limit of competition as a means of sourcing and replicating innovations and that sharing of information across organisational boundaries is a key enabler of the success and replication of innovations. Traditional hierarchical bureaucracies often have limited horizontal flows of information due to rigid regulations and incompatible information management practices or good old fashioned inter-organisational rivalries and competition.

Building capabilities and motivation to innovate

To help governments optimise their structures and functions to best support innovation it is important not only to consider the government functions which can affect the promotion of innovation but also how and in what ways they shape the environment for innovation. A useful starting point is to consider how and where innovation may originate, and the different institutional structures it must pass through before it becomes an implemented reality. Broadly speaking, the relevant units of analysis include individual members of staff, the teams that they work in, the units where their teams sit, the organisation where they work, and the whole of the public administration. Each of these units can be more or less innovative, both by generating innovative ideas and initiating innovation, and by creating an environment that supports (or hinders) innovations originating from elsewhere in the public sector. The degree of "innovativeness" at one level strongly influences innovation at the other levels, not necessarily in a linear relationship.

What explains the innovativeness at different levels? Two factors shape whether the public sector innovates or not: 1) capability to innovate, essentially whether the relevant level is able to innovate; and 2) motivation to innovate, whether the unit wants to innovate; and 3) opportunity to innovate, whether the enabling conditions are there to innovate.[2] Capability to innovate is shaped by resources, skills, knowledge and space to innovate; motivation is shaped by incentives, values, leadership and behaviour; and opportunity is shaped by creativity, autonomy and collaboration (Figure 1.2).

Figure 1.2. Central government functions' impact on capability and motivation to innovate

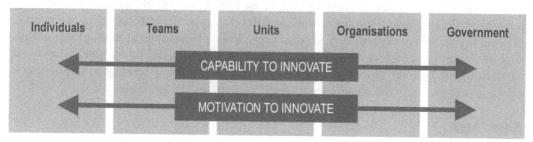

The government functions discussed above shape the public sector's capability and motivation to innovate. Table 1.1 sets out some of the ways in which this may occur. Although they are discussed separately in this section, these levers are rarely used in isolation but are often combined to achieve synergies and greater impact, for example combining prizes or awards with the provision of seed funds.

Table 1.1. How government functions influence the capability and motivation to innovate

	Capability to Innovate	Motivation to Innovate
Regulation	Are rules, processes and procedures blocking innovation? Are hierarchy and bureaucratic conventions impeding innovation?	Will challenging accepted practices be beneficial?
Budgeting	Funds for piloting and scaling up Flexibility to move resources	What happens to innovation dividends? How is innovation prioritised in budget allocation?
Human Resources	Discretion Autonomy Skills Professional and competency development Leadership support	Is there a system of rewards in place? Are innovation efforts systematically recognised? Is innovation included as criteria for career progression?
Innovation Organisations	Space to experiment Funds for investment Developing skills for innovation Support for using new techniques and methodologies	Is innovation a recognised priority? Are there fora to share and recognise success?
Risk	Knowledge of processes to manage risk and uncertainty Availability of required resources (skills and financial) for innovation to happen	How is innovation valued e.g. is there a recognise mandate for innovation?

By no means does this cover all relevant aspects of public sector innovation. There are clearly other elements of how the public sector is organised that will affect both its capacity, willingness and opportunity to innovate. Moreover, the approach set out above is not meant to imply that it is possible to develop a recipe for public sector innovation which, if followed, is guaranteed to yield results. Public sector innovation can be fortuitous, depending on a specific configuration of individuals, resources and personalities that mean that a purely government-focused perspective will just be one part of the equation. Nevertheless it is clear that governments can be proactive, by taking concerted and co-ordinated action across a number of policy levers to encourage innovation. As with all successful policies and reforms it is imperative that governments adopt an approach that matches their own priorities, circumstances and cultural norms.

Notes

1. The concept of public sector innovation as an explicit pursuit and subject of analysis is relatively recent so there is no universally accepted definition. Building on evidence from the work of the Observatory and international research, the following characteristics of public sector innovation emerge: 1) Novelty: innovations introduce new approaches in a defined context; 2) Implementation: innovations must be implemented, not just an idea; 3) Impact: innovation aim at better public results including efficiency, effectiveness, and user or employee satisfaction. For a discussion on the definition of public sector innovation see OECD (2015) and OECD (2014).

2. This approach draws on OECD research on how human resources shapes innovation (see Chapter 3).

References

Australian Government (2010), *Empowering Change: Fostering Innovation in the Australian Public Service*, Management Advisory Committee, Commonwealth of Australia, Barton, Australia, http://innovation.govspace.gov.au/barriers/.

Gallup Organization (2011), *Innobarometer 2010. Analytical Report: Innovation in Public Administration*, Flash Eurobarometer, European Commission.

OECD (2015), *The Innovation Imperative in the Public Sector: Setting an Agenda for Action*, OECD Publishing, Paris, http://dx.doi.org/10.1787/9789264236561-en

OECD (2014), "Measuring public sector innovation: Proposals for preliminary measurement guidelines", Working Party of National Experts on Science and Technology Indicators, 2 June 2014, Paris

OECD (2013), "Observatory of Public Sector Innovation: Identifying policy levers to promote innovation", 48th Session of the Public Governance Committee, 12-13 November 2013, OECD Conference Centre, Paris.

OECD (2011), *Together for Better Public Services – Partnering with Citizens and Civil Society*, OECD Publishing, Paris, http://dx.doi.org/10.1787/9789264118843-en

Chapter 2.

Dealing with regulations and procedures in public sector innovation[1]

Bureaucracy and red tape are often seen as the main barriers to innovation, particularly in the public sector. This chapter examines to what extent rules actually do inhibit innovation. Defining bureaucracy as a system of values as much as a system of rules and procedures, it considers how the wider bureaucratic context of risk aversion, silos, hierarchical organisations and lack of diversity can inhibit innovation rather than laws and procedures in the narrowest sense. The chapter examines some initiatives OECD governments have used to tackle barriers to innovation, from red tape reduction initiatives to behavioural insights. It discusses the challenge of using discretion to deal with use and procedures that seem to block innovation. It concludes with some considerations governments should apply to tackle both the specific rules and procedures which may be blocking innovation, and the wider context preventing civil servants from trying new approaches.

Introduction

Internal regulations and procedures are often mentioned as one of the main barriers to innovation (De Vries et al., 2014; Osborn and Brown, 2013). Part of the frustration seems to be caused by the perception that the rules have no other purpose than to preserve the status quo. This chapter examines the ways and extent to which internal regulations and procedures inhibit innovation in the public sector, and what approaches have been used to ensure that rules promote rather than inhibit innovation.

The evidence in both practice and academic literature of the reality of regulatory and procedural obstacles to innovation is still scarce. While the academic literature on public sector innovation has been growing steadily, the amount of systematic empirical research done in this field is still relatively small, at least compared to that on the private sector (De Vries et al., 2014; Potts and Kastelle, 2010; Vigoda-Gadot et al., 2008; Moore and Hartley, 2008). (See Annex 2.A1 for a review of the current literature).

Rules often seem to specify means – "employees can or cannot do this or that" – rather than ends – "we want to make sure / avoid that this or that happens". If opportunities to accomplish the same goals more effectively or efficiently present themselves, means-oriented rules become obstacles. Many international observers (European Commission, 2013; Lunn, 2014; OECD, 2015b) have voiced the concern that opportunities to improve the public sector are often impeded by bureaucratic obstacles that no longer adequately serve the purpose for which they were designed. Rigid application of obsolete rules and a lack of will to change the status quo stifle the production of public value through innovation.[2]

This is a serious concern. If government innovation is indeed held back by unnecessary constraints, it is important to better understand how, why and to what extent that happens, and to find out what can be done about it. The chapter is organised as follows. First, it identifies the most notable policy responses to the administrative burden reduction, distilling initial results and/or lessons. These approaches tackle problems generated by rules and procedures – intended in narrow sense (see Box 2.1) as opposed to those related to behaviours and attitudes around them – blocking innovation.

Box 2.1. Primary legislation, subordinate regulations and procedures: The narrow sense

- **Primary legislation**: laws, passed by parliament, with which all actors have to abide. With regards to innovation in the public sector, administrative law is of specific relevance.

- **Subordinate regulations**: these are approved by the head of government, by an individual minister or by the cabinet – that is, an authority other than the parliament. They specify requirements that need to be met in order to ensure an action is legal.

- **Procedures**: a procedure is a standardised process that presents a sequence of steps that need to be followed in order to reach a certain outcome.

Second, the chapter discusses the notion of "bureaucracy" as both a system of rules and a system of values, and tentatively describes emerging practices that specifically focus on bureaucratic obstacles standing in the way of innovation in the public sector.

Governments have responded to concerns about bureaucratic obstacles to innovation with various initiatives to improve the situation (OECD, 2008). This section highlights a number of relevant policy approaches and discusses the extent to which they can affect the creation, development and diffusion of innovation. It is not intended to be exhaustive, but rather gives an impression of the variety of approaches to removing or relaxing regulations and procedures.

Finally, the last section brings together the findings and formulates an answer to the question: what can governments do if innovation is (perceived to be) impeded by internal bureaucracy? It suggests approaches that individuals and institutions anywhere can apply to optimise the potential for innovation by looking critically at their organisational context.

Some of the practices discussed in the chapter are relatively new, and some have been around for some time or have faded. None of these practices have the sole purpose of removing bureaucratic obstacles, but some have this objective as one of their primary goals. Since none of these practices have been systematically evaluated in terms of their effectiveness in reducing barriers to innovation, it is hard to claim that these practices pose solutions to the (perceived) problem. However, they do provide interesting new ideas, experiences and questions that can help inform efforts to better understand the impact of regulation on advancing innovation throughout its lifecycle (Figure 2.1):

Figure 2.1. Approaches to rules and procedures that can drive the innovation lifecycle

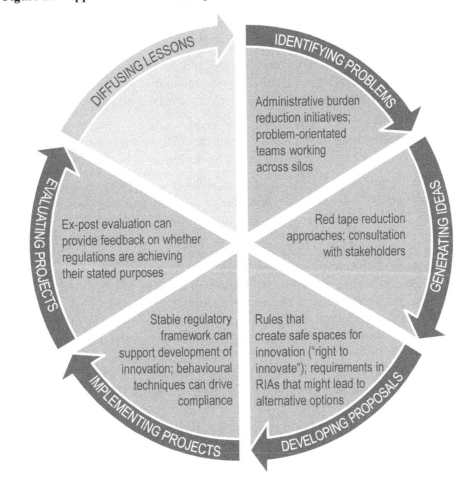

- **Identifying problems**: Red tape reduction programmes can help identify unnecessary administrative burdens which block innovation. Special units (e.g. digital transformation/ strategy/ delivery and behavioural units) working across administrative silos can also bring new approaches to problem solving and accelerate innovations. Early consultations with stakeholders (e.g. through advisory groups or consultation committees) in the rule-making process to jointly identify regulatory issues can help to identify factors inhibiting innovation.

- **Generating ideas**: By eliminating unnecessary bureaucratic procedures and internal waste, red tape reduction approaches can also create spaces for civil servants to refocus on core tasks and service improvements. Consultation with stakeholders in regulation reviews can generate new ideas on how to reduce barriers to innovation – especially if conducted at early stages. Innovative regulations that focus on outcomes and values rather than process compliance can provide opportunities to discover new approaches to problem solving.

- **Developing proposals**: Procedures can create safe spaces for innovation to occur, such as approaches involving exemptions from legislation or providing a "right to innovate". Requirements for built-in regulatory impact assessment (RIA) from the outset can result in identifying alternatives to regulation to achieve the desired objectives.

- **Implementing projects**: A stable regulatory framework (coupled with financial incentives such as innovation funds) can support the development and scaling up of innovations (see Chapter 4). The use of behavioural science can also strengthen compliance and help guide projects to achieve its intended results.

- **Evaluating projects**: Greater use and documentation of evaluation after implementation can help assess whether regulations are achieving their stated purposes and identify corrective measures that can be put in place.

This chapter is based on a review of the 21st century academic literature on the topic, as well as reports on emerging practices that aim to address the issue. It also builds on conceptual and empirical research by the author on dealing with bureaucratic obstacles.[3]

Within the context of this chapter it is impossible to explore in detail the many differences in legal and administrative practices, cultures and structures across countries that impact on the ability of the public sector to innovate. One major difference between OECD countries is whether their legal system is based on civil law or common law principles. A broad generalisation is that common law systems can be seen as more naturally supportive of innovation as they define only what is prohibited and the binding nature of case law provides for continued mutation of the law, whereas civil law systems often proscribe specifically what public sector actors can and cannot do and court rulings only have persuasive authority; rules can be changed only through legislation. As such, the way a public sector organisation approaches innovation may be influenced by the legal system in which they operate. However, these broad generalisations are evidently not a strong determinant of innovation given that many public sector organisations in common law systems struggle to innovate and there are examples of innovative public sector practices in civil law systems.

Another important distinction to make between countries is whether they are a federal or unitary country. In federal countries there are clearly defined roles and responsibilities for different levels of government and it is often prohibited for one level of government to act in the realm of the other. In unitary countries subnational tiers of government have more limited and specific capacities to act which have been granted to them by, and typically can only be changed by, a higher tier of government. The national tier of government also has the ability to act and intervene within the realm of the subnational authority. In both systems there is the potential to inhibit innovation. Federal systems may be seen as more insular, as there is less incentive for each tier, and administrations with a tier, to interact with each other as they have a defined and specific sphere of influence. In unitary systems there may be greater potential for conflict and disagreement as different tiers act in the same sphere of influence with competing objectives. However in both systems there is also the potential to enable innovation: in federal systems, subnational entities often show greater variation in practice as a result of their ability to make their own laws and rules, whereas in unitary systems variation at the subnational level is often the result of the need to achieve statutory outcomes despite fiscal/procedural constraints put in place by the national government.

This chapter does not focus in detail on either the legal system or the system of government, but considers regulation within the general framework of a liberal democracy under the rule of law designed around the basic principles of Weberian bureaucracy.

Policy approaches to red tape reduction

OECD member states have invested a lot in red tape reduction programmes (OECD, 2010).[4] In fact, over the past 12 years OECD members have focused most of their post-implementation evaluation programmes on reducing administrative burdens to business (OECD, 2015c). However, very few have applied the tools available to their own internal rules and procedures.

There are some programmes which have focused explicitly on public sector professionals and civil servants as well as citizens and businesses (Box 2.3). The assumption underlying cutting regulation to promote innovation is that it creates space for professionals in the public sector to spend more time on their core tasks, spend less time on administrative work and be more innovative in their organisations. For example, if social workers and medical professionals are less tied to protocols and standard procedures, they may be better able to create tailor-made solutions for complex cases, and develop more appropriate working methods to effectively and efficiently help their clients. This would be valuable for the client, more satisfying for the professional and more cost effective for the taxpayers (de Jong and Zuurmond, 2010a).

Multiple tools have been developed to detect, analyse and structurally remove red tape. The standard cost model (SCM) helps map administrative requirements and calculate their costs in time and money. These calculations have been used to identify opportunities for improvement and innovation, although they are primarily used for administrative burdens on businesses and citizens. Governments have also launched websites and toll-free numbers to report red tape in order to crowdsource examples of dysfunctional bureaucracy and suggestions for improvement. Some countries have used regulatory impact assessments to evaluate the "red tape" effect of new rules and regulations. Others have experimented with using more room for discretion and informal approaches to dealing with client complaints. This approach allows professionals to engage in more creative troubleshooting and problem solving than formal, legalistic procedures and protocols would (de Jong and Zuurmond, 2010b).

Box 2.2. Red tape reduction initiatives for the public sector

The OECD (2010: p.30) reports that several countries have made efforts to clarify rules and procedures, to reduce ambiguity, confusion and frustration for civil servants and professionals who are subject to legislation imposed by higher levels of government.

- France, for example, improved "codification". This refers to the process by which existing legislation is regrouped into specific areas under a single code. During this process, obsolete texts are removed (OECD, 2010).

- The United Kingdom has a "cutting bureaucracy for public services" initiative as part of its public sector reforms aimed at improving public services (NAO, 2009).

- In 2009 and 2010, the Mexican Ministry of Public Administration led an exercise to review the stock of internal regulations; by the beginning of 2011, this had resulted in the elimination of 67% of the internal regulatory instruments. They also published administrative handbooks to improve efficiency and effectiveness of the internal activities of the government, covering acquisitions, public works, human resources, financial resources, information and communication technologies, transparency, auditing, and control (OECD, 2011).

- The European Commission also aims to "identify inconsistencies, gaps and ineffective measures", including "regulatory burden related to how EU legislation is implemented at the national and sub-national level" through its REFIT Regulatory Fitness and Performance programme (European Commission 2013: p.19).

Bureaucratic barriers to innovation

In order to understand the role that regulations and procedures play in blocking innovation in the public sector, it is useful to take a broader look at the bureaucratic environment. In short, "bureaucracy" is both the internal rules and procedures, and the behaviour they generate. It arises from values that government and society want to uphold: rational decision making, integrity, effectiveness, efficiency, transparency, accountability, fairness, etc. (Peters, 2003; Etzioni-Halevy, 1985; Cels et al., 2012). When one explores the relationship between bureaucracy and innovation, one needs to consider the broader context that informs attitudes towards and behaviour around rules and procedures.

Research in the Netherlands has shown that it is often not the laws and regulations themselves that provide the barrier but the conservative interpretation of the rules that civil servants make (Kruiter et al., 2008; Cels et al., 2012). The laws and regulation may provide the space for innovation, but civil servants are not using it. This may be due to a lack of imagination, or they may be explicitly or implicitly discouraged from taking the initiative. Organisational cultures may either not value innovation – there is not an explicit statement of reward for innovation – or accountability for failure may be discouraging employees taking risks. The rewards for innovation may be much smaller than the sanctions for trying and failing. The broader context in which civil servants operate may present them with a reality that is not conducive to innovation, even when it is difficult to pinpoint the exact rules and procedures that stand in the way. The whole environment may feel rule-driven, strictly regulated and highly procedural. Thus, even if the rules leave room for innovation, civil servants may not feel it is possible, let alone desirable or imperative, to explore and use that room.

There is no consensus about what constitutes bureaucratic dysfunction. However when bureaucracies cease to uphold expected fundamental values, they become dysfunctional. Rules and regulations may be obsolete, or interpreted in too strict a manner. But when bureaucracies actually are protecting fundamental values of democratic governance and administration, and yet the results are not satisfactory, one should probably consider the underlying conflict in values. If an innovation is blocked by rules and regulation, it might be that the proposed novel practice would not sufficiently satisfy the values that the public want to see protected, or the innovator has not yet convincingly made the case that it will. The notion that there is an inherent negative causal relationship between governmental procedures and the capacity for innovation in the public sector appears to originate in a pejorative conception of bureaucracy.[5] To understand bureaucracy as an impediment to innovation, a nuanced and more sophisticated analytical approach is needed.

Bureaucracies are as much a system of values as they are a system of rules. Max Weber formulated characteristics of bureaucracy that are rooted in values that most people would agree with: rational decision making, integrity, effectiveness, efficiency, transparency, accountability and fairness (Peters, 2003: p.113). Table 2.1 lists these "Weberian" characteristics of bureaucracy. If one focuses on the concrete rules and procedures (in the right hand column) that have been put in place, one might get the feeling that bureaucracy primarily consists of or produces rules and procedures. If one focuses , however, on the values that these rules are seeking to uphold (in the left hand column), one has a better understanding that bureaucracy is all about upholding shared values of democratic governance.

Table 2.1. Weberian bureaucracy model: Underlying values and concrete rules and procedures

Underlying value	Weberian characteristic	Concrete rules and procedures
Stability, robustness, trustworthiness	Regulated continuity	Rules about documentation and archiving, formal paperwork, professional standards
Efficiency, rationality	Functional specialisation	Jurisdictional rules, business process design, professional authority
(Democratic) accountability	Hierarchical organisation	Rules about chains of command, accountability mechanisms, professional relationships
Effectiveness, professionalism, avoiding nepotism	Expert officialdom	Rules about job qualifications, recruitment, promotion, performance reviews
Integrity, accountability	Distinctions between public and private spheres	Rules about procurement, conflict of interests
Due diligence, accountability, transparency	Formalised documentation	Paperwork, informational requirements, rules about evidence of eligibility, etc.

The important thing to note here is that the values in the left hand column do not necessarily contradict the purposes of innovation. On the contrary: innovations often seek to make government more robust, efficient, accountable, effective, professional and transparent. In other words, if innovation is inhibited by rules and procedures, the following questions need to be asked first:

- Are the rules and procedures the best and only way to protect bureaucracy's underlying values or might they have become goals in and of themselves?

- Is the innovation challenging some specific rules and procedures or is it actually endangering the underlying values they are supposed to uphold and the public interests they are supposed to protect?

There is not a clear and common understanding of what the "bureaucratic obstacles" to innovation are. A number of recent surveys have measured the perception of the problem among public servants (Gallup Organization, 2011; ANAO, 2009; Patterson and Kerrin, 2009) and underscored the difference in definitions based on own respondent interpretation.

Expanding the definition of rules and regulations to include the broader context of bureaucratic organisations in the public sector helps to separate the impact of individual rules and regulations from what informs individuals' attitudes towards and behaviour around them. Box 2.3 discusses the four of the six key characteristics of the Weberian bureaucracy model listed in Table 2.1 to identify the tensions between the underlying principles and the attitudes underlying innovation.

Box 2.3. Tension between the characteristics of bureaucracy and innovation

Regulated continuity versus space for risk taking

Government has an obligation to its citizens to function consistently and reliably. This creates a desire for stability and control. Innovation may provide the opposite, in that it brings uncertainty and risk of failure. At the same time, government also has a certain obligation to provide public services in the most effective and efficient way possible. The bureaucratic principles of regulated continuity can function as a barrier to innovation as it creates a risk-averse environment (Eggers and Singh, 2009; De Vries et al., 2014: pp.19-20; Patterson and Kerrin, 2009).

Functional specialisation versus cross-silo collaboration

The tasks of bureaucracy are divided up in a manner that appears rational. Every task comes with specific authorities, resources and sanctions. Public sector bureaucracies typically have narrowly defined jobs and organisations dominated by individual professions (Borins, 2001). Part of the reason for this is to enable the efficient division of labour and to de-concentrate power. Many organisations' departments are ill equipped to tackle today's so-called "wicked problems" which extend beyond boundaries and require close collaboration and dynamic approaches. When an organisation fails to co-ordinate and collaborate, division of labour immediately fails to be efficient and may inhibit innovative solutions. This "silo system" has been identified as a main barrier to innovation (Bason, 2010; Australian Government, 2010; Walker 2008).

Hierarchical organisations versus diffused accountability

There is an elaborate, hierarchical authority system within each bureaucracy that assigns duties to every official, so that the means of control depends on obedience to higher levels of authority which might inhibit bottom-up innovation. The control function of hierarchy has the effect of discouraging people working in the frontline from coming up with approaches they think would be an improvement. This could mean frontline employees are less likely to step forward with their ideas because they anticipate not being heard (Kelman, 2005: p.17). Hierarchies may prevent the skills and knowledge that are gathered at the bottom of the organisation from travelling upwards (Sørensen and Torfing, 2012). However, studies indicate that many innovators still find a way to work with or around it. A study conducted in the United States found out that half of all (award-winning innovations or finalists innovations (51%) were not initiated at the top of the organisation (Borins, 2001). Half of the respondents to the question 18 of the Innobarometer survey saw the role of the manager as a significant factor in the capacity to innovate (Gallup Organization, 2011).

Box 2.3. Tension between the characteristics of bureaucracy and innovation *(cont.)*

Expert officialdom versus diverse and multi-dimensional skillsets

Because bureaucratic work is structured through regulation and functional specialisation, officials must be experts in applying rules technically and legally. This requires expertise on the part of employees, which demands targeted recruitment, selection and training. The Australian report on public sector innovation (Australian Government, 2010) notes that "there is a strong emphasis in the public sector recruitment on experienced administrators and regulators". Kelman (2005: p.25) observes that organisations often recruit after their own image, consolidating the nature of the workforce, reducing diversity and protecting the status quo. Such recruitment after their own image can lead to a public sector workforce that lacks diversity in skills and ideas, which can act as a barrier to innovation. Working with people from different backgrounds, with different areas of expertise and experience, is said to be a driver of innovation (Albury, 2005; Bason, 2010).

Policy approaches to reducing bureaucratic barriers to innovation

Governments have responded to concerns about regulatory obstacles to innovation, with various initiatives to improve the situation (OECD, 2008). This section highlights a number of relevant policy approaches, and discusses the extent to which they can affect the creation, development and diffusion of innovation. It is not intended to be exhaustive, but rather gives an impression of the variety of approaches to removing or relaxing regulations and procedures in the broader sense. It discusses more general attempts to make it easier to innovate in bureaucratic environments in the public sector, through approaches such as consultation, rule exemptions, innovation delivery models and behavioural insights

Stakeholder engagement

Engaging stakeholders in regulatory policy in making, implementing and reviewing regulations has become a widespread practice in OECD countries. Involving those who will be subject to regulations can help identify problems at early stage and ensure that rules do not stand in the way of or create barriers to innovation (OECD, 2015c).

OECD data show that while most OECD countries have systematically adopted formal stakeholder engagement practices, these are not evenly spread across the policy-making cycle. Most countries engage the stakeholders when developing new or amending regulations, and engagement often happens at the very end of the process (OECD, 2015c).

There is still only scattered evidence on whether stakeholder engagement processes in rule making enhance greater innovation by removing bureaucratic obstacles. Often such processes are connected to efforts to reduce administrative burdens. For example, the Danish Burden Hunters project and the Swedish Better Regulation Hunt are examples of more targeted, proactive approaches of using close co-operation with stakeholders to analyse existing regulatory burdens and to find ways on how to simplify existing regulations (OECD, 2015c).

Countries' experience with engaging stakeholders at the early stages of the project (also through online tools) indicates potential opportunities to identify new ideas that can feed into the decision-making, law drafting and planning processes.

Assessing the impact and evaluating regulations

The importance of taking into account the impact of regulations on innovation has gained increased traction and has increasingly been underscored at international level.[6] Regulatory impact assessment (RIA) supports the process of policy making by conducting an *ex ante* assessment of the implications of potential regulatory options. RIA can help identify where rules and regulations are overlapping or incoherent and provide a useful support for decision making (OECD, 2015c). RIA can be helpful when assessing requirements for innovative solutions – which may affect civil servants – when developing regulatory options.

Evaluation of regulations assesses the performance of regulations against stated objectives. OECD research underscores that evaluation is still a limited practice in many countries, and it is mainly carried out through the RIA process. While country practices remain sporadic in this area, better evaluation could significantly support better evidence-based decision making and create a sounder basis to foster innovative approaches in policy and services delivery.

Rule exemptions

A more radical approach, in some ways, is the phenomenon of targeted rule exemptions. These schemes focus on granting more discretionary authority to agencies or jurisdictions which can request exemption from a law that they feel inhibits their ability to innovate and improve their work in the public sector (European Commission, 2013). If they are able to argue this convincingly, they may be eligible for a *"licence to break the rules"* (Albury, 2005). One way to do this is to provide exemptions from legislation. Over a set time period, the effects of the exemption are monitored and evaluated (European Commission, 2013). Some countries' experience indicates that under certain conditions, rule exemptions can prove effective at eliminating unnecessary barriers to innovation and bottom-up experimentation, but they are not sufficient to sustain innovative approaches over time (Box 2.4).

Box 2.4. The Free Commune Experiment (Sweden)

One early example of rule exemption is the Free Commune Experiment (FCE) in Sweden, Denmark, Norway and Finland in the 1990s (DCLG, 2006). National governments exempted certain municipalities from national legislation and regulation in areas such as education, health care, childcare, social services, employment, trade and industry, the environment, and agriculture. The idea behind this initiative was that it would enable local government to come up with innovations that would lead to improvement. Consequently, these municipalities could perform an exemplary role in other areas. In an evaluation of the experiment in 2006, there was a net positive conclusion: "The experience of the FCEs suggests that granting relatively limited exemptions on a temporary basis to a sample of councils is an effective way of stimulating innovation and testing out new approaches at low cost and limited risk" (DCLG, 2006).

FCEs contributed to a more positive environment for innovation in public administration. The practical result was that legislation, which indeed turned out to be unnecessary or to provide extensive administrative burden, was removed or changed. This contributed to a more bottom-up innovation process (at state level at least). However, removing the rules turned out to be a necessary but not sufficient condition for innovation. A lack of funding and insufficient levels of resources for the creation and implementation of innovations served as additional barriers.

Box 2.4. The Free Commune Experiment (Sweden) *(cont.)*

Municipalities also experienced difficulties in co-operating with different levels of government and departments. Because the areas of legislation were so varied, there were many different departments involved, which had differing attitudes and interests towards this policy. Removing complex and cumbersome rules and procedures turned out to be a complex and cumbersome process in its own right.

Source: DCGL (2006), Free Communes Experiments: Lessons for Policy in England.

Another example is from the United Kingdom, where the same mechanism has been used to facilitate and foster innovation in public education from the early 2000s. Under the label The Power to Innovate, the Secretary of State for Education has the power to "temporarily suspend, or modify, education legislation that may be holding back - or even stopping - innovative approaches to raising standards". While results were mixed, the UK Department for Education claims that, overall, The Power to Innovate had a positive influence on the capacity of schools to innovate. In total, 32 orders were made affecting over 600 schools (Department for Education, 2011).

The limitation of this approach is that it does not address the wider problem of a risk-averse culture, which is why, for example, some of the Free Communes made a rather slow start in actually using their new authority. This also came up in the evaluation of The Power to Innovate, as schools were hesitant to step forward at first. Even when organisations achieve success with their innovations, this policy approach does not provide a process to help diffuse new practices.

Another interesting finding of the Power to Innovate study is that schools would typically apply for an exemption because they had an innovative idea. Often, it became clear during the process that the legislation already offered the freedom and flexibility for the idea to be implemented and an exemption was actually unnecessary. This is consistent with research from the Netherlands where, after in-depth field research in 13 cities, no single regulatory impediment to innovation was found, despite widespread concerns among these cities about suffocating regulatory pressure from the national government. As already discussed in this chapter, often it is not the formal regulations that provide obstacles, but instead people's interpretation of them. In those cases, red tape reduction, deregulation or rule exemption policies cannot help, unless the goal is to confront organisations and individuals with the actual amount of discretionary space they have, and clarify the boundaries of formal authority if necessary (Kruiter et al., 2008; de Jong and Zuurmond, 2010b).

Countries have experimented with regulation waivers for businesses to help them develop and test their ideas within existing regulatory framework. In the United Kingdom, the Financial Conduct Authority issues a regulatory sandbox allowing businesses to test innovative products, services, business models and delivery mechanisms in a live environment lowering barriers to testing within current regulations. The sandbox framework also allows businesses to request the FCA to waive or modify rules which have become unduly burdensome or are not achieving their objectives. The first cohort of the regulatory sandbox closed to applications on 8 July 2016. The FCA received a total of 69 applications from a diverse range of businesses in terms of sector, location and size. Applications from 24 firms met the sandbox eligibility criteria and were accepted to develop towards testing, including early-stage start-ups, challengers and incumbent firms (FCA, 2017).

Innovation delivery teams

A relatively new approach to promoting innovation is the innovation delivery team (Box 2.5). These are special units, for example, in a city administration, that work across silos and report directly to the mayor. The idea is that the unit functions as an innovation generator, facilitator and accelerator all at once. Using a data-driven, collaborative approach, and operating under the mayor's authority, the teams are deployed to take on particularly tough challenges in order to address pressing public problems. Examples of such problems are a homelessness epidemic in Atlanta, soaring homicides in New Orleans and failing public services in Louisville.

This approach is distinct from other efforts to remove barriers to innovation in at least three ways:

- First, the model is explicitly problem oriented. It asks the question: if innovation is the solution, what is the problem? In doing so, it raises the stakes and puts more pressure on any bureaucratic value trade-offs that might occur. The team is solving real problems and monitoring evidence of success and failure. That is a strong value proposition to which bureaucratic defensiveness may not have a good response.

- Second, the approach explicitly links innovation to the top of the organisation. In doing so, it acknowledges that only a superior authority can ultimately break through silos, encourage officials to use more of their discretionary authority and provide cover in order to mitigate risk aversion.

- Third, the model uses a process approach focused on continuous learning. It is based on the premise that one never knows in advance what kind of obstacles will come up or what kind of resistance will be generated by innovations. Having a team of dedicated professionals who stay close to the process and solve problems if and when they occur allows for a more tailored approach to navigating rules, procedures and other bureaucratic hurdles.

Box 2.5. How the innovation delivery model works

Originally coined by Michael Barber, who headed the Prime Minister's Delivery Unit in the Blair Government in the United Kingdom, this "delivery" approach in government has been adopted and further developed by a variety of governments around the world. Most notably, Bloomberg Philanthropies, founded by the former mayor of New York City Michael Bloomberg, has launched and funded innovation delivery teams in five American cities (Atlanta, Chicago, Louisville, Memphis and New Orleans). Mayor Bloomberg had experimented and refined the model in New York, where he created the Center for Economic Opportunity, an award-winning government lab that rigorously experiments with and evaluates novel approaches to poverty reduction, education and employment.

Box 2.5. How the innovation delivery model works *(cont.)*

Innovation delivery teams follow four basic steps:

- The team starts with a thorough investigation of the problem at hand. Here, they gain profound insights into the situation, how it came to be and who is involved. In Atlanta this problem assessment was based on interviews with local practitioners and national experts and the results of surveys and focus groups with homeless people performed by a local university.

- The second phase is about generating new ideas. The team seeks to work together across levels and departments within the municipality, as well as with external actors. In Atlanta, this phase involved an extensive brainstorming session.

- The most feasible solutions are gathered and operationalised in the next phase, preparing to deliver.

- The co-ordinated approach is launched and monitored in the final phase of delivery and adaptation. Results are assessed and programmes adjusted accordingly. In Atlanta, over 1 000 people were housed as a result, and a co-ordinated and structural approach was implemented to keep addressing the issue.

The initial results are very positive. The five US cities all report significant and convincing results. For example: In 2013, New Orleans reduced homicides by 20% compared to 2012, achieving the city's lowest murder rate since 1985, And Memphis leveraged the approach to fill 53% of the empty storefronts in key commercial tracts of the city, giving hope to small business owners and reinvigorating the city's core (Bloomberg Philanthropies, 2014).

The effectiveness of the delivery model is still being debated. Management literature has pointed to flaws related to the difficulty of combining very different mindsets for innovation and delivery. The approach is labour-intensive and expensive. It requires dedicated capacity and highly skilled team members, as well as unwavering commitment on the part of the political executive. In that sense, the innovation delivery model is a far from easy fix for inhibitive rules and procedures.

Behavioural insights

At its core, the application of behavioural insight to policy builds on the recognition that individuals are not as rational as they are expected to be in standard economic theory. Embedding experimentation into policy design and implementation can enhance the effectiveness of public policies (Lunn, 2014; OECD, 2015a). This understanding allows for a "culture of innovation" where the emphasis is on regulating differently, for example through requirements for summaries of essential information (Sunstein, 2011).

The use of behavioural insights has been a source of innovation, especially in policy implementation. It has been used to deregulate (reduce regulations and rules) as well as regulate better (rules that better achieve their outcome). While there are certain challenges with applying this tool to government, more and more work in this field is adding value to governments' understanding of underlying issues and policy problems that may not have a behavioural solution. The science is helping to create a culture and mindset that is more conducive toward using innovation to achieve policy objectives.

A mapping of applying behavioural insights to regulation conducted in 2014 showed that behavioural insights have been used to help consumers make choices that better meet their needs (Lunn, 2014):

- **Simplification of information and choices** has been used as a way to enable citizens to make better choices. The US Consumer and Financial Protection Bureau's "know before you owe" intervention made it a requirement for simplified disclosure of information on mortgages, credit cards and student loans to be made available to citizens.

- **Defaults and convenience** informed the 2007 Kiwisaver auto-enrolment policy which meant the default was for people to be enrolled into pension schemes, with the opportunity to opt out, leading to a 50% increase in pension coverage.

- **Debiasing and improving decision quality** interventions seek to counteract natural tendencies or biases that lead to suboptimal decisions. The US Environmental Protection Agency's regulation to include cost information on gallons per 100 miles and annual fuel costs in addition to the usual miles per gallon information addressed consumers' misunderstanding of the actual costs of fuel consumption (Larrick and Soll, 2008).

- **Salience** has long been used to attract people's attention, such as through the use of warning messages and pictures on cigarette packages and now certain food products. In the United States, it was found that alcohol purchases were reduced more by tax made obvious on the price tag than by an equivalent tax being levied at the till (Chetty, Looney and Kroft, 2009).

The first overview of behavioural economics and policy was published by the UK Cabinet Office in 2003. Behavioural insights were popularised as a policy discipline by Thaler and Sunstein in the 2008 book Nudge. The Obama administration began applying "nudges" on various policies related to the environment, savings and financial regulation. The UK's Behavioural Insights Team was set up in 2010 and began influencing government interventions such as on tax compliance. There are numerous other examples of early adopters, such as Colombia, Denmark and South Africa. Since then the application of behavioural insights by governments and regulators is increasing and many countries have set up such initiatives.

In 2016, the OECD collected over 100 applications of behavioural insights to policy and regulation (OECD, 2017). Evidence from this work shows that behavioural insights are used relatively late in the design of policy and regulation and mostly when a policy is already in place, to fine-tune and improve implementation and compliance. There is potential to do even more, with the potential for positive impacts on innovation inside government. At the end of the policy cycle, behavioural insights can be applied to evaluate the effectiveness of implementation. Behavioural insights can also be taken into consideration when designing and conducting evaluation of policy implementation (Figure 2.2).

Figure 2.2. Behavioural insights and the policy cycle

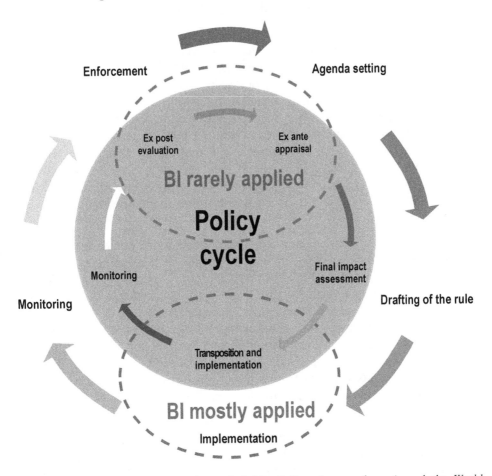

Source: OECD (2017), *Behavioural Insights and Public Policy: Lessons from Around the World*, http://dx.doi.org/10.1787/9789264270480-en.

Environment, culture and behaviour can create the perception of regulatory barriers

These features of the bureaucratic environment discussed above are not particularly conducive to innovation. Risk aversion, silos, hierarchical structures and a lack of diversity may have been consolidated in practice into rules and procedures which are acting as barriers to innovation. On the other hand, if no such specific rules and procedures can be found, it might well be that these features "live" in organisations as practice, behaviour and culture. As such, their existence is just as real and their influence may be just as big – it is just harder to pinpoint what the concrete obstacle is, and where it is.

This is important for those who want to remove regulatory obstacles for innovation. They may not need to look for actual rules and procedures, but rather assess the less tangible practice that results from codified and uncodified bureaucratic values and behaviour. Michael Lipsky (2010) warned that "to understand street-level bureaucracy one must study the routines and subjective responses street-level bureaucrats develop in order to cope with the difficulties and ambiguities of their jobs". Such ethnographic research is needed to better understand what is really going on in bureaucracies, and to develop new concepts and categories that help identify relevant patterns of bureaucratic culture and behaviour.

The use of discretion is one way to deal with rules and procedure that seem to block innovation. According to Ronald Dworkin (1977), "The concept of discretion is at home in only one sort of context; when someone is in general charged with making decisions subject to standards set by a particular authority. Discretion, like the hole in a doughnut, does not exist except as an area left open by a surrounding belt of restriction". Kruiter and de Jong (2008) studied the behaviour of frontline professionals who were tasked with creating tailor-made solutions for families with multiple problems (poverty, substance abuse, parenting issues, etc.). They found they always referenced the law, rules and procedures and agency handbooks available to service providers, but they rarely mentioned discretionary authority as a resource, even though discretion is an important feature of professional work.

Professionals who want to innovate typically first explore and seek to expand their discretionary authority: they seek to widen the hole in the donut. If they are still too restricted by the boundaries of their formal authority, they may start challenging those boundaries, and nominate them for discussion with their authorising environment. This could be called the exercise of leadership. Management can be described as the skilful and responsible administration of affairs within the boundaries of one's authority, while leadership is the pursuit of value creation beyond those boundaries. Both the maximum use of discretion and the transgression of formal boundaries are ways to deal with rules and procedures that seem to block innovation. The permission to question rules and, if they are considered a true obstacle, to challenge them, is a rule that itself nurtures an innovation culture and mindset.

But not everybody is willing to go there. The exercise of leadership requires a sense of purpose and personal courage, which is not present in – or rewarded by – every civil servant or public manager. But many people are even reluctant to use discretionary authority, as some research found (Kruiter and de Jong, 2008). All professionals in the public services they studied enjoyed some degree of discretion, but there was large variation in the ways in which and the extent to which they used it. Those who were reluctant to use it admitted high levels of anxiety around the lack of accountability and protection. They want to reduce the risks associated with making difficult decisions in a complex environment closely monitored by the public. Professionals under intense scrutiny may prefer clear guidelines and routines, even at the expense of freedom to act and tailor solutions to meet the needs of clients more accurately (Crozier, 1964). As a consequence, policy makers, managers and professionals attempt to fill the hole in the donut. Limiting discretion will not necessarily help the clients they serve, but it will protect the professionals working for the clients. Over time, in a more or less conscious process of institutionalisation, customs and norms evolve to become recognised organisational behaviour, which in turn then becomes formally entrenched in operating procedures and rules that legitimise some actions and prohibit others.

There are many reasons why public servants may be reluctant to use the leeway afforded by discretion and stick to the regulations. They may feel such decisions are easier to justify and less subject to administrative or legal attack. Regulations protect boundaries and turf and keep out competition. Regulations can provide a false sense of control in the sense that every possible scenario or option has been anticipated even if implementation is unworkable or the regulation too complex to follow as a result.

Regulatory compliance is a way of absolving the individual civil servant of any responsibility for acting in a way that focuses on actual outcomes ("doing the right thing") or expending additional effort ("going the extra mile").

Civil servants might also not feel at ease in managing the uncertainty, anxiety and vulnerability associated with innovation and change, so they consciously or unconsciously interpret – or make – the rules stricter than they really are or have to be. As a consequence, they become concerned about not being able to act in the best interest of their clients. Kruiter and de Jong conclude that these conflicting drives for both more regulation and more individual latitude reveal a deep discomfort with the use of discretionary authority. Therefore, in order to effectively deal with perceived regulatory impediments to innovation, one needs to look as closely at the perceptions as at the regulatory impediments themselves and the incentives and signals that internal rules and procedures send to civil servant and public officials more generally.

Conclusions and open questions

Complaints about internal rules and procedures as barriers to public sector innovation are often heard, repeated and amplified. Both the academic literature and reports from practice claim that this is a major problem that needs to be addressed in order to fulfil the public sector's potential to innovate, improve and create value for clients and society. This chapter has taken a more diagnostic approach to this problem. The mixed results from approaches reducing regulatory burdens and cutting red tape for citizens and businesses suggest that removing or relaxing rules and procedures is no easy task and requires careful analysis and handling of underlying value trade-offs or conflicts of interest (Kaufman, 1977; OECD, 2010; de Jong, 2014). Moreover, in many cases "the rules" are little more than a label that people apply to bureaucratic practice. In those cases, there is a need to investigate more carefully what exactly is going on, and at what level improvements would be possible and desirable.

This chapter has distinguished between the narrow definition of rules and procedures – laws, regulations and internal procedures – and rules and procedures in the broader sense, referring to the basic Weberian characteristics of the bureaucratic form of organisation. These characteristics include regulated continuity, specialised tasks, hierarchical structures and expert officialdom. There is a huge imbalance between the frequency of the claims that narrow rules and regulations inhibit innovation, and the empirical evidence that such is the case. This may be because enough systematic research has not yet been done and that future research will prove the claim to be valid, or it may be that when people complain about rules and procedures, they are actually referring to the broader bureaucratic environment. Some key characteristics of Weberian bureaucracy can be harmful to the practice of innovation, but it does not necessarily have to be that way. The characteristics of bureaucracy are rooted in values that still enjoy a broad consensus, such as efficiency, effectiveness, accountability, integrity and fairness. While concrete rules and procedures can be changed, it is clear that bureaucracies need to stick to their general principles, and certainly hold on to their underlying values. In any case, regardless of whether the obstacles that innovators encounter along the way are actual rules and procedures, or the perceived hostility or resistance of the bureaucratic environment, the concern is legitimate and needs to be taken seriously. The question is: what can governments do to remove both real and perceived obstacles to innovation?

A variety of different approaches have been tried. Tools and models used to reduce red tape for businesses could equally be applied to internal rules and procedures in governments. However, very few countries that have attempted to cut red tape for citizens and businesses have yet done so for their own officials and professionals. Rule exemption initiatives, focused on granting more discretionary authority to agencies or jurisdictions, can convincingly prove that the rules inhibit them from innovating and creating more value. The innovation delivery model, a novel approach to navigating the bureaucratic hurdles in municipal innovation, can provide a problem-centric, data-driven, cross-silo process with strong support from the political executive. Finally, behavioural insight approaches are built on the premise that science and evidence can support fewer and better rules that drive more innovative approaches. These approaches have not yet spread widely or matured fully, and therefore it is not possible to draw conclusions about their effectiveness or universal applicability. They provide proofs of concept, however, and with the rapid spread of more institutionalised approaches to promoting and enabling innovation, there will be more opportunities for the systematic evaluation of the effectiveness of each model.

Governments should assess the extent to which their employees feel – or claim to feel – inhibited in innovating, and then rigorously diagnose what it is that inhibits them, including the incentives and constraints created by internal and external rules. This can be done through targeted surveys with specific questions (more detailed than the typical surveys discussed in this chapter), focus groups and collaborative inquiry (connecting employees at all levels and across silos) and systematic review of rules and procedures (regulatory and business process mapping). If there are actual rules and procedures standing in the way, governments should find out if the rules are doing what they are supposed to do: protect the organisation from bad ideas and uphold the values of democratic governance and bureaucratic organisation. If not, they should try to rethink and rewrite the rules and procedures in accordance with their underlying values, but in a way that is more accommodating to novel practices. If there are no specific rules and or procedures standing in the way, they should try to find out what it is that keeps innovators from proceeding. All of the following hypotheses should be tested:

- **Phantom rules and procedures**: are employees imagining rules that are not there? Is it sufficiently clear what the rules and procedures are?

- **Unwritten rules and procedures**: are employees inhibited by the behaviours of others and by the organisational culture? Do some non-codified practices effectively limit innovation?

- **Discretionary deficits**: are people using their discretionary space maximally to innovate and push the envelope? If not, what is holding them back and what can the executive do to change this?

- **Excuses**: are people using rules and procedures, written or unwritten, as an excuse to avoid the hard work of making change? Are they rationalising fears, needs or personal interests and making up arguments to protect the status quo?

If rules and procedures are real obstacles to innovation and serve no other purpose than perpetuating their own existence, there is a case for eliminating them. But if the case is just a little bit more complex, and the pros and cons of rules and procedures are slightly more nuanced, it is more helpful to look at the broader picture and consider the situation in light of the values in which the bureaucratic organisation is rooted. Cutting rules left and right may actually do more harm than good and does not address the real issue. Innovation is a delicate art that deserves careful attention, strong support and perseverance. Fortunately, public organisations and their leaders are increasingly motivated and dedicated to making the practice of innovation a permanent component of their leadership strategies. Based on what is known about rules and procedures on the one hand, and drivers of innovation on the other, it seems that a positive opportunity-oriented approach, focused on building capacity to solve social problems, is more promising than a negative obstacle-oriented approach, focused on rules and procedures.

This diagnostic, opportunity-oriented approach needs to be accompanied by a more rigorous research agenda that addresses the gaping gap between what we really know about rules as impediments to innovation, and the general vituperations about bureaucracy that are so often heard and uncritically repeated in practice as well as in academic debate. Based on the research done for this chapter, three interesting avenues for further research include:

- **Empirical research on phantom regulation**. What happens after rules get cut? Do civil servants indeed become more innovative? As a result of the many initiatives identified and documented by the OECD to improve regulation in government, there are now many opportunities to do in-depth studies on the impacts of internal regulatory reform, as well as comparative case studies.

- **Controlled experiments on the effectiveness of various interventions and their impact on organisational behaviour**. If a government can be found that is willing to experiment with the level of structure imposed on civil servants, it would be very interesting to do a randomised controlled experiment among a population of similar government entities (municipalities or procurement departments, for example), where the treatment group works with a new set of rules and procedures (reduced or alternative) and a control group is monitored in parallel. Such a trial could test the hypothesis that there is a causal relation between the level of rules and procedures and the outcome variable – more initiative, or sustained efforts to innovate.

- **Comparative case studies of the innovation delivery model**. Recently, a growing number of cities have adopted the innovation delivery team model, promoted and facilitated by Bloomberg Philanthropies. This provides researchers with an opportunity to do systematic comparative case studies on the conditions under which this particular response to inert government bureaucracies is most likely to be successful.

- **Develop more in-depth research and provide practical advice on how to use and manage discretion to achieve public sector innovation.** This could lead to investigating the value of developing performance frameworks that allow civil servants to focus on outcomes and to manage risks. It would also develop better knowledge about what skills are needed to take decisions in a context of uncertainty.

It has taken almost the entire 20th century to construct robust, reliable and replicable models of bureaucratic organisation, to celebrate their merits and understand their limits. Government innovators and scholars around the world are now in the process of constructing and identifying models that address the undesirable outcomes associated with bureaucracy, while preserving and upholding its most important underlying values.

Notes

1   This chapter is based on a paper prepared for the OECD by Jorrit de Jong, Harvard Kennedy School of Government, United States

2   The OECD (2015b) defines innovation as a new way in which a public sector organisation operates to meet its mandate. It must aim to improve areas such as efficiency, effectiveness, quality, or user satisfaction. The key points in this definition are that innovation is approached 1) as a verb rather than a noun – it cares about the process of introducing new ideas; 2) as the application of concepts rather than the invention – it concentrates on novelty in a particular context; and 3) as a means to an end – it is about ideas that result in improvements, thus producing public value, not innovation for innovation's sake.

3   Excellent research support on the literature and practice review was provided by B.J. van Hiele.

4   According to Schultz (2004), red tape refers to "bureaucratic procedures that are seen as unnecessary, duplicative, or wasteful, thus contributing to delays and creating a sense of frustration". Barry Bozeman defines it as: "Rules, regulations and procedures that remain in force and entail a compliance burden but do not advance the legitimate purposes the rules were intended to serve." (2000: p.12)

5   While innovation as a term and as a phenomenon has built a positive reputation for itself, bureaucracy seems to have built a negative one. The two are often contrasted and even juxtaposed. Steve Kelman (2005) writes: "In popular discourse, bureaucracy has come to be a vituperation, usually referring to people and organizations devoted more to red tape, 'going by the book,' and pencil pushing than to achieving results". A more nuanced take on the issue would be to acknowledge that bureaucracy, as a form of organisation and a dominant paradigm for governmental action, has both merits and limits.

6   See recommendations arising from the Slovak Presidency seminar "Unleashing the power of innovation in the single market", 4 October 2016, Brussels, http://www.digitaleurope.org/Digital-Headlines/Story/newsID/536

References

Albury, D. (2005), "Fostering innovation in public services", *Public Money & Management*, Vol. 25/1, pp. 51-56.

Ammons, D.N. and W.C. Rivenbark (2008), "Gainsharing in local government", in D.N. Ammons (ed.) *Leading Performance Management in Local Government*, ICMA, Washington, DC, pp. 129-139.

ANAO (2009), *Innovation in the Public Sector: Enabling Better Performance, Driving New Directions*, Australian National Audit Office, Canberra.

Australian Government (2010), *Empowering Change: Fostering Innovation in the Australian Public Service*, Management Advisory Committee, Commonwealth of Australia, Barton, Australia, http://innovation.govspace.gov.au/barriers/.

Bason, C. (2010), *Leading Public Sector Innovation: Co-creating for a Better Society*, The Policy Press, Bristol.

Black, J., M. Lodge and M. Thatcher (2005), *Regulatory Innovation: A Comparative Analysis*, Edward Elgar, Cheltenham.

Blind, K. (2011), "The influence of regulations on innovation: A quantitative assessment for OECD countries", *Research Policy*, Vol. 41/2, pp. 391-400.

Bloom, P.N. and J.G. Dees (2008), "Cultivate your ecosystem", *Stanford Social Innovation Review*, Vol. 6/1.

Bloomberg Philanthropies (2014), *Transform Your City Through Innovation. The Innovation Delivery Model For Making it Happen*, Bloomberg Philanthropies.

Borins, S. (2014), *The Persistence of Innovation in Government*, Brookings Institution Press, Washington, DC.

Borins, S. (2002), "Leadership and innovation in the public sector", *Leadership & Organization Development Journal*, Vol. 23/8, pp. 467-476.

Borins, S. (2001), "Encouraging innovation in the public sector", *Journal of Intellectual Capital*, Vol. 2/3, pp. 310-319.

Carstensen, H.V. and C. Bason (2012), "Powering collaborative policy innovation: Can innovation labs help?", *The Public Sector Innovation Journal*, Vol.17/1.

Cels, S., J. de Jong and F. Nauta (2012), *Agents of Change: Strategies and Tactics for Social Innovation*, Brookings Institution Press, Washington, DC.

Chetty, R., A. Looney and K. Kroft (2009), "Salience and taxation: Theory and evidence", *American Economic Review*, Vol. 99/4, pp. 1145-1177.

Crozier, M. (1964), *The Bureaucratic Phenomenon*, University of Chicago Press, Chicago.

Damanpour, F. (1996), "Bureaucracy and innovation revisited: Effects of contingency factors, industrial sectors, and innovation characteristics", *Journal of High Technology Management Research*, Vol. 7/2, pp. 149-173.

DCLG (2006), *The Free Communes Experiments: Lessons for Policy in England*, Department for Communities and Local Government, London.

de Jong, J. (2014), *Dealing with Dysfunction: Innovative Problem Solving in the Public Sector*, Brookings Institution Press, Washington, DC.

de Jong, J. and A. Zuurmond (2010a), *De Professionele Professional. De Andere Kant van het Debat Over Ruimte voor Professionals*, Ministerie van Binnenlandse Zaken en Koninkrijksrelaties, Den Haag.

de Jong, J. and A. Zuurmond (2010b), *Een Aardig Begin. De Aanpak van Overbodige Bureaucratie in Nederland (2003-2010)*, Ministerie van Binnenlandse Zaken en Koninkrijksrelaties, Den Haag.

De Vries, H.A., V.J.J.M. Bekkers and L.G. Tummers (2014), "Innovations in the public sector: A systematic review and future research agenda", Public Administration, Vol. 94/1, pp. 146-166, www.lipse.org/upload/publications/VRIES_et_al-2015-Public_Administration%20(1).pdf

Department for Education (2012), "Power to innovate", Department for Education website, http://webarchive.nationalarchives.gov.uk/20130903192301/http://education.gov.uk/schools/leadership/schoolperformance/b0014624/power-to-innovate.

Department for Education (2011), *Powers to Facilitate Innovation. Annual Report for the Academic Year Ending 31 July 2010*, Department for Education, London, http://webarchive.nationalarchives.gov.uk/20130903192301/http://media.education.gov.uk/assets/files/pdf/p/power%20to%20innovate%20%20%20annual%20report%202009%2010.pdf.

DiIulio, J.J. (1994), *Deregulating the Public Service: Can Government Be Improved?*, Brookings Institution Press, Washington, DC.

Dougherty, D. and S.M. Corse (1995), "When it comes to product innovation, what is so bad about bureaucracy?", *Journal of High Technology Management Research*, Vol. 6/1, pp. 55-76.

du Gay, P. (2005), "The values of bureaucracy: An introduction", in P. du Gay (ed.) *The Values of Bureaucracy*, Oxford University Press, Oxford, pp. 1-13.

Dworkin, R. (1977), *Taking Rights Seriously*, Harvard University Press, Cambridge, MA.

Eggers, W.D. and S.K. Singh (2009), *The Public Innovator's Playbook: Nurturing Bold Ideas in Government*, Deloitte Research.

EPSA (2014), European Public Service Award website, http://www.epsa2013.eu/

Etzioni-Halevy, E. (1985), *Bureaucracy and Democracy: A Political Dilemma*, Routledge and Kegan Paul, London.

European Commission (2013), *Powering European Public Sector Innovation: Towards A New Architecture*, Report of the Expert Group on Public Sector Innovation, European Commission, Brussels.

FCA (2017), "Regulatory sandbox – Cohort one", Financial Conduct Authority website, www.fca.org.uk/firms/project-innovate-innovation-hub/regulatory-sandbox#cohort1.

Hartley, J. (2005), "Innovation in governance and public services: Past and present", *Public Money & Management*, Vol. 25/1, pp. 27-34.

Huber, C. and I. Munro (2013), "'Moral distance' in organizations: An inquiry into ethical violence in the works of Kafka", *Journal of Business Ethics*, Vol. 124/2, www.researchgate.net/publication/257942365_Moral_Distance_in_Organizations_An_Inquiry_into_Ethical_Violence_in_the_Works_of_Kafka.

Gallup Organization (2011), *Innobarometer 2010. Analytical Report: Innovation in Public Administration*, Flash Eurobarometer, European Commission.

Georges, G., T. Glynn-Burke and A. McGrath (2013), *Improving the Local Landscape for Innovation*, Ash Center Occasional Papers Series, Harvard Kennedy School, Cambridge, MA.

Gerth, H.H. and C. Wright Mills (1958), *Essays in Sociology*, Oxford University Press

Johns, C.M., P.L. O'Reilly and G.J. Inwood (2006), "Intergovernmental innovation and the administrative state in Canada", *Governance*, Vol. 19/4, pp. 627-649.

Kaufman, Herbert (1977), *Red Tape: Its Origins, Uses, and Abuses*, Brookings Institution Press, Washington, DC.

Kelman, S. (2005), *Unleashing Change. A Study of Organizational Renewal in Government*, Brookings Institution Press, Washington, DC.

Kruiter, A.J., C. Hijzen, J. de Jong and J. van Niel (2008), *De Rotonde van Hamed: Maatwerk voor Mensen met Meerdere Problemen*, Nicis Institute, Den Haag.

Kruiter, A.J. and J. de Jong (2008), "Providing services to the marginalized: Anatomy of an access paradox", in J. de Jong and G. Rizvi (eds.) *The State of Access: Success and Failure of Democracies to Create Equal Opportunities*, Brookings Institution Press, Washington, DC.

Larrick, R.P. and J.B. Soll (2008), "The MPG illusion", *Science*, Vol. 320/5883, pp. 1593-1594.

Lipsky, M. (2010), *Street Level Bureaucracy: Dilemmas of the Individual in Public Service*, Russel Sage Foundation

Lunn, P. (2014), *Regulatory Policy and Behavioural Economics*, OECD Publishing, Paris, http://dx.doi.org/10.1787/9789264207851-en.

Mergel, I. and K.C. Desouza (2013), "Implementing open innovation in the public sector: The case of challenge.gov", *Public Administration Review*, Vol. 73/6, pp. 882-890.

Moore, M. and J. Hartley (2008), "Innovations in governance", *Public Management Review*, Vol. 10/1, pp. 3-20.

NAO (2009), "Reducing bureaucracy for public service frontline staff", Briefing for the House of Commons regulatory reform committee, National Audit Office, www.nao.org.uk/wp-content/uploads/2012/10/0910_reducing_bureaucracy.pdf .

Nauta, F. and P. Kasbergen (2009), *OECD Literature Review: Public Sector Innovation*, Hogeschool van Arnhem en Nijmegen.

OECD (2017), *Behavioural Insights and Public Policy: Lessons from Around the World*, OECD Publishing, Paris, http://dx.doi.org/10.1787/9789264270480-en.

OECD (2015a), *Behavioural Insights and New Approaches to Policy Design: The Views from the Field*, Summary of an international seminar, 23 January, Paris, www.oecd .org/gov/behavioural-insights-summary-report-2015.pdf.

OECD (2015b), *The Innovation Imperative in the Public Sector: Setting An Agenda for Action*, OECD Publishing, Paris, http://dx.doi.org/10.1787/9789264236561-en.

OECD (2015c), *Regulatory Policy Outlook 2015,* OECD Publishing, Paris, http://dx. doi.org/10.1787/9789264238770-en

OECD (2013), "Innovation for better public services", GOV/PGC(2013)3/REV1, 48th session of the Public Governance Committee 12-13 November, Paris.

OECD (2011), "Regulation inside government in Mexico: Policies and framework", in *Towards More Effective and Dynamic Public Management in Mexico*, OECD Publishing, Paris, http://dx.doi.org/10.1787/9789264116238-6-en.

OECD (2010), *Why is Administrative Simplification So Complicated? Looking Beyond 2010*, OECD Publishing, Paris, http://dx.doi.org/10.1787/9789264089754-en.

OECD (2008), "Regulation inside government", GOV/PGC/REG(2008)15, Working Party on Regulatory Management and Reform, 21-22 October, Paris.

Osborn, S.P. and L. Brown (2013), *Handbook of Innovation in Public Services*, Edward Elgar, Cheltenham.

Patterson, F. and M. Kerrin (2009), *Innovation for the Recovery: Enhancing Innovative Working Practices*, Chartered Management Institute, London.

Peters, B.G. (2003), "Dismantling and rebuilding the Weberian state", in J. Hayward and A. Menon (eds.), *Governing Europe,* Oxford University Press, Oxford, pp. 113-128.

Potts, J. (2009), "The innovation deficit in public services: The curious problem of too much efficiency and not enough waste and failure", *Innovation: Management, Policy & Practice*, Vol. 11/1, pp. 34-43.

Potts, J. and T. Kastelle (2010), "Public sector innovation research: What's next?", *Innovation: Management Policy & Practice*, Vol. 12/2, pp. 122-137.

Rivera León, L, L. Roman and P. Simmonds (2012), *Trends and Challenges in Public Sector Innovation in Europe*, DG Enterprise, European Commission, Brussels.

Rosenblatt, M. (2011), "The use of innovation awards in the public sector: Individual and organizational perspectives", *Innovation: Management, Policy & Practice*, Vol.13/2, pp. 207-219.

Schultz, D. (2004) *Encyclopedia of Public Administration and Public Policy*, Facts on File, New York.

Shah, S and K. Costa (2013), *Social Finance: A Primer. Understanding Innovation Funds, Impact Bonds, and Impact Investing*, Center for American Progress, www.americanprogress.org/issues/economy/report/2013/11/05/78792/social-finance-a-primer/.

Sørensen, E. and J. Torfing (2012), "Introduction: Collaborative innovation in the public sector", *Innovation Journal,* Vol.17/1, pp. 1-14

Sunstein, C. (2011), "Empirically informed regulation", *University of Chicago Law Review*, Vol. 78/4, pp. 1349-1429.

Styhre, A. (2007), *The Innovative Bureaucracy: Bureaucracy in an Age of Fluidity*, Routledge Taylor & Francis Group, London and New York.

Teofilovic, Nada (2002), "The reality of innovation in government", The Innovation Journal, Vol.7/3, www.innovation.cc/scholarly-style/7_3_4_teofilovic_reality-govern ment.pdf.

Thaler, R.H. and C.R. Sunstein (2008), *Nudge: Improving Decisions About Health, Wealth and Happiness*, Yale University Press.

Vigoda-Gadot, E. et al. (2008), "Public sector innovation for Europe. A multinational eight-country exploration of citizens' perspectives", *Public Administration*, Vol. 86/2, pp. 307-329.

Walker, R.M. (2014), "Internal and external antecedents of process innovation: A review and extension", *Public Management Review,* Vol. 16/1, pp. 21-44.

Walker, R.M. (2008), "An empirical evaluation of innovation types and organizational and environmental characteristics: Towards a configuration framework", *Journal of Public Administration Research and Theory*, Vol.18/4, pp. 591-615.

Weber, Max (1922), *Wirtschaft und Gesellschaft*, J.C.B. Mohr, Tübingen.

Annex 2.A1.

Evidence from research on rule-based barriers to innovation

There is limited evidence in the literature of the reality of regulatory and procedural obstacles to innovation. Most sources are based on a conceptual or normative premise, offering a new perspective or admonishing practitioners, but lacking an evidence-based approach. Nonetheless, some important contributions have already been made in recent decades that can be seen as solid hypotheses about the factors contributing to or inhibiting public sector innovation.[1]

The academic literature seems to be in consensus about the negative relationship between rules and procedures on one hand and innovation on the other. Most studies identify stringent internal control, rigid mechanisms and formal procedures as major barriers to innovation (Box 2.6). But the literature is rarely very specific about *how* rules and procedures concretely inhibit innovation in the public sector.

Box 2.6. What does research say about rule-based barriers to innovation

- **Administrative controls and rules can constrain innovation.** Sandford Borins' longitudinal study on award-winning government innovators found that : "The largest percentage of obstacles were internal to the bureaucracy, encompassing more than 50% of all obstacles [...] The obstacles encountered reflect the tendency of innovations to challenge occupational patterns, standard operating procedures, and power structures" (Borins, 2014: p.90).

- **Tight regulations impede innovation.** A systematic review of the academic literature from the period 1990-2013 identified a general consensus and consistent observation that tight regulation hampers innovation (De Vries et al., 2014).

- **An ecosystem is necessary for innovation.** Empirical studies show that part of that ecosystem would be administrative structures that are conducive to innovation (Bloom and Dees, 2008).

- **The rigidity of regulations acts as obstacles to innovation.** While acknowledging that regulations and procedures are in place to control inappropriate behavior, their rigidity can stand in the way of innovation by not allowing the necessary flexibility (Eggers and Singh 2009).

- **Formal rules limit the development of service innovation.** A survey with English local authorities, gathering quantitative data on their perceptions of organisation and management, showed that formalisation (regulations and procedures in the narrow sense) was regarded as limiting the development of service innovations (Walker, 2008: p. 606).

- **Rules can poses obstacles to new providers in disruptive social innovation.** A study on "innovative jurisdictions" indicates that in most cases in which disruptive social innovation is difficult, rules, requirements and administrative hurdles act as barriers to entry for new providers (Georges, Glynn-Burke and McGrath 2013: p.16).

There is also a significant amount of practice-oriented "grey literature", produced by governments and think tanks[2] on the topic of obstacles to and drivers of government innovation. The 2010 Innobarometer study[3] reported rigid regulatory requirements as the most notable barrier to public administration innovation, after a lack of sufficient human and material resources (Gallup Organization, 2011). Sixty-five percent of the respondents considered regulatory requirements as being of medium or high importance. The 2012 cross-country report Trends and Challenges in Public Sector Innovation in Europe (Rivera et al., 2012) presents anecdotal evidence for organisational structures, internal bureaucracy and lack of an innovation culture as major barriers, but it is not clear how frequently these are real obstacles and to what extent they hamper innovation.

Australia has conducted specific research on the barriers to innovation in the public sector which led to identifying internal rules and procedures among the obstacles to innovation. The 2010 report Empowering Change: Fostering Innovation in the Australian Public Service points to public servants' sense of frustration with "approval processes". These processes were considered an inherent part of the public agencies' bureaucratic organisation and were regarded as inhibitors to creativity and flexibility, which are necessary features for innovation. Another significant obstacle mentioned in the Australia reports is legislation (Australian Government, 2010). One of the examples given was of using an Internet platform as a potential service delivery option; confidentiality and privacy laws seemed to have delayed the implementation of the innovation. However, that very example appears to be a case of a value trade-off between efficiency and user-friendliness on one hand and privacy protection and data security on the other. As such, although some might have seen it as an example of internal regulation standing in the way of innovation, in reality it reflects a fundamental value conflict to be resolved.

Another interesting source of data comes from the United Kingdom, where the Chartered Management Institute conducted a large survey among managers in multiple sectors on how organisations (public, private and not-for-profit) dealt with innovation, specifically in the light of the economic recession (Patterson and Kerrin, 2009). The results were consistent across the sectors: the top three barriers to innovation across the three sectors were lack of money, time and resources. Meanwhile "internal rules and procedures" were not even among the top 12. Hierarchical structures, the number 5 barrier, and lack of autonomy in job roles, ranked at number 10, might be related issues, but the general picture painted by this study is that the major obstacles to innovation are a lack of resources and opportunities.

All of these reports are generally based on the civil servants' perceptions of the problem. Respondents have been asked to give their assessments of the link between regulation and innovation in general. In addition, the questions are not very granular, for example not probing into what kind or regulation was inhibiting innovation, how often and to what extent procedures were limiting it. What they measure is the perception of rules as obstacles in general. What is not clear is to what extent the respondents' perception of the problem is consistent with reality: they may see more regulation or less discretionary space than there really is. On the other hand, if they perceive the regulations and procedures to be real obstacles, then effectively they become obstacles, in the sense that they actually shape civil servant behaviour. The perception becomes a reality and subsequently a self-fulfilling prophecy.

Another aspect that often remains vague is at what phase of the innovation life-cycle regulations and procedures are inhibitive and in what conditions they could instead drive innovation. Black et al. 2005 pointed out a misalignment between conditions for innovation needed by initiators (decentralisation and flexibility) versus those needed by adopters (centralisation and formalisation). The Innobarometer research indicates that the single most important driver of innovation was the introduction of new laws and regulations that led to organisations having new responsibilities and/or new methods of service provision. Bason (2010) goes even further and suggests that governments may actually want to create procedures to drive innovation. In many public sector organisations there are few or no formal processes for conducting the innovation process. He implies that procedures could also play a positive role in innovation processes by creating some sense of safety for innovators.

In conclusion, neither the evidence from the academic literature nor the data from the practice literature on public sector innovation convincingly support the claim that rules and procedures in the strict sense pose a major or frequent obstacle to innovation. In order to get a more precise idea of what it is about the regulations and procedures that inhibits innovators, more precise concepts and characterisations need to be used and more systematic and in-depth research needs to be done. It would be interesting to learn in specific cases, or from specific groups of innovators, how exactly rules and regulations were an obstacle, and then go into further detail. Was it the law, and if so which one? Was it a regulation imposed by the executive branch, and if so which one? Was it the procedure, and which aspect of it made it an obstacle? Is it the clarity of the law, the length of the process, the paperwork? These are questions that need to be asked to determine which aspect is actually the problem.

To draw the general conclusion that rules and regulations in the narrow sense have a direct negative effect on innovation in the public sector would be too drastic and not do justice to the complexity of the work of innovation. However, consistent concerns expressed in surveys show the enduring *perception* of regulation and procedures as a barrier to public sector innovation. These concerns may very well be legitimate and merit further research.

Notes

1   This may change, now that innovation as a continuous and sometimes institutionalised practice has become more prevalent. If more governments innovate in more areas, more frequently, social scientists have more opportunities to do comparative, longitudinal and large N studies. More systematic quantitative and qualitative research will yield more empirical evidence of relationships between the variables – like drivers and obstacles – than identified by previous research. As of yet, we do not have a corroborated body of knowledge.

2   In the private sector literature there is more research – and advice – on how to structure the innovation process. See for example the work by Utterback (1996), Tushman and O'Reilly (2002), and Govindarajan and Trimble (2005). Much attention is paid to how innovating affects existing business processes and how existing business processes react to innovation.

3   The Innobarometer study conducted by Gallup for the European Commission covered data from 27 member states of the European Union, Norway and Switzerland for the European Commission (Gallup Organization 2011). A telephone survey of 4 000 public organisations aimed to gain insight into the innovation strategies are used throughout the EU. Question 18 of the survey asked: "Since January 2008, how important were the following factors in preventing or delaying your organization's efforts to develop or introduce new or significantly improved services, communication methods, processes or organizational methods?"

Chapter 3.

Incentivising staff and building capacity for innovation

Public employees are central to all stages of public sector innovation, and how they are managed can be fundamental to enabling organisations to innovate. This chapter links theory and practice to explore how human resource management (HRM) can affect organisations' capacity to innovate. Starting from the premise that employees need ability, motivation and opportunity (AMO) in order to perform, it explores what this means for innovation for each of these aspects. The chapter then considers the kinds of HRM practices which might affect employees' AMO to innovate. Case studies from a number of OECD countries offer examples of awards and recognition programmes, learning in networks, schemes to increase employees' mobility across sectors, and holistic HRM approaches to innovation. It then considers the implications for HRM approaches to leadership, work organisation, recruitment and selection, performance management, training and development, and compensation, which together may start to form the basis of a system of HRM for innovation. Finally, it considers some of the tensions that may arise as such a system is put in place and concludes with questions for further investigation.

Introduction

People are at the core of public sector innovation. Ideas for new services and business activities are sparked in the minds of civil servants, political leaders, service users and members of the broader community, and are developed and brought to scale through the dedication of many various professionals and stakeholders at different stages of the process. Civil servants and public employees are central to every stage, and therefore how they are managed can be fundamental to enabling organisations to innovate.

The OECD's definition of public sector innovation (OECD, 2015) positions the workforce as central not only to implementing reforms, but to bringing forward innovative ideas and working them through every stage of the process. Research on public sector innovation suggests ideas are often initiated by middle managers or frontline staff (Borins, 2014), leading some experts to reflect that, "Increasingly, innovation is as much a 'bottom-up' and 'sideways-in' process as a 'top-down' process" (Hartley, 2006).

Eurofound (2012) suggests that employee-driven innovation "depends strongly on employees contributing their knowledge, expertise, creativity and commitment to the process". The management challenge is to harness the creative problem-solving potential of the workforce to enable more employee-driven innovation. Managers and leaders can establish the conditions needed to support employees to innovate, champion and lead employee-driven innovations, and rally the resources required to support the innovation process.

Academic research suggests that human resource management (HRM) practices can affect the capacity of organisations to innovate. The factors proven to have an impact in certain circumstances include communication networks; rewards and incentive structures; managerial and leadership styles; organisational practices related to the attraction, selection, training and compensation of employees; and job design factors such as the use of teams and delegation of decision rights (Laursen and Foss, 2013). However, most authors suggest that the underlying causal mechanisms are not well understood.

Figure 3.1 maps examples collected from OECD countries of ways HRM can support public sector innovation onto the innovation lifecycle. Good two-way communication across organisational levels may help to identify problems which are apparent on the front line but may not be clearly visible to those at the top. Ideas contests and other engagement forums can be used to source ideas for improvement from employees. Staff skills needed for research and prototyping can be strengthened and deployed to develop proposals. Successful implementation then requires careful change management, making use of networks and mobility programmes, while innovation awards can help to disseminate experience and share lessons learned to inspire others. Furthermore, human resources (HR) tools are essential to create the conditions needed for any innovation to begin at all – by building a capable workforce and establishing an organisational culture that supports innovators at all levels of an organisation.

Figure 3.1. How human resource management can support the innovation lifecycle

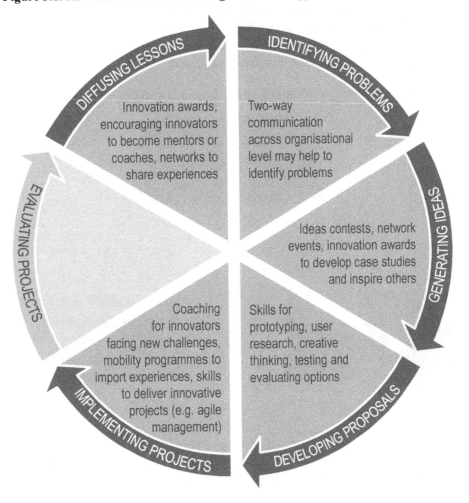

This chapter links a number of established theories of HRM and organisational performance with cases gathered from HRM specialists in OECD member countries. These examples help to illustrate how OECD countries are organising their public workforces to better address their innovation challenges. This chapter does not empirically test the impact of these practices. Only time will tell if they are maintained and deemed to be successful or not.

The chapter starts by presenting and discussing the research framework used, organising its discussion of the literature around three themes, motivation and opportunity for innovation. This is followed by a brief description of the cases collected, categorised into competitions and awards, learning in networks, mobility programmes, and holistic and integrated HRM strategies. The chapter then returns to the framework to consider the challenges each of the HRM practices might encounter and suggests paths for future work in this area.

The research model: Human resource management practices for innovation

Public organisations' workforces are central to public sector innovation and so one of the goals of public HRM should be to support employees to contribute to innovation. It is a well-established theory of employee performance that employees require the ability, motivation and opportunity (AMO) to do their jobs well (Boxall and Purcell, 2011; Figure 3.2). Therefore increasing the innovative capacity of the workforce requires addressing employees' ability and their motivation to innovate, and giving them the opportunity to put these abilities and motivation to work.

Figure 3.2. The ability, motivation and opportunity (AMO) model of performance

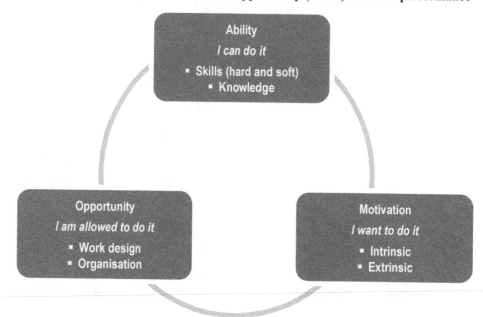

Ability can be defined in terms of skills and knowledge. The skills and knowledge needed to innovate will depend on the sector and the type of innovation desired. Abilities are held by individuals but need to be considered and balanced at the team and organisation level, for example through strategic workforce planning and competency management.

Motivation can be defined as a willingness or desire to do a good job. Motivation can be deeply personal, based on one's beliefs and values, and can also be highly relational, influenced by an employees' relationship with their peers, managers, organisational leadership and their perception of their organisation.

Ensuring that capable and motivated employees have the opportunities to innovate is a matter of organisational development. Factors influencing this variable include the design of teams and work units, the flexibility of working arrangements, the availability of resources and time, freedom and autonomy, regulatory context, and job descriptions and role clarity.

The following sections explore these factors in more detail.

Ability to innovate

As mentioned above, abilities are generally thought of in terms of skills and knowledge. Knowledge can be explicit or tacit while skills can be certified or acquired informally. Governments today are increasingly expanding their concept of ability to include behaviour within broader competency frameworks that better identify the range of abilities a person should possess to excel not only in their current post, but in the wider organisation and throughout the course of their career (OECD, 2011a).

In a narrow sense, abilities affect an employee's performance in the post they occupy. However, innovation may require taking a broader view, to include a wider range of abilities that the individual brings to work every day, including some that may not be required to fulfil their immediate position but which could benefit the organisation. Building a more innovative workforce may require thinking beyond employees' individual job descriptions to harness all of the abilities they bring to their workplace in a constructive and developmental way.

Innovation is not a skill or ability in itself, but the combination of a variety of elements that come together at the right place and time. The OECD's work on skills in the labour force identifies three types of abilities needed for innovation (2011b):

- **Subject specific**: the technical skills and knowledge associated with the subject area being innovated – computer programming skills for developing software innovations, medical knowledge to innovate in the health sector. In a public sector context, this might include policy analysis skills in a specific field (such as tax policy, housing policy or educational policy), financial analysis, or big data analytics.

- **Thinking and creativity**: the ability to ask the right questions, to identify the gaps and develop creative solutions and approaches to help fill these gaps. This includes the ability to look across seemingly disparate data, cases, problems and processes to identify common threads and connect the dots. Imagination and curiosity are drivers. These are more difficult to assess using traditional selection and assessment methods, and are not easily developed in traditional classroom-based learning environments.

- **Behavioural and social**: recognising that innovation is a team sport places a high level of significance on teams' ability to work in partnerships, communicate, negotiate, network and collaborate within and across organisational boundaries. Leadership is required to draw out the right skills in the team and a level of confidence is needed to take the kinds of risks that result in learning and growth.

Dyer, Gregersen and Christensen (2011) identify five skills which contribute to innovation. The most fundamental, "associative thinking", describes how one synthesises new information and makes connections across concepts. "Put simply, innovative thinkers connect fields, problems, or ideas that others find unrelated" (Dyer et al., 2011). The rest of the skills support associative thinking. They are: questioning (even more than answering), observing (implies being close to those you serve and the world around the service), networking (to find and test ideas among people with "radically" different views), and experimenting (holding convictions at bay and testing hypotheses). Furthermore, Dyer and colleagues suggest that these skills can be learnt and developed.

HRM can support the acquisition and development of innovation skills into an organisation in two ways. First, it can ensure the organisation hires employees with the right profile to support innovation. This means opening positions to external sources of recruitment; selecting people based on their "polyvalent" skills and their fit with the organisational culture and values, and providing employment security. Second, organisations can develop innovation skills within existing teams, and long-term orientation and the participation of employees in the design of training activities can help build innovation capacity (Jiménez-Jiménez and Sanz-Valle, 2008).

In early 2016 the OECD started work on identifying the skills that support and enable public sector innovation. In May 2016, an initial mapping was presented at a joint session of the Working Party on Public Employment and Management and the National Contact Points for the OECD's Observatory of Public Sector Innovation. The OECD is using stakeholder feedback and further research to refine the model. Box 3.1 outlines its second iteration.

Box 3.1. A preliminary model of skills for innovation in the public sector

The OECD's initial mapping, developed in collaboration with Nesta, was based on research with innovators in government and comprised over 40 separate skills and competencies for public sector innovation. To provide a more tangible and usable product for officials, the OECD has used stakeholder feedback and further research to develop a second iteration based on a six core skills areas. To increase levels of innovation in the public sector, it is important not just to hire in specialists with strong capability in these skills, but also ensure that all officials have a basic awareness in each skill area.

- **iteration**: incrementally and experimentally developing policies, products and services

- **data literacy**: ensuring decisions are data-driven and that data isn't an afterthought

- **user centred**: public services should be focused on solving and servicing user needs

- **curiosity**: seeking out and trying new ideas or ways of working

- **storytelling**: explaining change in a way that builds support

- **insurgency**: challenging the status quo and working with unusual partners.

Motivation to innovate

While ability determines what the workforce is capable of doing, motivation determines what the workforce will try to do when given the chance. In some ways motivation can make up for lack of skill as highly motivated people will be more likely to transfer skills from other domains, or invest more effort in acquiring the necessary skills (Amabile, 1997).

Motivation can be thought of in individual terms, as an element of one's personality. It is also highly relational – people can be motivated to do things because they are inspired by others. Motivation forms the basis for goal-directed action – or, more precisely, the willingness to behave in a certain way – and is therefore a state that can be influenced. Motivation includes influencing the thoughts and emotions that form the basis for a willingness to behave in a certain way, for a specific period and with a certain intensity in order to achieve a specific goal.

In this sense, work motivation can be influenced by the work environment, task design, organisational culture and management. While some individuals may arrive at a job with a higher degree of intrinsic motivation than others, this motivation can be nurtured or smothered by their organisational surroundings (for an overview see Mumford, 2000).

Motivation is a key input to a wide range of performance outcomes at the personal and organisational level. Even if employees have all the abilities required to perform, they will only apply these abilities if it is valued by the organisation. Hence, organisations must offer the right incentives to motivate the right behaviour (Boxall and Purcell, 2011).

Motivation is closely linked to the concept of employee engagement. Since motivation constitutes at first only a willingness to act, the question arises of when the motivated person actually goes on to act in order to achieve goals. An engaged employee will gear his/her behaviour towards achieving goals as effectively as possible. Motivation and decision making are therefore two processes that underlie engagement. Multiple studies have found that engagement is significantly correlated to improved organisational outcomes, including performance and innovation (Box 3.2). For more detailed analysis on employee engagement see *Engaging Public Employees for a High-Performing Civil Service* (OECD, 2016).

Box 3.2. Employee engagement and innovation

Engagement shows a clear, significant correlation with performance and customer satisfaction, according to research primarily conducted in the private sector (see Bakker, 2011; MacLeod and Clarke, 2011).

A representative study of 314 companies on behalf of the German Federal Ministry of Labour showed a clear relationship between organisational culture, quality of work, employee engagement and business success. The study presented evidence of a significant relationship between employee engagement and profit and levels of sickness absence of the companies. The positive correlation between engagement and performance is due to people's positive and optimistic attitude, which boosts creativity and solution orientation; good health, which allows the person to mobilise all of their energy; the active seeking of feedback and support; and the positive infection and inspiration of others in their environment (Bakker et al., 2014).

A United Kingdom initiative, Engage for Success (Rayton et al., 2012), cites the following evidence linking engagement to profit, customer satisfaction, productivity and innovation:

- **Innovation**: data and research correlate high engagement scores with innovation. Engaged employees show more personal initiative and innovative work behavior. They tend to be more involved and socially connected to their work, which allows more opportunity to contribute to improvement and innovation. Gallup data indicate that 59% of engaged employees said that their job brings out their most creative ideas, against only 3% of disengaged employees.

- **Customer satisfaction**: a range of private studies prove a strong link between engaged front-line customer-facing staff and customer indicators such as satisfaction, loyalty and advocacy (customers who actively promote a company to their contacts). The link between engagement and client impact is also found in the public sector. For example, one study shows that 78% of highly engaged public sector employees say they are able to make an impact on public service delivery, while only 29% of disengaged employees feel the same way. Data from the UK National Health Service suggest higher employee engagement is correlated with more patient satisfaction, and even lower patient mortality.

- **Productivity**: research indicates strong links between employee engagement and behavior associated with a more productive workforce. Engaged employees perform their tasks better, more efficiently and with fewer errors. Aside from working productively, engagement is also highly correlated with higher employee retention and well-being. Research by some private consultancy firms suggests that disengaged employees can be up to four times more likely to leave an organisation. Research also shows that engaged employees show higher levels of well-being all around, experience less work-related stress, and are less often absent.

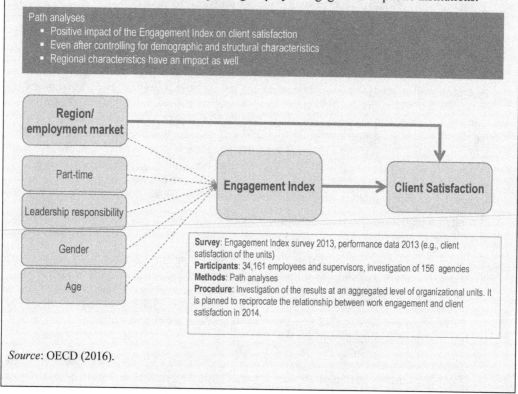

Box 3.2. **Employee engagement and innovation** *(cont.)*

- **Profit**: private consultancy firms have looked at large samples of surveyed employees, often in multiple countries and consistently show that companies that score within the highest quartile for employee engagement perform far better on a range of financial indicators including total net income, one-year operating margins, revenue growth, and shareholder value.

The OECD's 2016 report *"Engaging Public Employees for a High-Performing Civil Service"* looks at the role of employee engagement in government performance and includes case studies and good practices for improving employee engagement in public institutions.

Path analyses
- Positive impact of the Engagement Index on client satisfaction
- Even after controlling for demographic and structural characteristics
- Regional characteristics have an impact as well

Region/employment market

Part-time

Leadership responsibility

Gender

Age

Engagement Index

Client Satisfaction

Survey: Engagement Index survey 2013, performance data 2013 (e.g., client satisfaction of the units)
Participants: 34,161 employees and supervisors, investigation of 156 agencies
Methods: Path analyses
Procedure: Investigation of the results at an aggregated level of organizational units. It is planned to reciprocate the relationship between work engagement and client satisfaction in 2014.

Source: OECD (2016).

Motivated and engaged employees are considered to be better at their jobs: they put in more effort to achieve outcomes, and are willing to push for positive change in their workplaces by committing extra energy above and beyond the minimum required by their job descriptions.

Motivation is also considered to be deeply personal – what motivates one person may discourage another, and this adds to its complexity. At the most basic level, people are motivated to do things they perceive will produce a beneficial outcome. At the individual level, it is common to distinguish between intrinsic and extrinsic motivation. With intrinsic motivation, the reward comes from the activity itself. Frey and Osterloh (2002) identify three kinds of intrinsic motivation. The first kind is when people do an activity because it brings them pleasure. In the second, it is the completion of the activity that brings pleasure, such as crossing the finish line of a marathon or meeting an important deadline. The third kind of motivation is when people act to comply with internally held standards. This last category includes values-based standards, such as community service, commitment to family and ethical fairness. With extrinsic motivation, people act because of a reward that is separate from the act itself. The most common example is financial payment for services rendered.

Research often concludes that intrinsic motivation is much more useful for motivating creativity and innovation than extrinsic motivation. In fact, some authors (Amabile, 1997; Fernandez and Moldogaziev, 2012) suggest that extrinsic motivation, especially in the form of rewards for short-term performance, can result in a narrower view of the task and can cause employees to avoid innovative ways of doing things (see Box 3.3).

Box 3.3. Amabile's componential theory of creativity

The componential theory of creativity, and the research that underlies it, suggest a number of management implications for the motivation for creativity in business and the effect of the work environment on that motivation:

- Because human motivation is so complex and so important, the successful management of creativity for the next century must include management education about the types of motivation, their sources, their effects on performance and their susceptibility to various work environment influences.

- We cannot hope to create a highly and appropriately creative workforce simply by "loading up" the intrinsic and the extrinsic motivators in the work environment, without paying attention to the type of extrinsic motivators and the context in which they are presented.

- Because a positive sense of challenge in the work is one of the most important predictors of creativity, it is imperative to match people to work that uses their skills, stretches their skills and is clearly valued by the organisation. As much as possible, all work should be designed to maximise its intrinsically motivating aspects.

- Organisations must demonstrate a strong orientation toward innovation, which is clearly communicated and enacted, from the highest levels of management, throughout the organisation.

- Organisations should orient themselves toward the generation, communication, careful consideration, and development of new ideas. This includes fair, constructive judgment of ideas, non-controlling reward and recognition for creative work, mechanisms for developing new ideas, and an active flow of ideas. It excludes turf battles, conservatism and excessively negative criticism of new ideas.

- Work groups should consist of diversely skilled individuals with a shared intrinsic motivation for their work and a willingness to both share and constructively criticise each other's ideas. These groups should be led by supervisors who clearly set overall goals for projects, but allow operational autonomy in achieving those goals. Performance feedback should be highly informational and work focused.

- People should be given at least adequate resources to carry out their work, and at least minimally sufficient time to consider alternative approaches.

Source: Amabile (1997).

According to Foss et al. (2009), intrinsic motivation relates positively to the following three elements, each with their own work design considerations:

1. The perceived meaningfulness of work, which relates to the concept of **task identity** – the degree to which an employee is empowered to undertake a package

of work from beginning to end. An employee who is responsible for the end-to-end design and delivery of a project is more likely to be motivated than one who simply contributes to one small phase.

2. Level of responsibility taken for work outcomes, which relates to the concept of **autonomy** – whether the employee is empowered to decide when and how to carry out the tasks to achieve agreed-upon outcomes. The more autonomy they have, the more personal responsibility employees will take for the outcomes and the more motivated they will be to complete the job well.

3. The results of work efforts, which relates to the concept of **feedback** – how the employee receives direct and clear performance-relevant information as the task is carried out. This can be both inherent to the job, as in the case of teachers seeing their students improve, or it could be external, coming from managers or the stakeholder community.

Extrinsic motivation does not necessarily need to limit intrinsic motivation. Some forms of extrinsic motivation are shown to increase intrinsic motivation and creativity: reward and recognition for creative ideas, well-defined project goals, and frequent, constructive feedback.

Some have suggested that those who decide to join the government workforce often do so because they are intrinsically motivated to serve their countries and improve their communities (Perry, Hondeghem and Wise, 2008). This public service motivation is driven by a sense of altruism and prosocial behaviour. Research, although limited, generally supports the idea that people with high levels of public service motivation seek jobs in public organisations. The concept of public service motivation suggests that not all private sector motivational practices may have the same relevance in public sector institutions.

Opportunity to innovate

Even when a workforce is made up of highly capable and motivated individuals, they may not effectively and efficiently achieve their goals if they have no opportunity to do so. Considering opportunity shifts the focus away from the individual and towards the organisation of work and the structures that organisations use to align resources with objectives.

First, employees need to be appropriately matched to a job that reflects their skills and passions, and to stretch their abilities to provide a level of challenge requiring creativity. This requires a good knowledge about employees and their assignments.

One of the job characteristics most consistently attributed to innovation is autonomy (Shalley and Gilson, 2004). Employees need a level of freedom in the way they plan their time and approach their tasks to feel as if they have the opportunity to address their tasks creatively. Clear goals and expectations can frame this autonomy to provide some structure which can benefit both managers (to regulate action), and employees (to structure their time and work).

Resources are essential for innovation. Having enough time is critical, as experimentation and creative design generally take longer than using existing processes as they usually require thinking up alternatives, testing them, learning and course correction. However, managers have to strike a balance: too many resources can also lower creativity by making individuals too comfortable (Shalley and Gilson, 2004).

People are essential to innovation and the way people are organised into teams and connect through networks seems to be a significant factor in developing innovative capacity within the workforce. Teams should be mutually supportive, but with a diversity of perspectives and backgrounds. Diversity can lead to more friction and conflict, which, if managed constructively, can lead to more creative outcomes. Managing diversity to build a more inclusive and innovation-oriented culture is a growing challenge among OECD countries and is being addressed in parallel OECD research.

People also need a supportive organisation to inspire learning. Learning organisations are often invoked in the context of organisational design, providing opportunities for employees to learn and an organisational culture that motivates learning-oriented behaviour. HRM practices associated with learning organisations include support for training, payment for skills, transparent career paths, supportive management and opportunities for informal learning. The OECD (2010) defines learning organisations as those characterised by high levels of autonomy in work combined with high levels of learning, problem solving and task complexity. This study correlates innovative organisations with employee discretion in solving complex problems. See also discussions in chapter 7 on data information and knowledge management supporting innovation.

The same OECD report summarises two further ways that the organisation of work can provide opportunities to innovate. First, work can be organised to stimulate interaction among diverse actors, within and across organisation boundaries. Second, organisations can delegate responsibility for solving problems to a wide range of employees, thereby building competence at lower levels. See also discussion in chapter 5 on different types of organisations supporting innovation.

Supporting public sector innovation: Case studies from OECD countries

If HRM practices affect employees' ability, motivation and opportunity then it is likely that particular forms or groups of HRM activities would affect the strength and type of AMO, and the balance between the three elements. Figure 3.3 depicts the exploratory research model employed for this project. The left hand side shows the people management levers, while the right hand side shows the goal of AMO for innovation. The middle column reflects the specific types of HRM approaches that contribute to the outcomes on the right, as emerged from the cases collected. OECD countries were provided with a similar model, but the box in the middle included a number of hypothetical ideas for specific HR practices that countries might employ to stimulate innovation. Countries were asked to supply cases that they had used to increase AMO for innovation.

Figure 3.3. HRM for innovation research model

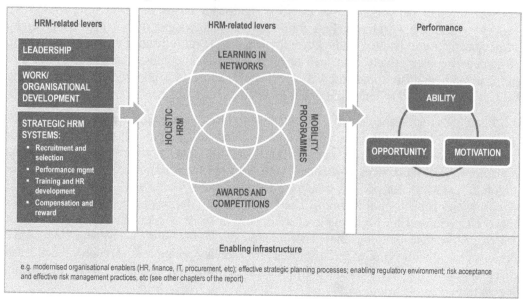

The OECD's Working Party on Public Employment and Management sent out a request to countries to volunteer cases. This resulted in 21 case submissions from 13 countries: Australia, Austria, Belgium, Canada, Finland, Germany, Israel, Korea, Poland, Spain, Sweden, Switzerland, and the United Kingdom. These cases were submitted to illustrate processes and tools in use, and do not represent all of the HRM for innovation taking place in OECD countries. Annex A3.1 provides detailed descriptions of some of the cases submitted.

The cases can be categorised in various ways. Almost half (10) of the cases involved HRM practices and programmes with a clear focus on promoting innovation in the public sector. These include, for example, innovation awards (Australia), innovation training courses/programmes (Austria), and networks developed specifically to nurture innovation in the public administration (Belgium, Finland and Spain). A subset of these cases focuses on sourcing innovative ideas from employees. These include ideas competitions (Austria), workshops with a range of public employees to build future vision of the workforce (Finland), and the use of web 2.0 tools to engage staff in leadership competency development (Canada).

The rest of the cases did not target innovation directly, but are HRM practices that are hypothesised to have a positive impact on innovation by promoting innovation-oriented behaviour. These include, for example, mobility programmes, which encourage internal and external mobility, and cross-sector assignments (Austria, Canada and Korea); training and development programmes for young employees which include the development of critical thinking and creative problem solving skills (Germany and Israel) and management approaches to better align human talent with organisational objectives (Belgium, Germany, Sweden, Switzerland and the United Kingdom).

An analysis of the cases revealed the following broad groupings: awards and recognition, learning in networks, mobility management, and HR management tools which include holistic HRM approaches and staff engagement methods. It should be noted that not all cases sit perfectly within just one of these categories. For example, awards often create networks of winners and networking often supports mobility.

However, for the sake of clarity, each of the cases will be discussed within only one category.

Awards and recognition

Innovation awards were an early tool used by some governments to motivate public sector innovation, with the first coming on line around 30 years ago. According to Sandford Borins,[1] awards for successfully implemented innovations have five objectives: 1) to reward and recognise successful innovators; 2) to stimulate more innovation in public sector organisations; 3) to make innovators aware of one another and thereby help to develop a sense of community among them; 4) to provide information for use in case studies and statistics for those studying innovation; and 5) to improve the public's perception of the public sector. Poland and Australia both provided cases of awards celebrating innovation.

Australia's **Awards for Excellence in Public Sector Management** incorporate innovation in two ways. First, innovation in the design and/or delivery of products, services and processes is one of the four criteria that all submissions are assessed against – the others are stakeholder service and satisfaction; transparent leadership, planning and governance; and people management and change management. Second, the shortlisted excellence nominations are reviewed against additional criteria for a separate innovation award. To receive the award, the nomination must 1) meet the defined threshold for innovation; 2) be linked to an organisational strategy or a response to a significant organisation issue or risk; 3) involve co-design with key stakeholders (internal or external); and 4) result in a demonstrable difference to the relevant product, process or service and its delivery.

Poland's **Contest for the Best Innovative Practices in Public Management** is meant to identify and then promote champions of change by identifying both institutions and leaders of innovation in the public sector. Good submissions are collected to create a database of various good management practices in the Polish public sector, thereby enabling the spread of good practices ranging from information technology (IT) management, HR and strategic management to procurement, the involvement of citizens, and service delivery. The contest also addresses a common perception that the bureaucratic administration is outdated and to increase trust in government. The contest aims to 1) show that change and modernisation are possible within the public administration; 2) link successful managers with others; 3) strengthen and promote successful managers and institutions through recognition and positive feedback; and 4) inspire the public sector.

These award schemes are based on the assumption is that recognising and awarding successful innovation can motivate and inspire public employees to undertake similar activities within their own organisations. The high level of importance placed on the awards and the presence of ministers and high-ranking senior officials at award ceremonies sends a clear message that innovation is a priority for the governments of Poland and Australia. In the Australian example, the fact that innovation is used both as a key component of the wider excellence awards, and as an award on its own, gives it a double impact. The clear message is that excellence in management and innovation are consistent with each other and that innovation should be a central consideration of all public management. This may indirectly help provide more opportunity for innovation. Another important feature of the Australian scheme is the use of an integrated model for innovation, awarding points for the processes used and not just the final outcome. It sends a clear message that innovation is not just about outcomes, but needs to be linked to organisational strategy and employ co-design methods. This links innovation to particular competencies (abilities) to be developed. Poland's model stands out for its clear intention to bring innovators together to inspire and learn. In this way it builds ability by developing a learning community.

Ideas awards are another kind of innovation award. Ideas awards often work within an organisation to source ideas for improvement and innovation. Various schemes exist to motivate staff to suggest concrete improvements to the effectiveness and/or efficiency of service delivery or to improve working conditions. They can be a useful way of engaging employees at all levels and all geographical regions. Winners generally receive support to implement their idea, public recognition from senior management and occasionally financial incentives.

For example, Austria's Federal Chancellery has implemented an **Ideas Management Scheme** to enable and encourage staff to contribute their ideas and suggestions for improving day-to-day work processes, with a modest financial reward for successful ideas. Proposals are expected to offer concrete solutions to identified problems. Staff can submit proposals directly from the Chancellery home page and receive a nominal bonus of EUR 15 if the submission is accepted after a preliminary assessment of the underlying idea. After a subsequent in-depth evaluation, proposers may then be awarded a cash bonus depending on how ready the proposal is to be implemented, its novelty, feasibility and usefulness, as well as its reach within the Federal Chancellery. The maximum bonus is EUR 1 000, while unsuccessful submissions that show the submitter's genuine desire to make a positive contribution may be awarded a recognition bonus of up to EUR 75.

Such ideas generators can be a useful source of innovative ideas by giving staff at all levels the opportunity to contribute to innovation. This can be particularly useful in organisations characterised by multiple levels of hierarchy and/or geographical dispersion, where frontline staff are removed from the decision-making levels. It is important for such schemes to have a highly structured and transparent multiple-factor evaluation approach so that staff know what is expected of an idea and how best to describe and sell it to the relevant decision makers. Also interesting (and perhaps controversial) element of the Austrian scheme is the use of bonuses for unsuccessful ideas, to motivate, recognise and compensate staff for taking the time to think through an idea and submit it, regardless of its eventual success.

Innovation-oriented networks

A number of countries have established innovation networks with the intention of enabling communication and collaboration across organisational boundaries in both structured and free/informal ways. Nowadays, there is an understanding that good citizen-centred policy and service design rarely sits under the jurisdiction of a single office or institution, but often sits at the intersection between traditional policy silos and can often extend across jurisdictions and even across sectors. The primary aim of the examples of networks submitted for this project is to stimulate learning, which is central to innovation. Networks also strengthen cross-departmental working to better identify public challenges, optimal solutions and effective implementation.

The cases collected here differ greatly in a variety of ways. Some are maintained within one ministry and are designed to promote greater interaction across silos within that ministry and others take a cross-government view. Some are structured learning or orientation programmes with clear membership and others are more loosely associated and informal in nature.

The German Ministry of Labour and Social Affairs' **Junior Staff Orientation Programme** falls at the formal end of the spectrum. The programme is for freshly recruited young staff members who need to be retained and supported over the long term, because they are potentially the experts and leaders of the future. After an initial 18 months of networking, training, mentoring, discussions with senior executives and site visits, an active alumni network ensures continuity through broader network meetings and seminars. The main goals are to support new employees; develop their methodological, interpersonal and management skills; and to establish and maintain social networks that will facilitate and foster their potential for innovation, making the ministry more attractive to potential employees. The programme results in better co-operation across directorates-general. Such co-operation helps increase interaction, improve the flow of information and develop creative ideas across existing hierarchies and across teams.

The programme recognises that networking is in itself an essential skill that potential innovators need to develop. Two principles – trust and reciprocity – are key assets and the glue that binds networks together. By strengthening teamwork, conflict management and communication skills, developing horizontal thinking and improving negotiation skills for working in groups and projects, junior staff and alumni learn to build trusting relationships, co-operate with colleagues from other divisions or departments, and create new and innovative ideas. By focusing on new entrants, the network can help to establish a culture of sharing and co-operation from the start, rather than trying to correct a situation later. If participants establish bonds and positive experiences early on in their careers, this can improve their ability as well as their motivation to work across boundaries. Management are challenged to ensure that members of the network are given time and opportunities to leverage (and be leveraged by) it and to avoid the creation of an elite group with special access to networking that others don't have.

Israel's **Civil Service Cadet Program** also aims to build and train a management cadre that will catalyse change in the civil service. Each year, a cadre of cadets are identified, screened and recruited into a six year training and placement track, after which each cadet is placed in a key position in the civil service. Candidates are selected through a competitive multi-stage screening process that examines their personality, values, capacity to catalyse change, teamwork and leadership skills, and their desire and capacity to help mobilise the civil service to the next level. Systemic and integrative training lasts two years and combines synergetic professional and academic components. Cadets have the opportunity to learn topics theoretically in the classroom and afterwards be able to observe and experience them on the ground, accompanied by various methods such as study visits all over the country and abroad; encounters with people, organisations, perspectives and ideas within society; simulations; case studies; workshops and peer learning.

After the two year training period, cadets are placed in a government ministry to work in two positions of influence over four years, during which time they build their network and work with other cadets and people in positions of influence, authority and leadership to catalyse change. Currently, cadets are placed in more than 20 ministries and sub-governmental organisations in 5 different content clusters: HRM, social (health, welfare and education), regulations and economy, environment, and governance and macro. In order to ensure the best fit between the public sector's needs and the interests and capabilities of the cadets, cadets are exposed to various civil service fields during the training stage and gradually matched to placements based on which content cluster would be most suitable and through modules of internships within the civil service.

The programme's focus on group learning across policy domains during their training and placement phases enables cadets and alumni to develop networks beyond their own policy focus. The programme builds core leadership abilities such as vision and long-range thinking, constructive thinking, ability to cope with lasting uncertainty, continuous learning, and performance orientations. Graduates can maintain these abilities through their ongoing network.

In contrast to the structured elite training-oriented networks of the German and Israeli examples, Finland's **Government Change Agent Network** is a loosely organised and self-directing team of experts from different ministries, with different backgrounds, education and expertise. While diverse, all participants recognise the need and will to build up a working culture based on a "whole of government" mind set and "cross-silo" ways of working. In practice this is being implemented by building a new kind of working culture in many different ways: common discussions, supporting and launching new initiatives, writing blogs, giving expert statements, and starting new experiments, as well as supporting and bringing innovative approaches to the preparation of all new issues and projects. The biggest value of the Change Agent Network lies in its unofficial character. At the same time, this is the most challenging factor in keeping the network alive.

Networking is a way of overcoming many of the rigidities of bureaucratic organisations, by giving staff the opportunity to interact with a wider range of peers and employees with different views, ideas and information than they would otherwise. The informality of the Change Agent Network stands in contrast to the official bureaucracy. The themes of the network, which are culture change, removing resistance, quick experiments, widespread sourcing and co-ordination of action, further challenge core traditional bureaucratic values. This raises questions as to how such a network finds space to exist within or alongside a bureaucracy, and how this can provide a resource to managers for change and reform.

Spain's **Social and Knowledge Ecosystem** also prioritised semi-informal communication, favouring communities of interest connecting various actors, thereby allowing the linking of talent and encouraging public innovation. It is a project of Spain's National Public Administration Institute (INAP). The main objectives of this project are to create and disseminate transformative learning and high quality knowledge; to promote transparency and open government; to boost innovation within the public administration and to foster exemplary practice, legitimacy, autonomy, efficiency and responsibility. It does this through three tools: a professional network, a knowledge bank and an innovation bank of good practice. The project is aimed at public employees of all public administration levels and also citizens.

This example uses networks as a way of accessing the full range of competencies and motivations an individual brings to their job, including those beyond the narrowly defined requirements of their position. From the individual perspective, it offers them the opportunity to put a broader range of their abilities and motivations to work. From an organisational perspective, it suggests that skills can be sourced through horizontal networks when they don't exist within the vertical bureaucracy. The knowledge and innovation banks supplement this concept.

Belgium's **Innovation Learning Network** aims to coach innovative projects, and to create an environment where civil servants can help and learn from each other to become better at innovation processes. The objectives of the network include better organisational outcomes and practices (e.g. co-creation with users) and learning for individual civil servants. The participants, civil servants from different government organisations, are encouraged to become better at understanding the goals of government and society, management incentives, recognising restrictive patterns, co-creation with all kinds of stakeholders, encouraging passion, multidisciplinary working, following trends and getting things done more efficiently. The network currently operates in 14 government organisations, with 20 projects and about 50 civil servants.

This network is designed to develop and share innovation abilities. By bringing together those who have knowledge with others, there is a peer learning effect through coaching and knowledge sharing. The project orientation of this network may help to structure the focus of the networking activities. One challenge may be how employees can manage to balance the demands of the learning network with those of their regular posts.

Austria uses **Cross-Mentoring Programmes** to give staff the opportunity to build their personal networks and expand female employees' potential to reach management positions. The programme develops networks through mentoring, with a specific focus on female employees who wish to enter the management cadre. In the course of the programme, experienced senior managers support female civil servants from other federal ministries to develop professionally and advance their careers. The mentors pass on their knowledge and experiences, give advice on career planning, and facilitate the mentees' entrance into professional networks. Since mentors may be male or female, the programme not only supports female mentees, but also encourages men in management positions to develop openness towards female careers, overcome their own prejudices and rethink common role clichés.

While this programme is not focused directly on innovation, diversity in teams has been shown to correlate with innovation; therefore any effort to increase the diversity of management in the public sector should result in increased opportunity for innovation. The focus on building mentees' networks is also significant as it establishes the role of networking in career and personal development, but can also have a spillover effect if networks can later be drawn upon to improve and innovate.

Mobility programmes

Another group of HRM practices submitted to the project aims to increase the mobility of public servants both within and across sectors. Giving employees and leaders opportunities to work outside of their home organisation is assumed to offer opportunities to develop new insights and build new skills by giving the individual a more horizontal understanding of policy issues and allowing them to look at things from outside their narrow sector perspective. Mobility can also increase the exchange of ideas and problem-solving approaches. Mobility programmes can be used to send public sector employees on secondment outside organisations for a limited time, ultimately benefiting the home organisation when they return with new ideas and experiences. They can also be used to bring employees into public sector organisations from other organisations or other sectors, with competencies and perspectives developed elsewhere. This is hypothesised to support innovation by increasing the diversity of experience and perspective employees bring to bear in solving problems.

Interchange Canada enables the Government of Canada to temporarily exchange employees with all other sectors of the economy, domestically and internationally. Assignments are for the purpose of knowledge transfer, acquiring specialised expertise, and/or professional development. Interchange Canada has been used to facilitate exchanges between the federal government and the provinces or territories, private business, non-profit organisations, academia, and aboriginal organisations both within Canada and internationally.

Interchange assignments can be used to develop leadership competencies through the use of assignments to organisations which need specific experience to bridge a skills-building gap. Interchange Canada also serves as an excellent means of temporarily attaining skills unavailable in the home organisation and to build and transfer knowledge, enhancing the capacity of both government and other sectors.

Korea's **Open Position System** and **Job Posting System** both enable the appointment of qualified persons who have been selected through open recruitment to the Senior Civil Service and director positions across organisations. The Open Position System recruits both inside and outside the public sector for positions that require specific expertise, while the Job Posting System recruits staff from within the public sector but across agencies for policy development and management positions.

Korea also maintains a Personnel Exchange System, which is a one-to-one exchange programme moving public servants between administrative agencies and other public organisations for a limited period. Its goals are to improve professional understanding across different agencies through personnel exchanges; to remove departmental partitions by building a mutual co-operation system; to actively respond to changes in the administrative environments and demands for convergent administration; and to enhance the capabilities of the public workforce by providing extensive experience and opportunities for development.

Together, these programmes reinforce the Korean government's openness and competitiveness, so that it performs well and provides a better service to the public. The Open Position System and the Job Posting System enable the recruitment of talented people while the personnel exchanges improve job performance by allowing participants to directly experience other working methods and organisational cultures. In order to overcome any reluctance to participate in personnel exchanges, participants are given a one-step higher grade in their performance assessments and are assigned a desired position when returning after the exchange.

Austria's **Mobility Management Programme** enables needs- and skills-oriented personnel deployment in the civil service. The Federal Chancellery set up the Mobility Management Service in 2012 to help to balance internal labour supply and demand by matching excess staff from one area with vacant positions in another, as well as supporting staff members who wish to change careers. Using the Civil Service Job Exchange and Career Databank (the key instruments for mobility, along with the necessary legal framework), the Mobility Management Service tries to find suitable staff for all federal ministries from among those interested in changing jobs. The result is effective and efficient personnel management which goes hand in hand with promoting staff members' specific knowledge, strengths and interests.

Holistic and integrated HRM strategies

A fourth group of case studies submitted to the project integrates disparate HR functions into a framework to support staff to innovate. Fundamental to many of these is a recognition that employees are a heterogeneous group each with their own needs. Enabling employees to better match working conditions and HRM tools to their individual needs should allow them to maximise their work contributions, which in turn can enable more innovation. For example, Sweden's common values provide a foundation for values management which may enable the development of trust and work autonomy within a diverse workforce. Germany's employment agency uses a lifecycle approach to ensure that employees have the right supports at each phase of their career to maximise their work contribution. Belgium is using a combination of tools to modernise the workplace and encourage more flexibility and individualised working environments, while Switzerland's multiple career paths for lawyers enables a more individualised career that matches their personal motivations and abilities. The United Kingdom has provided a mini case study showing the link between holistic HRM and innovation on the ground, placing a variety of tools within the context of an actual innovation in employment services. Finally, two countries – Canada and Finland – highlight innovative employee engagement approaches to modernising HRM to better enable organisations to meet current and future challenges.

Sweden's **Common Basic Values for Central Government Employees** clarifies the value system that stems from the constitutionally based principles of equal value for all people, the rule of law and good service to citizens. The values documents have been recently updated and summarised by the government's Council for Skills Development. Since all government agencies are independent employers, Sweden has rather high mobility between sectors, so employees' knowledge of and respect for these basic values and principles needed to be improved both on recruitment and when developing central government activities. Central government employees often have a high degree of independence in their work. In many areas, the law or regulations may leave scope for interpretation. It is at such times, when civil servants have to rely on their own judgement, that the central government's basic values play a particularly important guiding role.

Values-based management can be an important tool to enable greater autonomy and mobility across sectors, both of which are considered to be preconditions for innovation in organisations. The more open and position-based the recruitment system, the more likely an organisation is to have people from diverse backgrounds working alongside each other. Clarifying and working through values-based learning is therefore an important tool to ensure that diversity is aligned towards a common set of goals and criteria for judgement-based decision making. This enables greater autonomy, since teams and individuals can be better trusted to make sound judgements based on common understandings.

The German **Employment Agency's Lifecycle Approach** to HRM is an intergenerational approach to enhancing staff's abilities. It focuses on competence, health and engagement to promote lifelong learning and well-being in the workplace. It is made up of a variety of measures which, as a whole, support the individualisation of HR management and also support talent management. These include a competency-based and modular HR development system open for career opportunities and competency development at every age; reintegration programmes for workers who return after prolonged absence due to, for example, parental leave; family services to help employees care for family members; various flexible working time models; telework and mobile working options; an engagement index to measure and better understand the workplace climate and management requirements; and a knowledge transfer programme to stimulate intergenerational learning and maintain corporate knowledge. This lifecycle approach is also supported by corporate health management to face the challenge of longer working lives, recognising that engaged and healthy staff should be able to contribute to innovation at any age.

This holistic approach is a clear example of the need to think in an integrated and strategic way about HRM and innovation. It is unlikely that an award or a network or a mobility programme on its own will have a significant impact on developing innovation capacity, but it may contribute significantly as one element in a broader HRM strategy. Using an engagement index to measure the impact of the HRM tools and processes, as well as leadership and other elements of the workplace, is essential to understanding the effects of different approaches. Finally it is interesting to note that engagement was also used in the development of the system through a series of HR Future Conferences, a practice also employed by Finland (see below).

Belgium's **New Ways of Working** initiative is about the creation of a more dynamic workplace where new ways of working have been implemented to promote practices such as desk sharing, home working, increased focus on results and more flexible ways in which teams are structured and work. The business objective was to become an attractive and sustainable federal public service in order to achieve three main HR challenges: to find talented people, to retain the right people and to make people happy. It consisted of five new programmes: 1) result orientation through team objectives; 2) dynamic and modular office spaces; 3) digital e-working solutions to enable more efficient collaboration; 4) client orientation; and 5) communication and change management.

The flexible e-enabled approach is expected to enable a more innovative workforce by allowing staff to collaborate with each other and interact with clients in a way that suits the employees' personal needs and the specific demands of their work. The combination of team-driven results-oriented management, flexible working environments, client orientation and change management for staff support should provide a significantly more innovative approach to work design than is commonly associated with government bureaucracy.

Switzerland's **Career Guidance for Lawyers** addresses a broad-based need to be able to offer people a variety of career paths. The idea was to offer individually differentiated development possibilities, which do not have to culminate in a hierarchical management position. Using the example of the position of lawyer which is common to all departments, the scheme recorded the concrete expectations and guidance for the professional development of this category within the federal authorities. It grouped these into four types of career paths where each implies a different approach to training and development, mobility, and eventual management responsibilities. The four career types identified provide clear evidence that most lawyers in the federal administration do not aspire to the classic paths of promotion but wanted to gain in-depth specialist knowledge or broaden their skills profile.

Enabling employees' careers to develop in line with their own skills and motivation is important for ensuring the right people are placed in positions that enable them to best contribute to organisational goals, including innovation. The assumption that all employees should eventually either become managers or find their career development stalled contradicts the modern understanding that management is a skill set in and of itself and that good specialists don't necessarily make good managers, and nor do they all want to become managers. This is a clear example of how organisational structures such as career paths can hinder or enable employees in their search for positions that match their motivation and abilities.

The United Kingdom's **Movement to Work** is a cross-sector initiative. Its objective is to reduce youth unemployment through quality work experience and learning. Collectively, it will deliver 6 000 work placements in the civil service during 2014/15. Implementing this programme at a time of limited financial and human resources has required the HR community charged with making the programme a success to take a number of innovative approaches to work organisation. This has included making use of various networks to share insights and co-ordinate implementation. A holistic and coherent people strategy has enabled the programme to be integrated with attempts to tackle issues including an ageing workforce, improving social mobility through employment and exploring bias towards experience over potential in recruitment and selection. This has helped to turn Movement to Work from a corporate social responsibility programme into a meaningful and tangible part of delivering the civil service's business strategy. Partnerships with public and private sector organisations have also been an innovation that has led to success.

This case provides a tangible example of how networks, flexible teams and cross-organisational co-operation can be used to implement a specific innovation with tangible results for the public sector and society more broadly. Developing the programme further will require building and using networks within each sector of the UK economy. The UK civil service has already begun to work closely with counterparts in the National Health Service on this. It will also rely on effective working relationships between the HR and commercial communities of each organisation to involve the supply chain and therefore increase the number of placements they can offer. This will represent an innovative and significant partnership between corporate functions in order to support a societal agenda.

In order for HRM to remain responsive to the diverse needs of the workforce it supports, it also needs to innovate. Cases from Finland and Canada highlight the use of innovative co-creation tools to innovate and update their HRM policies and practices. Finland's **Towards Year 2020 Initiative** is a co-creation process driven by the Ministry of Finance with other ministries and state agencies to update and clarify the state's management and personnel policy and working methods to meet future challenges, improve productivity and effectiveness, and achieve cost savings. To this end, the Ministry of Finance organised three workshops under the themes Towards New Leadership, Towards New Working Methods and Towards New HRM Practices. The aim is to crystallise outcomes and spread the message widely to the state administration in a new, inspiring way. The aim is also to get the main messages included in the next government programme for 2015-19.

Canada's **Key Leadership Competencies consultations** were launched as part of an initiative to review and renew the Key Leadership Competencies (KLCs) which form the foundation for the recruitment, learning and development, and performance and talent management of executives in the Canadian federal public service, so that they better respond to the new environment. The initiative to refresh these competencies used a very open, democratic and innovative consultation. To engage with public servants in a non-hierarchical fashion, the policy centre made use of two concurrent initiatives: 1) a government-wide engagement effort launched by the head of the public service; and 2) the introduction of a new internal social media tool. Through its consultation, the policy centre simultaneously engaged with and promoted a tech-savvy and high-performing work culture by "crowdsourcing" its consultation.

Canada approved a KLC profile for executives and senior leaders in the public service in October 2014. The new profile maintains the classic leadership competencies: create vision and strategy, mobilise people, uphold integrity and respect, and achieve results. The profile also includes two new competencies: collaborating with partners and stakeholders, and promoting innovation and guiding change. A comprehensive set of examples of effective behaviours was developed for each of the Deputy Minister, Assistant Deputy Minister, Director General and Director roles. These indicators were validated by a representative sample of executives at all levels of the public service. The new KLC profile continues to be integral to the performance and talent management of federal public service executives and forms the basis for revised assessment and learning products.

Towards a human resource management strategy for public sector innovation?

What do these cases and the literature review tell us about the kinds of HRM that may help develop the ability, motivation and opportunity to innovate in the workforce of OECD governments?

First, the cases confirm the first statement of the OECD's call to action for public sector innovation (Chapter 1): people matter. OECD countries recognise their employees are fundamental contributors to innovation. This is apparent both in HRM practices that aim to improve people's AMO for innovation and those which recognise that holistic and supportive HRM is a precondition for effective innovation.

If we return to the left-hand side of the framework in Figure 3.3 there are implications for each of the HRM levers it identifies:

Leadership

Leaders steer organisations, set goals, and play a significant role in developing the organisational culture and climate. They impart and embody the values of the organisation on a tacit level. Leadership in this context can include not only senior management, but any exertion of influence, whether by managers, project leaders, unions or employee organisers. In fact, potentially every employee in an organisation could (and should) play a leadership role in one form or another.

One of the themes that come out of the examples and discussions held with leaders in OECD countries is the need for collaborative forms of leadership, dispersed throughout an organisation. For innovation to flourish, "top leaders" may no longer have a monopoly on leadership and instead see their role as that of delegation and facilitation. The European Commission's expert group report on public sector innovation envisions the public manager of the future as an entrepreneur: "As a public entrepreneur, one's emphasis must shift to a more pro-active stance in pursuit of collaborative problem-solving and unleashing new opportunities." This means leaders who "challenge assumptions", "focus on outcomes" and co-design solutions with end-users, "lead the unknown" by experimenting on a small scale with potential innovations, and "envision a concrete future" by making innovation tangible (European Commission, 2013: p. 30).

Leaders in the public sector face particular challenges, including the relationship between political and administrative leadership; the multiplicity of sometimes vague and conflicting goals, interests and dependencies; and a more constrained legal environment to maintain democratic accountability and citizen trust (Petrovsky, 2010). This suggests that any discussion of leadership should not consider personal leadership competencies and styles, but also the regulatory and institutional elements that both support and constrain leadership.

Box 3.4. Ability, motivation and opportunity for innovation: The role of leadership

- Leadership helps build innovation **abilities** as leaders play a key role in developing and reinforcing an innovation-oriented learning culture and can align recruitment and selection with innovation priorities.

- Leadership can **motivate** innovation by modeling and rewarding innovation-oriented behaviour. Employees are generally motivated by leaders whom they respect and trust.

- Leadership can create **opportunities** for innovation, opening doors and removing barriers for people and projects that they support. Leaders who trust in their staff's abilities can provide them the autonomy they need to innovate and make space for learning through trial and error.

Work organisation

Organisations structure roles and relationships in order to accomplish tasks. "Work organisation" encompasses the assignment of tasks and responsibilities, and the structuring of people into units and teams. This includes job descriptions, organisational charts and hierarchies; the design and use of teams; and the flow of responsibility and accountability. Traditional hierarchical bureaucracies in the public sector have a very structured approach to work organisation, in contrast to policy networks where a variety of groups come together for a specific purpose and form ad hoc structures for particular tasks. Today, information and communications technology (ICT) collaboration tools enable people to work in distributed and virtual teams. This calls for new forms of work organisation that take into account the changing nature of work and public sector work environments, as well as expectations and working methods.

Research suggests that the organisation of work can have a significant impact on innovative capacity. For example, analysis of the European Survey of Working Conditions shows that innovation is positively correlated with teamwork, autonomy, employee engagement and commitment, and flexibility (OECD, 2010; Eurofound, 2012). In other words, giving teams the autonomy to make their own decisions and structure their own work can give them the opportunity to innovate. Working in teams brings together wider perspectives, knowledge and skills than one worker would have access to on their own. Engaging staff in the decisions of the team, unit or organisation may also boost their motivation to innovate.

Recently, a number of researchers have been discussing bundles of HRM and managerial practices that rely heavily on teamwork, autonomy and flexibility under the label of High Performance Work Systems (Boxall and Macky, 2009). These generally include high involvement work practices, where managers delegate decision making to teams (usually process-oriented decisions – how to meet goals – not which goals to meet); and high commitment to employment practices, which seek longer, motivated attachment to organisations. Innovation is likely to be positively driven by work designs that empower staff to work with end users and network with peers to find novel solutions to pressing problems.

Quite a number of the cases the project collected reflect the importance of work organisation, particularly among the innovation-oriented networks. Working across horizontal networks supplements the traditional top-down hierarchy of bureaucracy and supports staff to expand their resource base and interactions in a way that can redefine how they structure their work. The UK's Movement to Work showed this in action, with cross-departmental networks implementing an innovation and ensuring its success.

Box 3.5. Ability, motivation and opportunity for innovation: The role of work organisation

- Work organisation can ensure that **abilities** are matched to tasks and responsibilities (e.g. through job profiling). Work organisation can also help to get the right skills mix in teams tasked with innovation-oriented projects, or to share skills that are in short supply through skills pools, for example.

- Work organisation can affect **motivation** by designing jobs and tasks that provide appropriate levels of meaningfulness and feedback to motivate innovation. For example, designing projects so teams have responsibility for seeing a project through to completion and structured interaction with the beneficiaries of the project can promote a greater sense of motivation and desire to innovate.

- Work organisation probably has the most direct impact on **opportunity** to innovate by structuring work around problem solving and giving employees safe spaces to learn by doing, as opposed to working on an assembly line.

Recruitment and selection

Recruitment and selection systems bring people with skills and competencies into the organisation. Bringing the right people with the right competencies together to accomplish work is at the heart of recruitment and selection. If innovation is the desired outcome, then it can be assumed that hiring a certain profile of staff would help to build innovative capacity.

As discussed at the start of this chapter, innovation is not a single skill, but requires a combination of technical and behavioural skills and competencies. Current work by the OECD is looking at the skills needed by public sector innovators in six related areas: iteration, data literacy, user centricity, curiosity, storytelling and insurgency. It can be more difficult to design recruitment processes that test for these often softer kinds of skill clusters than to test for standard experience and knowledge. This may imply the need to think of recruitment in two layers: the first looking at hard skills (experience and knowledge, especially for specialists) and the second looking at the existence of – or development potential for – behavioural skills sets. This implies the need to incorporate behavioural testing into selection processes and to train all recruiting managers in these techniques.

The literature suggests that diversity of ideas is positively correlated with innovative problem solving (Eurofound, 2012; OECD, 2010), and this implies that selecting for innovation is not just a question of selecting for the right skill, but the right balance of skills, competencies and perspectives: diversity of gender, ethnicity, age, experience and educational background needs to be considered. Mobility programmes to move staff across ministries, levels of government and even across sectors can be one way to enable such recruitment and diversity. However it should be noted that diversity alone will not result in more innovation unless efforts are made by managers to ensure an inclusive work environment where different ideas and opinions are given voice and support.

Recruitment is most directly tackled in the cases discussed through mobility programmes, which enable management to use a wider range of tools to bring people with skills into organisations and build teams with the right skills and level of diversity to support innovation.

Box 3.6. Ability, motivation and opportunity for innovation: The role of recruitment

- Recruitment and selection builds innovation **ability** by bringing people with the skills profiles, competencies, values, and mindsets needed into the organisation.

- Recruitment and selection processes can also assess candidates' **motivation** to innovate, thereby selecting people who may have more intrinsic motivation to contribute to public sector innovation.

- Recruitment and selection may have an impact on **opportunity** from a manager's perspective as they build their team, particularly when they are competing in a tight labour market for particular qualities that are in high demand.

Performance management

Performance management processes are intended to encourage employees to perform to their highest potential. A narrow view of performance management systems usually includes some kind of formal assessment, rewards and sanctions. Performance management systems often include discussion of staff development and learning plans to help employees improve their performance and advance through their career. A broader view may include all incentives that motivate staff to adopt certain behaviours, including innovation, or conversely to maintain the status quo. This could include working conditions, career path structure and job stability.

Fostering innovation relies on establishing approaches that incentivise safe risk taking and embrace early experiments as part of the learning process. It has been argued that the public sector is risk averse (see Chapter 6), in part due to its particular balance of rewards and sanctions. In the private sector, multiple small failures can be balanced out by large successes. In the public sector this kind of balance is more difficult to achieve. Developing performance objectives that encourage safe risk taking may be one way to do this. Creative safe spaces to experiment and learn from the results, for example in a laboratory setting, could also help (see Chapter 5). Valuing innovation as a competency against which to measure performance requires rethinking what it means to perform well in an innovative organisation and a careful assessment of the multiple incentives that are active in an organisational context. It may also require considering which positions should be made more accountable for innovation and how (for example, linking innovation objectives to service delivery outcomes for certain groups of professionals).

Among the cases submitted and discussed here, formal performance management is addressed in Canada's leadership competency framework, as these competencies form the basis for performance management discussions. The management of performance in a broader sense is central to a number of them, especially the holistic management approaches which aim to support employees to maximise their contribution to the organisation's overall performance, including innovation. For example, Belgium's New Ways of Working enables more flexibility and thereby more effective and efficient working, while Switzerland's multiple career paths for lawyers allows a different understanding of performance for different types of people. Sweden's values management gives employees a clearer understanding of what performance should entail and recognises that in the public sector, performance can sometimes mean balancing contradictions and conflict between values, which can itself be a source of innovation.

Box 3.7. Ability, motivation and opportunity for innovation: The role of performance management

- Performance management can help to build **ability** to innovate by helping to identify training and development needs and aligning career development with innovation-oriented objectives.

- Performance management can **motivate** innovation by rewarding innovation-oriented behaviour, and taking care not to discourage appropriate risk taking and learning by doing.

- Performance management can also help to create more **opportunities** to innovate when employees are encouraged to use performance discussions to raise perceived limitations to innovation within their working environment and come up with solutions.

Training and development

People are dynamic and grow throughout their careers. Learning is increasingly essential for public sector jobs as employees are asked to take on new projects, address new challenges and keep up with fast-changing technologies. Learning happens in structured ways, through courses, seminars, trainee rotation programmes and increasingly through online platforms. Learning also happens on the job, as managers slowly stretch their employees' activities into new areas that require new knowledge development and a growing range of skills, such as when a high performer begins to manage a team.

Learning is at the heart of innovation and an innovative organisation can incorporate it into all working considerations. This could mean taking advantage of a wide range of learning opportunities within and beyond the organisation, to build skills, knowledge and spark new ideas. While courses in a variety of areas related to innovation and creative problem solving may help, they are probably not enough. Incorporating learning into work means rotating staff through a variety of tasks to build their competencies; taking advantage of external conferences, partnerships and opportunities to share ideas with others; and using the performance management and assessment process as an opportunity to discuss learning needs and potential.

When it comes to training for innovation, a number of public service schools are designing innovation programmes for senior management that take them beyond their day-to-day managerial responsibilities, builds their networks and gives them the opportunity to look at problems from new perspectives. While there is no perfect formula for innovation training, good programmes recognise that traditional classroom methods need to be stretched to take people outside of their comfort zone and ask them to look at traditional problems and work in new ways, from new perspectives, with new tools and with new partners. This might be done by teaching participants how to iterate through evaluation, adjustment, reallocation and benefit realisation; by focusing on tools for problem solving rather than on rules and procedures; by creating lab-like environments where participants can test tools and skills in a safe environment; by addressing organisation and personal values; by looking at how innovation can address societal problems and government priorities and encouraging participants to make these linkages to outcomes and showing them where it has been done elsewhere. In short, training for innovation demands innovative training.

Learning, training and development are reflected in all of the cases above, even though very few employ traditional classroom training methods. Learning happens in networks by interacting with people from other backgrounds, organisations, perspective or expertise. Learning happens through mobility by exchanging staff between organisations and sectors. Learning is also at the core of awards and recognition programmes which enable staff to learn from the success of others. Finally, learning and development are core to any holistic HRM perspective, such as that promoted by Germany's Employment Agency which takes a lifecycle approach to identify learning opportunities at different career stages and which emphasises knowledge transfer opportunities between, for example, older and younger generations of employees.

Box 3.8. Ability, motivation and opportunity for innovation: The role of training and development

- Training and development is one of the most important tools to build a public workforce's **ability** to innovate, especially in career-based civil services where recruitment is generally limited to lower-level employees who are expected to develop throughout their careers.

- Training and development can have a significant secondary impact on **motivation** as employees take pride from mastering new skills and are motivated to put them to use once learned.

- Training and development can also increase **opportunity** as new skills open doors to new experience, while often learning opportunities bring together staff from a range of areas who share ideas and build networks, which can develop into opportunities for new collaborations elsewhere.

Compensation

Compensation is a fundamental component of HR and needs to be considered in broad terms: not just pay but also benefits and time. This are includes issues related to performance pay, but also to "total compensation", a concept employed by the United Kingdom, which includes recognition and work-life balance considerations. Compensation also brings in elements of working conditions and fairness and justice (internal and external comparisons). Compensation is also linked to performance management incentives, especially where pay is linked to performance.

Using financial compensation to motivate and/or reward innovation is a complex area with little evidence of success. For example, there appears to be a growing amount of research that challenges the effectiveness of performance-related pay in the public sector, and particularly for tasks involving creativity and teamwork (Weibel et al., 2010). Part of the problem may be related to the balance between individual and team incentives, and the effects of internal competition on knowledge sharing and co-operation. If innovation is a team activity which relies on open knowledge and data, it is very difficult to design a pay for performance system that does not pit one individual or group against another and thereby limit information sharing and networking. In the private sector some pay systems allow everyone to benefit from the firm's performance through, for example, profit sharing systems. This does not clearly translate to the public sector. Innovation awards may be one approach to achieving similar outcomes.

Pay can, however, generate disincentives for innovation. Between 2008 and 2013 compensation for civil servants was frozen or reduced in 75% of OECD countries (OECD, 2016). These and other cost-control measures have resulted in a measurable loss of trust and commitment within the civil service and an increase of stress and job intensity. This implies that pay adjustments, especially when perceived as unfair, result in a working environment less conducive to innovation, and therefore likely act as a disincentive.

None of the cases submitted directly referenced compensation, but there is a clear link to awards programmes which recognise and reward innovation primarily through non-monetary means. While Austria's ideas contest includes some financial compensation, the amounts are so low that the real motivator is likely to be the recognition associated with the compensation and not the small awards themselves. Switzerland's career path for lawyers is, in a sense, related to compensation if it is suggesting that careers equal development and associated salary raises should not necessarily be tied to one path up the hierarchy. Giving staff the opportunity to advance in their careers as specialists may provide an organisation with better-compensated specialists who are supported to promote innovation and not just manage teams.

Box 3.9. Ability, motivation and opportunity for innovation: The role of compensation

- Compensation could affect a workforce's **ability** to innovate from an organisational perspective as it may relate to the attractiveness of hard-to-find skill sets.

- Compensation most directly impacts **motivation** as it is the most fundamental external motivator for work. However the link between compensation and innovation is not clearly defined in the literature and does not relate easily to performance-related pay.

- Compensation can impact **opportunity** if reward systems are not calibrated for the kinds of work organisation required. For example, pay for performance that rewards individual effort can limit opportunities for knowledge sharing and teamwork.

A holistic system of HRM for innovation?

Taken together, the various practices highlighted in this chapter begin to form the elements of a potential system of HRM for innovation. Learning networks, innovation awards, and mobility brought together in holistic HRM systems by flexible managers and transformational leaders could go a long way towards supporting more public sector innovation if organisations can negotiate the management challenges discussed above.

However, the literature and theory suggest that there are a number of key HRM elements that have not been highlighted in our case studies that are likely to complement more and better HRM for public sector innovation. These include increased use of autonomous teams and other work design features, careful recruitment and selection practices that prioritise innovation-related skills, and group-oriented rewards for performance. This is not to suggest that these don't exist in OECD countries, but they were not highlighted in the country examples.

Furthermore, many of the country examples mentioned organisational culture as an enabling or limiting factor, often in the context of implementation challenges. Organisational culture is generally understood as the deep-seated values and beliefs, often unwritten, which guide normative behaviour. It is often said that HRM tools need to be aligned with organisational culture to be effective. Many of the tools and elements of workforce management highlighted in the collected examples and other high performance work practices require a work culture built on trust, which enables people to share ideas and information.

Organisational culture is often blamed when corporate management tools that have been cascaded through a large organisation end up, in practice, "paying lip service to the formal requirements while perpetuating existing behaviour" (Kidson, 2013: p.18). At the same time, setting out to change an organisational culture is not easy. Kidson suggests that culture be treated as a consequence, not a cause. This involves making clear what is to be valued and ensuring consistent alignment of processes and behaviours.

One key element of culture is how organisations treat risk and whether employees feel empowered to experiment and to learn from their experiments. Eurofound suggests that this "can be cultivated through making time, space and communication channels available and appointing and rewarding senior individuals who are prepared to engage in this process" (Eurofound, 2012). It would be useful to know if, and how, OECD countries are addressing culture and risk in their organisations.

What is clear from the cases collected and the discussions that followed, is that while HRM practices are important for enabling the development of a workforce that possesses the ability, motivation and opportunity to actively use and expand their scope of discretion in a way that contributes to innovation, on their own they will not be enough. Innovation needs leadership and management at all levels, including the development of future leaders at the organisational and team level. Organisational development needs to match HRM processes and systems to provide opportunities. Culture matters greatly as both an input and output of success.

Looking at HRM for innovation in the context of previous work on public employment and HRM at the OECD, we may be beginning to identify a new frontier for HRM and public employment policy in OECD countries. The framework in Figure 3.4 offers a first glance at the how these concepts relate. Its foundation is a human resources system based on professionalism and integrity. This is a prerequisite for enabling the autonomy and discretion required to build a culture of innovation. Strategic HRM is a set of top-down processes which help to plan and ensure capacity to deliver operationally. However, to build a workforce for innovation, some countries go beyond strategy to actively engage the workforce, their knowledge and ideas. This requires an HRM built around the individual (and team) and their full sets of competencies, motivations and engagement and suggests a path forward for research and experimentation in OECD countries. One in which the OECD is excited to play a supportive role as this sphere becomes further defined.

Figure 3.4. An HRM for public sector innovation?

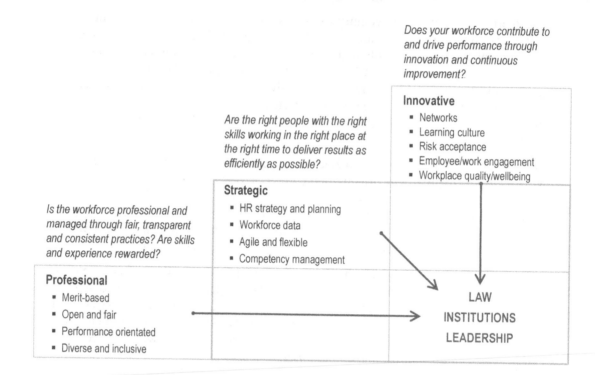

Concluding considerations: Management trade-offs and opportunities for future exploration

This chapter has begun to explore the abilities, motivations and opportunities public servants need to be active partners in a more innovative public sector. Without public servants playing an active role in innovation, it will not achieve its potential to drive the effectiveness, productivity and inclusive growth sought from today's public policies. This means looking at how the workforce is managed, and particularly the kind of practices that can lead to a more capable, motivated workforce with the opportunities required to contribute to innovation. The cases collected through this project suggest that OECD countries are taking this task seriously and together point towards a number of the elements that might constitute an integrated HR approach to addressing the public sector innovation challenge.

It is important to recognise that these practices are not all easy to implement, and are not without their own risks. Effective leadership is needed at various levels, often in ways that diverge from traditional command and control leadership competencies. Eurofound (2012) suggests that obstacles to implementing innovative HRM tools include the reluctance of middle managers to give up power, lack of skills among line managers to use the tools, and reluctance among employees to take on the additional responsibilities implied by the use of these tools. The tensions identified below should provoke discussion and consideration of the trade-offs and contradictions that leaders may need to consider and resolve if they seek to maximise the ability, motivation and opportunity for innovation in their workforce.

Bottom up versus top down

HRM tools that give employees responsibility to innovate, either at the individual employee level or by providing teams with autonomy, require leaders to listen, be open to challenge from below, and be able to muster resources to implement good ideas and innovations. This bottom-up approach to innovation can be powerful when done well, but can have detrimental consequences if handled badly as negative experiences can engender cynicism in staff and reduce their motivation to participate in future innovation.

Horizontal versus vertical

Similarly, the focus on networking requires a different understanding of management and leadership – one that focuses on empowering staff to work across organisations and encourages the sharing of information rather than on controlling people and information. In the future, an organisation's value will depend less on the knowledge it holds and authority it exerts, and more on its ability to connect, find and mobilise external resources for its mission. This requires the kind of leadership that can corral groups of stakeholders not directly under any authority. This can mean a challenge to traditional command-and-control bureaucracies and suggests a greater level of agency and entrepreneurial behaviour at various levels than is traditionally expected. Not only does this require leadership that is more flexible and open to bottom-up and outside-in possibilities of work and team design, but it also places additional responsibilities and expectations on all employees. Networking and partnership development/maintenance is itself a skill that needs to be developed and promoted, and takes time away from other tasks.

People development versus organisational development

The previous two tensions suggest that developing a more innovative workforce is not likely to lead to a more innovative organisation if the organisation is not flexible enough to give staff the opportunity to put their motivation and abilities to use. This means that any discussion of HRM for innovation needs to include aspects of organisational development which support cross-boundary collaboration. We've captured this in the context of work organisation on the left hand side of the model in Figure 3.3, and opportunity to innovate on the right side (Figure 3.4). The link is also clearly captured in the examples of holistic HRM models that were submitted, such as Germany's Employment Agency's Lifecycle Approach and Switzerland's Career Guidance for Lawyers which redesigns career paths to better accommodate individuals' motivation and abilities.

Autonomy versus stress

At the individual level, it is also important to recognise that asking staff to be innovative may place additional stress on them and increase their work intensity, particularly as it may imply giving them more autonomy and responsibility over decision making, problem solving and results. In such cases it is important to ensure that staff are ready for increased responsibility and are supported in taking on new challenges. Promoting networking and mobility may also increase stress. For staff to be active members of a horizontal network takes time and resources out of their already busy schedules. Moving staff between ministries can be stressful as an employee is required to develop a new set of social connections and learn a range of unwritten codes to become a successful participant. This reinforces the need to think holistically about HRM and ensure that individuals and teams are supported in appropriate ways so that innovation tools act as enablers and not just as burdens.

Holistic versus individual tools and practices

Another tension that emerges from this discussion is the need to think simultaneously in terms of holistic strategies and systems, and of individual practices. It is unlikely that any one practice added on top of a legacy HRM system will make much of a contribution on its own. An award, while a step in the right direction, is likely be more powerful when combined with a range of other elements such as a databank of recent innovations, a network of innovators associated with previous years' awards and coaching based on the proven best practice of previous winners.

Formal HRM versus informal and cultural

Formal HRM systems sit within an organisational culture with its own sets of unwritten rules, expectations and professional codes. It is often said that the biggest challenge to developing a more innovative public sector is changing the organisational culture into one that accepts more risk and promotes innovation as a value. It has also been said that culture does not change by setting out to change culture, but instead by clarifying expectations and modelling appropriate behaviour from the top down. There is a tendency to actively manage formal systems as they can be identified and monitored, whereas the informal cultural factors are often overlooked, although arguably they are of equal or greater importance. The OECD's work on the measurement of employee engagement in OECD countries provides examples of how some countries actively measure and manage organisational culture through the eyes of their employees (OECD, 2016).

Steady state versus innovation and change

Culture and shared public values strengthen public sector organisations, but may also come into conflict with each other. Public sector organisations have long valued stability and predictability which enable citizens to know what services to expect from their government and how to access them. Skilled managers have to not only be effective and responsive to these values, but also to innovation. This raises the question of when innovation should be used to complement stability and continuity, when it should replace it, and when it should take a back seat. At times the two will have to co-exist in order to allow reform and delivery to happen at once. How to give each one their due recognition as necessary and complementary without value judgement as part of a dynamic transitional process? It also raises the question of which parts of the workforce should be involved in innovation and at which stage of the process. If innovation requires different skills than steady-state delivery, then who should be involved and when? If one accepts that there is a time and place for innovation (not everywhere and not all the time) then the outcome of HRM for innovation may turn out to be less innovation for innovation's sake, but with innovation taking place when and where it is needed.

Efficiency and austerity versus slack; fear versus motivation

These last two tensions point to the question of innovation in times of austerity. Much of the motivation to launch the public sector innovation agenda at the OECD was directly related to the impact of the financial crisis on governments, which were looking for new ways of delivering essential services at a time of fiscal consolidation. However, the tools here and the report by the OECD (2016) clearly show that innovation will not happen without engaging the workforce. Employees need time to network, time to test ideas and to learn from experiments. If all the organisation's resources are being devoted to meeting minimum production targets, then there will not be time or space for innovation. Innovation requires some slack in the system to provide staff with the opportunity to innovate and time to develop the right abilities.

Furthermore, the motivation to innovate requires a level of trust in the organisation. If employees are afraid of losing their jobs, or of losing the quality of their workplace due to the outcome of their innovations, they will likely be less motivated to think creatively and honestly. Furthermore, if employees don't trust their organisation to deliver on their ideas, they will be less motivated to contribute. This places a great deal of responsibility on managers, not only to motivate creativity (transformative leadership) but also to balance this with transactional leadership (focus on outcomes and targets), healthy leadership (ensuring a healthy work environment with manageable stress levels to ensure staff have the time and energy to contribute to innovation) and authentic leadership (trust in the individual leader to make commitments that she or he can and will follow through).

The exploratory nature of this chapter suggests that there is much we do not yet know. The OECD can work with governments to begin addressing some of the following questions:

- What abilities are required to innovate in the public sector and how can these be acquired, developed and best be used? How can recruitment be better aligned to softer skills such as creativity and teamwork, which are essential for innovation? How can organisations undertake capability reviews with respect to public sector innovation so that they can get a clear picture of which individuals are equipped with which skills? How can workforce planning tools and processes be best aligned to the public sector innovation challenge?

- What motivates civil servants and how can this motivation be harnessed by public organisations? How can formal systems and incentives be aligned to promote innovation-oriented behaviour? How can senior management develop and reinforce an innovation-oriented organisational culture in public sector organisations, and strike the right balance between top-down and bottom-up innovation? How can middle managers be equipped with the right skills to motivate their employees and support employee engagement?

- How can public employees be given the opportunities to contribute to meaningful innovation? How can their ideas and experience be harnessed and built upon? How can work be (re)designed to balance the need for autonomy and safe risk taking?

The OECD and member countries could collect data and evidence to help answer many of these questions. For instance:

- A definition of skills for innovation, and innovation skills audits could help more clearly identify and understand the distribution of these skills across civil services. The OECD is working with member countries to more clearly define these skills, and structure interventions to help to promote them in public sector contexts.

- Employee surveys can be a powerful tool to understanding innovation-oriented opportunities and challenges from the perspective of employees. Asking questions related to employee's perception of innovation and their organisations' openness to new ideas can help to identify areas where organisational culture may be more or less conducive to innovation. This can allow targeted management actions. The OECD is working with member countries to identify questions that may allow for international comparison of employee views.

- Analyses of public sector entities could give a deeper insight into which forms of work organisation give employees opportunities for public sector innovation and where these are implemented. Such an approach would likely be required at organisational level as such policies are rarely identified centrally.

Note

1. Remarks made at the international conference on public sector innovation held at the OECD 12/13 November 2015.

References

Amabile, T.M. (1997), "Motivating creativity in organizations: On doing what you love and loving what you do", *California Management Review*; Vol. 40/1, pp. 39-58.

Bakker, A.B. (2011), "An evidence-based model of work engagement", *Current Directions in Psychological Science*, Vol. 20/4, pp.265-269.

Bakker, A.B., Demerouti, E. and Sanz-Vergel, A.I. (2014), "Burnout and work engagement: The JD–R approach", *Annual Review of Organizational Psychology and Organizational Behavior*, Vol.1, pp.389–411.

Borins, S.F. (2014), *The Persistence of Innovation in Government*, Brookings Institution Press, Washington, DC.

Boxall, P. and K. Macky (2009), "Research and theory on high-performance work systems: Progressing the high-involvement system", *Human Resource Management Journal*, Vol. 19/1, pp. 3-23.

Boxall, P. and J. Purcell (2011), *Strategy and Human Resource Management*, third edition, Palgrave Macmillan.

Dyer, J., H. Gregerson and C.M. Christensen (2011), *The Innovator's DNA: Mastering the Five Skills of Disruptive Innovators*, Harvard Business Review Press, Boston.

Eurofound (2012), *Work Organisation and Innovation*, European Foundation for the Improvement of Living and Working Conditions, http://eurofound.europa.eu/sites /default/files/ef_files/pubdocs/2012/72/en/1/EF1272EN.pdf.

European Commission (2013), *Powering European Public Sector Innovation: Towards A New Architecture*, Report of the Expert Group on Public Sector Innovation, European Commission, http://ec.europa.eu/research/innovation-union/pdf/psi_eg.pdf.

Fernandez, S. and T. Moldogaziev (2012), "Using employee empowerment to encourage innovative behaviour in the public sector", *Journal of Public Administration Research and Theory*, Advance Access published 23 May 2012.

Foss, N.J. D.B. Minbaeva, T. Pedersen and M. Reinholt (2009), "Encouraging knowledge sharing among employees: How job design matters", *Human Resource Management*, Vol. 48/6, pp. 871-893.

Frey, B. and M. Osterloh (2002), *Successful Management by Motivation: Balancing Intrinsic and Extrinsic Incentives*, Springer, Berlin.

Harter, J.K., F.L. Schmidt and T.L. Hayes (2002), "Business-unit-level relationship between employee satisfaction, employee engagement, and business outcomes: A meta-analysis", *Journal of Applied Psychology*, Vol. 87/2, pp. 268-279

Hartley, J. (2006), "Innovation in governance and public services: Past and present", *Public Money & Management*, Vol. 25/1, pp. 27-34.

Jiménez-Jiménez, D. and R. Sanz-Valle (2008), "Could HRM support organizational innovation?", *The International Journal of Human Resource Management*, Vol. 19/7, pp. 1208-1221.

Kidson, M. (2013), *Civil Service Capabilities: A Discussion Paper*, Institute for Government, www.instituteforgovernment.org.uk/publications/civil-service-capabilities.

Laursen, K. and N.J. Foss (2013), *"Human resource management practices and innovation"*, prepared for M. Dodgson, D. Gann and N. Phillips (eds.) *Handbook of Innovation Management*, Oxford University Press.

MacLeod, D. and N. Clarke (2011), *Engaging for Success: Enhancing Performance through Employee Engagement*, United Kingdom Government, http://dera.ioe.ac.uk/1810/1/file52215.pdf.

Mumford, M.D. (2000), "Managing creative people: Strategies and tactics for innovation", *Human Resource Management Review*, Vol.10/3, pp 313-351.

OECD (2016), *Engaging Public Employees for a High-Performing Civil Service*, OECD Publishing, Paris, http://dx.doi.org/10.1787/9789264097490-en

OECD (2015), *The Innovation Imperative in the Public Sector: Setting an Agenda for Action*, OECD Publishing, Paris, http://dx.doi.org/10.1787/9789264236561-en.

OECD (2011a), *Public Servants as Partners for Growth: Toward a Stronger, Leaner and More Equitable Workforce*, OECD Publishing, Paris, http://dx.doi.org/10.1787/9789264166707-en.

OECD (2011b), *Skills for Innovation and Research*, OECD Publishing, Paris, http://dx.doi.org/10.1787/9789264097490-en.

OECD (2010), *Innovative Workplaces: Making Better Use of Skills within Organisations*, OECD Publishing, Paris, http://dx.doi.org/10.1787/9789264095687-en.

Perry, J.L, A. Hondeghem, and L.R. Wise (2008), "Revisiting the motivational bases of public service: Twenty years of research and an agenda for the future", paper prepared for presentation at the International Public Service Motivation Research Conference, 7-9 June 2009, Bloomington, Indiana http://sihombing17.files.wordpress.com/2010/01/revisiting-the-motivational-bases-of-public-service.pdf.

Petrovsky, N. (2010), "The role of leadership", in R.E. Ashworth, G.A. Boyne and T. Entwistle (eds.), *Public Service Improvement: Theories and Evidence*, Oxford University Press.

Rayton, B., T. Dodge and G. D'Analeze (2012), *The Evidence: Employee Engagement Task Force "Nailing the Evidence" Workgroup*, Engage for Success, http://engageforsuccess.org/wp-content/uploads/2015/09/The-Evidence.pdf.

Shalley, C.E. and L.L Gilson (2004), "What leaders need to know: A review of social and contextual factors that can foster or hinder creativity", *The Leadership Quarterly*, Vol. 15/1, pp. 33-53.

Weibel, A., K. Rost and M. Osterloh (2010), "Pay for performance in the public sector: Benefits and (hidden) costs", *Journal of Public Administration Research and Theory*, Vol. 20/2, pp. 387-412.

Annex 3.A1.

Innovation Cases

Awards and recognition (cases from Australia, Austria and Poland)

The Australian Awards for Excellence in Public Sector Management

The Australian Awards for Excellence in Public Sector Management aim to encourage and recognise better practice and innovation in all levels of government in Australia. These awards focus on specific initiatives and are designed to honour the achievements of public sector work groups, units and teams rather than individuals. They are open to all public sector organisations in Australia, including federal, state, territory and local government bodies. Nominations can also incorporate private sector or community third party delivery organisations.

The awards are in three areas: sustainable excellence in public sector management, collaboration (joint nomination across agencies or levels of government) and innovation. Initiatives are judged against four criteria: 1) stakeholder service and satisfaction; 2) transparent leadership, planning and governance; 3) people management and change management; and 4) innovation in the design and/or delivery of products, services and processes. Assessment for the awards is conducted in two stages. First, teams of independent volunteer assessors drawn from across the public sector assess the nominations using a common methodology. In Stage 2, a committee of eminent judges reviews the assessors' recommendations and selects the award winners – judges include retired high-ranking public servants (chief executive and deputy level), academics practising in the field and specialist public administration consultants.

In practice, an innovative proposal is considered to be any non-trivial application of new or improved methods: it is the process of developing and applying novel products, processes, technologies and management practices to create significant value for stakeholders. It is not solely restricted to "big bang" changes or inventions. It applies not only to technologies but to processes as well, since innovations in processes can equally lead to significant improvements.

While innovation is a criterion applied to the overall Award for Excellence, and thereby incorporated into the process as a whole, there is also a separately assessed Innovation Award. Each of the shortlisted excellence nominations is reviewed against the following additional criteria to determine the recipient of the innovation award:

1. Does the nomination meet the defined threshold for innovation?

2. Is the innovation linked to an organisational strategy or a response to a significant organisation issue or risk?

3. Did the innovation involve co-design with key stakeholders (whether internal or external)?

4. Has the innovation resulted in a demonstrable difference to the relevant product, process or service and its delivery?

Austria's Ideas Management Scheme

Austria's Ideas Management Scheme was implemented in the Federal Chancellery to enable and encourage staff to contribute their ideas and suggestions for improving day-to-day work processes. Successful ideas receive a modest financial award. A proposal can be of material use (for example reducing costs, increasing efficiency, optimising processes or saving resources), or of purely immaterial use (such as improving communication). Proposals are not considered if they only involve minimal changes and they are expected to present concrete solutions to identified problems.

Staff can submit proposals directly from the Chancellery home page and so they do not need to go through traditional hierarchical channels of communication. All accepted proposals are described on the home page and implementation is tracked for all to monitor. Staff have submitted 77 proposals since 2008, of which 20 were eventually rejected, but received a recognition bonus, and 7 were adopted and received a cash bonus; of the latter, 6 have been implemented.

A staff member who has submitted a proposal receives a nominal bonus of EUR 15 if the submission is accepted after a preliminary assessment of the underlying idea. Based on the subsequent in-depth evaluation, the proposal may then be awarded a cash bonus depending on its readiness for implementation, its novelty, feasibility and usefulness, as well as its reach within the Federal Chancellery. The maximum bonus is EUR 1 000, with the actual amount awarded calculated by means of a utility table. If a proposal is rejected after in-depth evaluation, but still showed that the submitter had tried to make a positive contribution, the submitter may be awarded a recognition bonus of up to EUR 75.

Poland's Contest for the Best Innovative Practices in Public Management

Poland's Contest for the Best Innovative Practices in Public Management is the culmination of the pilot edition of the Academy of Public Institutions Management. It is being implemented by the National School of Public Administration, in co-operation with Mazovia Governor's Office, the Social Insurance Institution and the Centre for Dialogue and Analysis THINKTANK. The predominant purpose of the Academy was to enable an effective and broad exchange between Polish public administration institutions of best practice and innovations in the field of management. Within this framework, the Academy organises regular lectures, workshops and panel discussions on public sector management themes ranging from public e-services to social participation, led by important mentors and experts. All events are transmitted online to reach a large audience.

The contest is meant to identify and promote champions of change by identifying both institutions and leaders of innovation in the public sector. The winners are chosen by a jury which consists of management experts from public and private sectors. The first edition of the contest was organised in 2014 and the results of the first round were very promising and exceeded expectations. In total, the National School of Public Administration received 51 applications. Jury experts praised the scope of change and innovation in many quality applications. As a result of the contest, the School not only identified the champions of innovation but will also create a database of various good management practices in the Polish public sector, thereby enabling the spread of good practices ranging from IT, HR and strategic management, to procurement, the involvement of citizens and service delivery.

The contest is also expected to have an impact on the public perceptions and to increase trust in government. Public administration in Poland is often criticised for being not innovative, incapable of change or unresponsive to clients' and citizens' needs. The motivations for the contest are:

- showing that change and modernisation are possible within the public administration

- linking the successful managers with others who are planning to create change or would like to know what works and what does not work within other organisations by establishing a network of innovative managers in public administration

- strengthening and promoting successful managers and institutions through recognition and positive feedback

- inspiring the public sector by presenting and considering approaches used in private companies and third sector organisations.

The contest is expected to continue over the coming years. The best practices were distributed in a publication prepared jointly with THINKTANK. Some of the entrepreneurial managers will also be invited to the panel discussions and following workshops organised by the Academy in 2016.

Learning in networks (cases from Finland, Spain, Belgium, Germany, Israel and Austria)

Finland's Government Change Agent Network

Finland's Government Change Agent Network was founded in 2013 and is open to all civil servants working in government ministries. The network is a loosely organised and self-directing team of experts from different ministries, with different backgrounds, education and expertise. While diverse, all participants recognise the need and will to build up a working culture based on a "whole of government" mind set and "cross-silo" ways of working. The network is also willing to test and adopt modern, explorative and digital ways of working. Its participants are all volunteers, i.e. they are not nominated to represent any particular point of view or ministry in the network.

In practice the network's mission is being implemented by building a new kind of working culture in many different ways: common discussions, supporting and launching new initiatives, writing blogs, giving expert statements, and starting new experiments, as well as supporting and bringing innovative approaches in to preparation of all new issues and projects.

In implementing government strategies, ministries need to take an agile and smart approach that cuts across administrative boundaries, making it easier to link up with other relevant stakeholders in society, and making the best possible use of their wide range of skills and expertise.

The biggest value of the Change Makers Network lies in its unofficial character. At the same time, this is the biggest challenge to keeping the network alive. However, the future of the network seems positive. It is already widely recognised and its informal and unofficial nature is accepted. Little by little it has taken "to the tables" where decisions are being made; either as a network or through its members representing new, open- and broad-minded approaches

The future of the network will be characterised by the following themes and actions:

- getting rid of unnecessary resistance to a culture of new approaches and ostensible efficiency

- from planning to quick experiments

- taking advantage of the power of networks and the wisdom of crowds

- with common objectives to common activities.

Spain's Social and Knowledge Ecosystem

Spain's Social and Knowledge Ecosystem is conceived of as a new model of semi-informal communication, favouring communities of interest connecting various actors, thereby allowing the linking of talent and encouraging public innovation. It is a project of Spain's National Public Administration Institute (INAP). Its main objectives are to create and disseminate transformative learning and high quality knowledge; to promote transparency and open government; to boost the innovation within the public administration and to foster exemplary practice, legitimacy, autonomy, efficiency and responsibility in the public administration. It does this through three tools: a professional network, a knowledge bank and an innovation bank of good practice. The project is directed at public employees of all public administration levels and also citizens.

The project hopes to use informal networks as a way of tapping into the potential of human actors beyond the day-to-day requirements of their relatively rigid job posts. By linking people with similar interests and abilities across bureaucratic silos, the project expects to detect talent that can be a precursor to innovation inside government. In this way, INAP hopes to contribute towards an inclusive talent management strategy which enables people to leverage networks beyond their team to build their personal and professional capacity, building a working system based on a social chart, not an organisational chart. This is a good example of the link between HRM and organisational development.

Belgium's Innovation Learning Network

Belgium's Innovation Learning Network aims to coach innovative projects, and to create an environment where civil servants can help and learn from each other to become better at innovation processes. The participants (civil servants from different government organisations) are encouraged to become better at understanding the goals of government and society, management incentives, recognising restrictive patterns, co-creation with all kinds of stakeholders, encouraging passion, multidisciplinary working, following trends and getting things done more efficiently. Innovative civil servants have been interviewed to ask how innovation could be stimulated. They considered that innovative projects should be supported by coaching and knowledge sharing.

The network's objectives include better organisational outcomes and practices such as co-creation with users, and learning for individual civil servants. It currently works in 14 government organisations, with 20 projects and about 50 civil servants.

Germany's Junior Staff Orientation Programme

Germany's Junior Staff Orientation Programme is a programme for junior staff development at the Federal Ministry of Labour and Social Affairs. Its focus is on freshly recruited young staff members who need to be retained and supported over the long term, because they are potentially the experts and leaders of the future. Since the launch of the programme some 300 employees have taken part. The result is a network that is fit for the future and benefits not only the junior staff but the whole organisation.

The main goals are to support new employees; develop their methodological, interpersonal and management skills, and to establish and maintain social networks that will facilitate and foster their potential for innovation, making the ministry more attractive to potential employees. This is accomplished via 18 months of networking, training, mentoring, discussions with senior executives and site visits. An active alumni network ensures continuity through broader network meetings and seminars.

The programme is a network with a training and development focus. Its emphasis is on strengthening co-operation, teamwork and networking; and strengthening staff's methodological and interpersonal skills. It recognises that Germany needs highly skilled employees and executive staff who know how to use and benefit from networks. Today, the key skills junior staff should have are the ability to work in a team, viable self-management and effective communication skills. Employees' commitment, creativity and capacity for innovation largely depend on their degree of motivation and their skills.

The programme results in better co-operation across directorates-general. Such co-operation helps increase interaction, improve the flow of information and develop creative ideas across existing hierarchies and across teams. Junior staff, alumni and mentors use the network to build up contacts within the ministry, informally share information and to support and learn from each other. Two principles – trust and reciprocity – are key assets and the glue that binds the network together. By strengthening teamwork, conflict management and communication skills; developing horizontal thinking and improving negotiation skills for working in groups and projects, junior staff and alumni learn to build trusting relationships, co-operate with colleagues from other divisions or departments, and create new and innovative ideas. This process has more lasting effects than individual measures delivered by external educational institutions, because staff members are more motivated to change their social behaviour, improve their skills and their ways of communicating to reduce misunderstandings if they have the opportunity to get involved in shaping the approach.

Israel's Civil Service Cadet Program

Israel's Civil Service Cadet Program intends to build and train a management cadre that will catalyse change in the civil service. Each year, a cadre of cadets is identified, screened and recruited into a six year training and placement track, after which each cadet is placed in a key position in the civil service. The first cohort of the renewed programme began in August 2012, and there are now 4 cohorts, each consisting of approximately 30 cadets.

In an era when the pace and the nature of change are rapidly evolving, the public sector must develop the capacity to identify, sort, train, place and develop its civil servants in a way that will better prepare them for making decisions that are relevant to the complex challenges of the 21st century. To do this, the programme consists of three stages:

1. Identifying foxes rather than hedgehogs: candidates are selected through a competitive multi-stage screening process that examines their personality, values, capacity to catalyse change, teamwork and leadership skills, and their desire and capacity to help mobilise the civil service to the next level. The recruitment process looks for candidates who possess qualities of "foxes" – a distinction made by Isiah Berlin in *The Fox and the Hedgehog*. According to Berlin, a person with fox-like characteristics, will cope easily with constantly changing reality, is flexible and open to absorbing new patterns of thought and action, and has the ability to cope with long periods of uncertainty. This is as opposed to "hedgehogs" who tend to examine reality through one unifying principle.

2. Systemic and integrative training: this lasts two years and combines professional and academic experience within five core clusters: 1) generating multidisciplinary learning; 2) shaping public policy; 3) learning and integrating leadership models among people who are influential within the public sphere, focusing on adaptive leadership and leading in groups; 4) deepening understanding of Israeli society, the Jewish people and the regional and global arenas; and 5) acquiring a set of management tools. These clusters are integrated in three concurrent tracks: the academic track, the professional track (practical experience through practicums and rotation programmes), and the personal and team development track (the network of graduates).

3. The placement model to create a network of diverse opportunities: this consists of a four-year period during which cadets are placed in government ministries based on their capabilities and the state's needs. The goal is that during this period, the cadet will work in two positions of influence, either on national assignments as determined by the government, within policy planning departments and ministerial cabinets, or in national knowledge centres, assisting the Director-Generals of ministries and/or strengthening ministries challenged by ageing leadership or which are in need of reinforcement.

The programme is expected to affect employees' ability to innovate through several aspects including:

- providing knowledge and tools to a management cadre who will be leading change in the civil service

- generating a multidimensional perspective of Israeli society, including familiarisation with the diverse layers of Israeli society

- instilling an understanding of the processes of change in the public sector in Israel and worldwide (in local and central government and in national and international institutions), and familiarisation with key models in this field

- teaching different management methods and providing a critical examination of the role of the manager and the leader in the civil service (from the definition of the problem, to presentation of alternatives based on an analysis of the problem, and ultimately, implementation on the ground)

- advancing personal and professional empowerment, including dealing with ethical dilemmas.

The programme is expected to improve motivation by using intrinsic rewards which include the six-year training and placement track, and guidance into key positions in the civil service. It is important to emphasise that from the beginning, the programme targets people who are motivated to work in the civil service of Israel since they seek to catalyse changes from inside the public system.

The programme develops and cultivates the following values and capabilities in the cadets:

- Vision and long-range thinking.

- Constructive thinking: analysing the context and acting accordingly and being able to examine the significance of events by constantly moving between different spheres of knowledge. Understanding the realities in times of constant change.

- Ability to cope with lasting uncertainty.

- Nimble-mindedness and quick thinking and creativity, methodological discipline, and focus.

- Continuously learning while improving and building a toolbox.

- Eagerness to expand knowledge and insights, while identifying the relevant knowledge to use in different frameworks.

- Performance orientation/activism: ability to translate plans into action that adheres to a high standard while reflecting attention to detail, with or without direction from above; systemic thinking; familiarity with the structure and complexities of the public sector; use of the best technological and pedagogical systems available (such as simulations and e-learning).

Austria's Cross-Mentoring Programme

Austria's Cross-Mentoring Programme aims to develop networks through mentoring, with a specific focus on female employees who wish to enter the management cadre. In the course of the programme experienced managers such as directors and directors general act as mentors and support female colleagues from other federal ministries interested in developing professionally and advancing their careers. The mentors pass on their knowledge and experiences, give advice on career planning and facilitate the mentees' entrance into professional networks. The fact that mentors may be male or female brings about another positive effect: not only women do women have the chance to give career guidance and build networks, but men in management positions are encouraged to develop openness towards female careers, overcome prejudices and rethink common role clichés.

Within the supporting programme, there are several networking meetings open to all mentors, mentees and personnel developers. To engage even more in networking, mentees may organise peer groups dealing with different relevant topics.

Since 2005 about 750 participants have taken part in the programme.

Austria's Federal Academy of Public Administration

Austria's Federal Academy of Public Administration views itself as a "driver of public administration innovation" as it enables staff to improve their skills and qualifications, develop and optimise their careers, and improve organisational development. In addition to a wide variety of training and development programmes and activities, the academy offers a number of courses and seminars directly focused on improving the innovation capacity of Austria's public sector. These include:

- Innovation – Thinking public administration anew: This seminar focuses on the principles of innovation management based on practical examples. It includes: defining innovation, methods and tools of innovation, concepts and developments in the EU and OECD, presentation of national and international examples, open innovation, and working on case studies. It is aimed at civil servants working in the fields of HR and public innovation, executives, and staff members with an interest in the development of new ideas.

- Public administration innovations – "Learning Journeys". This offers executives and organisations an opportunity to learn about different innovation methods and to get tailor-made consulting for specific innovation projects in their working environment. Participants aim to learn from each other, set up networks and exchange know-how with experts. These workshops assist organisations wanting to implement successful change processes. It is aimed at public organisations at federal, regional and municipality level.

- Service design – Customer orientation. This addresses a growing concern among public administrations to focus on service and consumer orientation, using service design to assess and organise services and processes from the customer's perspective in order to enhance their effectiveness, efficiency and usability. Service designers work together with companies and people from various disciplines. Its aims are to both improve services and to improve citizens' awareness of services.

- Co-operation with NGOs. This seminar presents three concrete co-operation projects between the Ministry of Agriculture, Forestry, Environment and Water Management and NGOs. The aim is to assess and critically analyse the potential of this form of co-operation. The seminar sheds light on the various fields of activities and tasks of NGOs; financial conditions of projects; between the poles of administration, politics and civil society; new opportunities versus risks; and the motivations for participants to set up co-operation in their field of activity.

Mobility programmes (cases from Austria, Canada and Korea)

Austria's Mobility Management Programme

Austria's Mobility Management Programme is a key instrument for needs- and skills-oriented personnel deployment which also supports employees in pursuing career changes. The Federal Chancellery set up the Mobility Management Service on 1 April 2012 to manage the federal civil service's internal labour market. It helps to balance labour supply and demand within the civil service by matching excess staff from one area with vacant positions in another, as well as supporting staff members who wish to change their careers. Using the Civil Service Job Exchange and Career Databank (the key instruments for mobility, along with the necessary legal framework), the Mobility Management Service tries to find suitable staff for all federal ministries from among those interested in changing jobs. The result is effective and efficient personnel management which goes hand in hand with promoting staff members' specific knowledge, strengths and interests.

The Job Exchange and Career Databank allows civil service staff looking for a career change to set up individual career profiles, listing their qualifications, know-how, skills and experience, as well as their preferred fields of work and the ministries they would like to work for. They can also do this anonymously. In any case, contact is made using the contact details given in the respective career profile. Many civil service managers have come to value "brain exchange", having recognised the benefit of staff rotation, i.e. the know-how employees bring from other areas of public administration, putting it to good use in their day-to-day work. Mobility is therefore increasingly being seen as enhancing human capital, and consequently becoming standard practice.

Since the implementation of the Mobility Management Service, various government departments have used it to search for staff. In total, it has received more than 1 100 requests from government departments to fill a variety of jobs. About 200 employees have successfully changed jobs.

Interchange Canada

Interchange Canada enables the government of Canada to temporarily exchange employees with all other sectors of the economy, domestically and internationally, while maintaining a link to the employee's home organisation. Assignments are for the purpose of knowledge transfer, acquiring specialised expertise, and/or professional development. Interchange Canada has been used to facilitate exchanges between the federal government and the provinces or territories, private business, non-profit organisations, academia, and aboriginal organisations both within Canada and internationally.

Interchange assignments can be used to develop leadership competencies through the use of assignments to organisations which need specific experience to bridge a skills-building gap. Interchange Canada also serves as an excellent means of temporarily attaining skills unavailable in the home organisation and to build and transfer knowledge, enhancing internal capacity both within government and in other sectors.

There were 645 active Interchange Canada assignments in the 2015/16 fiscal year. Approximately 40% of these were core government employees assigned outside the core government, and the remaining 60% were external employees assigned into the core government. Approximately 60% of the total assignments involved other levels of government (provinces/municipalities) or government agencies. About 7% involved the private sector, and the rest involved non-governmental organisations.

Korea's Open Position System and Job Posting System

Korea's Open Position System and Job Posting System are two ways of appointing qualified people to the senior civil service and director positions, which play a crucial role in key government policy decisions. The Open Position System recruits from both inside and outside the public sector for positions that require expertise and the Job Posting System recruits from within the public sector. There is a significant correlation between both systems and the AMO of employees. According to surveys conducted in 2009 and 2011, personnel who took the positions through these two systems reported that their abilities and achievements have increased.

Korea's Personnel Exchange System

Korea's Personnel Exchange System is a one-to-one exchange programme moving public servants between administrative agencies and other public organisations for a limited period. Its goals are to improve professional understanding across different agencies through personnel exchanges; to remove departmental partitions by building a mutual co-operation system; to actively respond to changes in the administrative environment and demands for convergent administration; and to enhance the capabilities of the government human resources by providing extensive experience and general development of abilities of individual public servants.

Personnel exchange improved participants' ability to perform their jobs by allowing them to break out of their narrow perspective about their existing work and directly experience the work details, working methods and cultures of different organisations, which improved their understanding of other organisations.

Some staff were reluctant to participate in personnel exchanges due to concerns about job assignment and performance assessment, adapting to new organisations, and economic or living issues due to moving to a different city. To address these issues, Korea has improved the system to give staff a one-step higher grade in their performance assessment compared to the grade before the exchange, assign them a desired position when returning after exchange, support consultation with a mentor, and provide incentives for moving to a different city such as housing subsidies and housing support allowances. Furthermore, Korea has made every effort to encourage interest in exchanges in the civil service community by holding workshops to share information and experiences among existing participants.

To further develop the practice, the Korean government has plans to systematise personnel exchange around collaboration, mutual use of expertise, policy-field link areas, and to diversify the exchange methods by including unilateral exchanges as well as one-to-one mutual exchanges.

Holistic people-centred HRM (cases from Belgium, Germany, Sweden, Switzerland, the United Kingdom, Finland and Canada)

Belgium's New Ways of Working

Belgium's New Ways of Working initiative is about the creation of a more dynamic workplace where new ways of working have been implemented to promote practices such as desk sharing, home working, increased focus on results and more flexible ways in which teams are structured and work. The business objective was to become a "sexy" and sustainable federal public service in order to achieve three main HR challenges: to find talented people, to retain the right people and to make people happy.

The initiative implemented five programmes:

1. Culture shift and results orientation, with a focus on motivating staff members and promoting team spirit, initiative taking and personal development. This programme integrated the concept of team objectives through enhanced accountability of supervisors and an optimised evaluation methodology.

4. Dynamic offices create modular working and living areas. Offices are no longer assigned to people; agents choose the workplace that is best suited to the assignment they are carrying out ("dynamic office"). They totally vacate their workstation at the end of the day to allow a colleague to use it the following day ("clean desk"). Special attention is paid to the concepts of welfare and design.

5. Digitisation and e-working provide Federal Personnel Service (FPS) staff members with ergonomic, reliable, high-performance tools to enable them to work efficiently together and well as concrete solutions to better manage the lifecycle of paper and electronic documents.

6. Client orientation provides quality services and increases accessibility and responsiveness, for greater public satisfaction.

7. Communication and change management support all programmes and themes. Better communication facilitates greater clarity, transparency and participation.

The German Employment Agency's Lifecycle Approach

The German Employment Agency's Lifecycle Approach to HRM is an intergenerational approach to enhancing the work ability of its staff and focuses on competence, health and engagement to promote lifelong learning and well-being in the workplace. Promoting lifelong learning helps support all measures to promote sustainable change and innovation. The approach is made up of a variety of measures which, as a whole, support the individualisation of HR management and also support talent management. These include a competency-based and modular HR development system open for career opportunities and competency development at every age; reintegration programmes for workers who return after prolonged absence due to, for example, parental leave; family services to help employees care for family members; various flexible working time models; telework and mobile working options; an engagement index to measure and better understand the workplace climate and management requirements; and a knowledge transfer program to stimulate intergenerational learning and maintain corporate knowledge.

By establishing a programme to promote work ability (competence, health and engagement), HR management contributes towards building an innovation-friendly environment. It tackles the most challenging issues, such as career downturns during parental leave, by supporting leadership through dialogue-based instruments and tapping into staff potential at every age. Strengthening mental health and well-being in the workplace mainly requires addressing leadership and collaboration issues and requires "healthy leadership". This type of leadership addresses the emotional aspects of working relationships between superiors and their staff. The main risk is not making a shift in leadership training. Individualised HR management is a major leadership challenge. Leaders must be prepared to lead mixed-age teams and to go for more transformational leadership. At the same time, the Bundesagentur für Arbeit is taking action to also strengthen leaders' resilience and health.

The major challenge was to design the framework and to create acceptance within the organisation for an integrated or holistic management approach at the start. It was a long road to transfer the concept into practice and raise awareness that this might be the right way to avoid past mistakes. Leaders must be convinced that such activities are intended to support them to perform successfully and to achieve their targets. It was, and is, very important to invest time in developing the concept, but even more time to developing and discussing the right implementation strategy. It is more difficult to shape thinking patterns than to change structures and standards. The right methods need to be used to bring organisational development and HR development together as interactive players.

In this context, a key success factor turned out to be increasing participation and getting all stakeholders involved to build on their experiences with best and worst practices, and to let them participate in developing the concepts (hence, so-called "HR future conferences" were used). It was also very effective to test each concept (such as the family service) and to gain more experience and information about users' needs and the relevant process steps before developing the final concept. It was also very helpful to bring leaders together with leaders from different organisations, either from the private or the public sector, to learn why these institutions had invested in similar policies. The project used networks, platforms and forums to share common experiences and to gather further ideas.

Sweden's Common Basic Values for Central Government Employees

Sweden's Common Basic Values for Central Government Employees clarifies the value system that stems from the constitutionally based principles of equal value of all people, the rule of law and good service to citizens. The values documents have been recently updated and summarised by the government's Council for Skills Development. One specific reason for publishing these documents is Sweden's position-based recruitment system based on merit and skills. Since all government agencies are independent employers, Sweden has rather high mobility between sectors. So both at the time of recruitment and during the development of central government activities, knowledge of and respect for these basic values and principles needed to be improved.

The regulation of government agencies' activities is based on the legal foundations that apply to all central government agencies. These can be summarised in six principles, which together make up the common basic values of central government activities:

- Democracy – all public power proceeds from the people.

- Legality – public power is exercised in accordance with the law.

- Objectivity – everyone is equal before the law; objectivity and impartiality must be observed.

- Free formation of opinion – Swedish democracy is founded on the free formation of opinion.

- Respect for all people's equal value, freedom and dignity – public power is to be exercised with respect for the equal worth of all and for the freedom and dignity of the individual.

- Efficiency and service – efficiency and resource management must be combined with service and accessibility.

By necessity, these principles are formulated in a general way. It is up to civil servants and their management to clarify what they mean in the context of their particular activities. Different principles may sometimes be in conflict with each other. It is then a matter of carefully weighing up alternatives that remain within the law and do not disregard important values.

Central government employees often have a high degree of independence in their work. Many times they may discover that the law or regulations leave scope for interpretation. It is at such times, when civil servants have to rely on their own judgement, that the central government's basic values play a particularly important guidance role.

In order to promote the values and increase their use as a management tool, the council arranges seminars at a national level, inviting representatives from all agencies to attend. The seminars are recorded and displayed on the council's website. The council also uses a "train the trainers" model which has seen 130 employees trained in methods of working with values at the agency level. The agency also uses case studies to support internal discussions about sensitive situations and dilemmas.

Switzerland's Career Guidance for Lawyers

Switzerland's Career Guidance for Lawyers addresses a broad-based need to be able to offer people specialist career paths. The idea was to offer staff individually differentiated development possibilities, which did not have to culminate in a hierarchical management position. Using the example of the position of lawyer which is present in all departments, the scheme recorded concrete expectations and guidance based on the professional development of this occupational category within the federal authorities.

Employees and line managers agreed that current development paths for lawyers beyond assuming management functions have not yet been clearly defined. For the most part, qualified specialist staff did not see systematic advancement from the point of view of a specialist or horizontal career. Employees would like more support from line managers and more transparency about opportunities for further career development.

Staff were interested in four overall types of career patterns. Promotion-oriented generalists attach a great deal of importance to their role as managers to structuring management relations along very collegial and supportive lines. Self-development and balance-oriented generalists have a meticulous approach to work and an attention to linguistic detail, quietly working away out of the limelight and drawing their job satisfaction less from deepening their understanding and more from the rich variety of their work as well as its communicative and co-operative dimensions. Balance-oriented specialists appreciate the specialist advisory work occurring behind the scenes, but also actively seek social and technical exchanges with colleagues, superiors and co-operation partners from other offices. Idealistic specialists get immense delight from the specialist intellectual challenges in their work and a high degree of satisfaction from working as highly competent, autonomous and at the same time very solution-based specialists and advisers.

Each of these four profiles suggests a particular approach to training and development, mobility and eventual management responsibilities. Identifying the different career types provided clear indications that the majority of lawyers in the federal administration probably did not aspire to the classic paths of promotion, but want to gain in-depth specialist knowledge or broaden their skills profile. They have great willingness, for example, to acquire new knowledge on task switching and activity changes, job rotation or job enrichment and to move at right angles to the classic paths of advancement. The same approach could also be used for development paths in other jobs such as personnel specialists, IT specialists and engineering technical experts.

The UK's Movement to Work

The United Kingdom's Movement to Work is a cross-sector, employer-led initiative. Its objective is to reduce youth unemployment through quality work experience and learning. The UK civil service is one of 15 founding employers of Movement to Work. A range of departments within the civil service committed to Movement to Work placements during 2014 with even more joining from 2015. Collectively 6 000 work placements will be delivered in the civil service during 2014/15. Implementing this programme at a time of limited financial and human resources has required the HR community charged with making the programme a success to take a number of innovative approaches to work organisation.

During 2014 the HR community in the civil service has been working collaboratively in a number of different ways, including working with HR colleagues in other sectors.

Within the civil service a working-level network was developed with responsibility for implementing Movement to Work Each department has a lead contact responsible for implementing their department's commitment. This network has increased in maturity, sharing insights and developing an approach for new organisations coming on board. The group has explored and escalated practical issues, such as a low risk appetite for reduced security clearance limiting access to buildings or computer systems. The group has also played an increasingly strategic role in Movement to Work by making sensible and insightful links with other organisational priorities such as age diversity in the workforce and addressing capability gaps. All of these insights have strengthened the business case for Movement to Work, by identifying benefits for different stakeholders. The infrastructure and processes built through the efforts of this group, had delivered over 3 000 work placements at the halfway point of 2014/15.

As the civil service is a federated organisation comprised of autonomous departments, gaining commitment and engagement from departments in order to deliver the work placements has been heavily based on influence from the centre of the organisation and by peer influence between HR Directors. The organisation of HR in the civil service has been conducive to this, with strong networks of departmental HR Directors who can be directed by the Head of Civil Service HR. This governance and accountability has been important for gaining engagement and pushing for progress.

HR leaders have been instrumental in implementing Movement to Work as a coherent strategy for the organisation. Identifying and bringing together relevant topics including the ageing workforce, improving social mobility through employment and exploring the bias towards experience over potential in recruitment and selection has helped to turn Movement to Work from being a corporate social responsibility programme into a meaningful and tangible part of delivering the business strategy for the civil service. This will, in turn, help to gain commitment from outside of HR.

Exploring and committing to partnerships with other organisations has been a further success. Accenture, a management consultancy, are providing an online skills academy for young people and the Chartered Institute of Personnel and Development (CIPD) are delivering a pilot employability mentoring scheme for young people through their members (HR professionals). These partnerships have been cost neutral, responding to interest from other organisations in undertaking a proof of concept with a big employer.

Outside of the civil service, at a programme level, the business case for Movement to Work has been refined and has undergone several iterations over the last year. HR directors from each organisation have shared their experiences with colleagues in other organisations at fortnightly meetings. These meetings included sharing success stories and testimonials and developing an approach to quality assurance. Organising the secondment of civil servants into the programme to help drive progress and to bring back expertise and insight from a variety of organisations has also strengthened this learning and sharing.

Finland's Towards Year 2020 Initiative

Finland's Towards Year 2020 Initiative is a co-creation process driven by the Ministry of Finance with other ministries and state agencies to update and clarify the state's management and personnel policy and working methods to meet future challenges, improve productivity and effectiveness, and achieve cost savings. In knowledge-based work, productivity growth cannot be achieved by doing more, but doing things in a new way. Therefore, thinking and acting in a new way should be reflected in the operational culture, relationships with the customers, expertise and leadership as well as in new practices in performance management and working habits, and more customer-friendly approaches to other players in society. To seek new solutions to so-called "wicked problems", civil servants should be willing to take more risks and start quick experiments and be prepared to replace old, outmoded ways of doing things.

To this end, the Ministry of Finance organised three workshops under the themes Towards New Leadership, Towards New Working Methods and Towards New HRM-practices. The aim is to crystallise the outcomes and spread the message widely to state administrations in a new, inspiring way. The aim is also to get the main messages included in the next government programme for 2015-19.

Together, these workshops are oriented towards establishing a new working culture in the state as an employer and as a working community. The main messages are:

- Public sector organisations' capacity to change is based on an enabling mindset and customer-oriented course of action, enabling leadership, up-to-date expertise, and highly motivated and healthy personnel.

- Public sector productivity is enhanced by digitising work and services and by acting smarter in every possible way.

- Digitisation opens up totally new possibilities to work and serve customers in the public sector.

- It is mainly a question of a new kind of balance between redefined responsibilities and increased level of freedom for individual workers.

- While work in the public sector is constantly changing as "free from time or place", the workshop emphasised the importance of guidance through common and understandable. This is a challenge to existing leadership skills and HR practices, which traditionally emphasise target setting at an individual level, rather than at a team or working community level.

- HR has to be seen as an enabler of the new working culture and new ways of working.

Canada's Key Leadership Competencies consultations

Canada's Key Leadership Competencies consultations were launched as part of an initiative to review and renew the Key Leadership Competencies (KLCs) that had been in place since 2005. The KLC profile forms the foundation for the selection, learning and development, and performance and talent management of executives in the Canadian federal public service. They needed to be updated to better reflect the new environment. The 2005 competency profile was comprised of four competencies: 1) values and ethics; 2) strategic thinking; 3) engagement; and 4) management excellence.

The 2005 KLC profile had been developed using the critical incident technique and in-depth conversations with senior public servants. In contrast, the initiative to refresh the KLCs used a very open, democratic and innovative consultation. To engage with public servants in a non-hierarchical fashion, the policy centre made use of two other initiatives running at the same time: 1) a government-wide engagement effort launched by the head of the public service; and 2) the introduction of a new internal social media tool. By using Web 2.0 tools for consultations, the policy centre was able to reach far and wide, and simultaneously engaged with and promoted a tech-savvy and high-performing work culture by "crowd sourcing" its consultation. In addition to this wide-reaching crowdsourcing approach, consultation efforts also deliberately engaged with stakeholders ranging from aspiring leaders looking to make it into the executive ranks, to the current cadre of executive leaders, and with very senior and retired public servants. The policy centre also consulted with recognised public policy experts from the private sector and academia to validate the proposed KLCs. This was one of the first occasions that such broad consultations had been conducted for the development of a human resources policy instrument within government. The KLC profile approved in October 2014 consists of a preamble that sets out the fundamental expectations of leadership within the Canada's public service and six competencies and their accompanying definitions: 1) create vision and strategy; 2) mobilise people; 3) uphold integrity and respect; 4) collaborate with partners and stakeholders; 5) promote innovation and change; and 6) achieve results. It is a product of these innovative consultation methods, and serves as a living example of the innovation and collaboration benchmark set for public service leaders.

One of the benefits of the broad consultations on the KLC profile is that it has led to increased buy in from those who are directly affected by it. The policy centre was also able to increase stakeholder engagement and generate a high degree of enthusiasm for the new KLCs across the Canadian public service. This level of engagement would never have been possible using more traditional methods.

While not without its challenges, the consultation proved itself to be a highly effective and cost-effective way to engage. Participation levels confirmed that public servants want to be engaged and to be engaged meaningfully. Web 2.0 technologies enabled a small team to reach other public servants and subject matter experts from coast to coast to coast in real time, without incurring travel costs. Another key insight is that this initiative would not have been successful were it not for the support of senior leadership who were willing to take the leap of faith required to implement this approach, and to take the risk of sharing content, broadly and openly for consultation.

Chapter 4.

The role of the budget process in promoting public sector innovation[1]

As OECD countries face continuing pressures to do more with less, public sector innovation increasingly offers a means of improving performance across government. Drawing on the OECD's extensive research on budgeting reforms across member countries, alongside in-depth case studies, this chapter examines the impact of budget processes and particularly the role of central budget authorities (CBAs) in supporting public sector innovation. The chapter considers how strategic outcome goals, fiscal frameworks, spending reviews, financial incentives, flexibility and performance management can serve to support (or hinder) innovation. It considers what conditions need to be in place for fiscal austerity to give rise to innovative ways to reduce spending, and how funds and other incentives can be used to encourage innovation. It considers the balance between granting the flexibility line agencies need to pursue innovation and the need for fiscal accountability, and the role of performance management and evidence in finding that balance. It concludes with some measures that budget agencies should consider in order to sustain public sector innovation.

The statistical data for Israel are supplied by and under the responsibility of the relevant Israeli authorities. The use of such data by the OECD is without prejudice to the status of the Golan Heights, East Jerusalem and Israeli settlements in the West Bank under the terms of international law.

Introduction

OECD countries face growing pressures to deliver more with less. This has prompted reforms in management and policy delivery, and budget processes have evolved to accommodate these new prerogatives with renewed focus on fiscal rules, expenditure frameworks and performance-informed budgeting. While public sector innovation can certainly support value for money and public sector performance, its disruptive features – including bottom-up and cross-cutting elements - are more challenging to the traditional top-down budget process. This raises the question of whether budget processes could better support public sector innovation, and if so how.

The rules and procedures of public sector decision making structure both the incentive and the capacity to innovate. In particular, the budget process is central to nearly everything that the public sector does, thanks to its critical role in allocating scarce resources among competing priorities and needs. Compared to other management areas (such as human resource management), there has been relatively little research exploring how the different dimensions of budgeting affect the inclination and capacity to innovate in OECD countries. Given the way many innovation efforts have grown out of the period of austerity following the global crisis – necessity being the mother of invention – the relationship between budgeting and public sector innovation is not neutral. Is innovation primarily seen as a way for sector agencies and ministries to do better with less resources, or is it a way for central budget authorities (CBAs) to identify additional sources of fiscal consolidation? How does each view affect the incentives to innovate? And how can budget processes and procedures be better structured to take into account an understanding of the dynamics of public sector innovation?

This chapter addresses the particular roles that the budget process and the central budget agency play in innovation in OECD countries. It examines important features of the budget process likely to have an impact on the capacity and incentives to innovate, including overall fiscal health, the budget flexibility provided to managers, budget rules and investment strategies for innovation. The chapter also reviews the innovation record of OECD countries, as reflected in recent public management reforms and new models of service delivery. Finally, it examines the role played by fiscal consolidation in defining space for innovation.

As in Chapter 3, the pathways of influence for budgeting on the innovation process can be captured through the common framework of ability, motivation and opportunity:

- Ability: does the budget provide agencies with the fiscal space, skills and platforms to scale up new ideas to achieve their broader adoption in government and the economy?

- Motivation: does the budget provide incentives and pathways to innovate, mitigation of risks, and ways to use savings to invest in new delivery systems?

- Opportunity: does the budget provide frontline workers and agencies with flexibility and room to experiment?

The chapter draws on the OECD's extensive databases and research on budgeting and management reforms across all member countries. These include the Observatory of Public Sector Innovation, the periodic OECD state of public finances surveys into members' fiscal strategies, the OECD's surveys of budgeting practices and procedures, and its individual country budget reviews, complemented by desk research and a literature review. This included access to a large survey of senior public sector managers in 19 European countries done under the auspices of the EU Coordinating for Cohesion in the Public Sector of the Future (COCOPS) project.

Finally, this work relies on in-depth case studies of six OECD countries that offer a mix of different fiscal positions, political regimes, governance structures, innovation records and budgetary practices. The case countries cover Denmark, France, the Netherlands, Portugal, the United Kingdom and the United States. The case studies are based on interviews with senior central budget and political officials, selected line ministry staff, dedicated innovation groups and independent observers such as national audit officials and academic researchers on budgeting and management.

The research indicated that the impact of the budget process and institutions on public sector innovation depends on the features of the budgeting process and how they come to support the innovation lifecycle, from identifying problems to diffusing tested innovations (Figure 4.1).

Figure 4.1. How budget arrangements support the innovation lifecycle

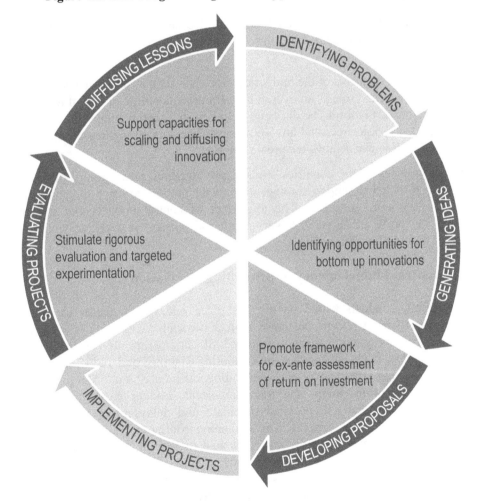

- **Generating ideas:** while top-down approaches ensure high-level goals are aligned with budgetary considerations, budgetary and performance frameworks can promote the bottom-up identification of service gaps and areas where interventions can be carried out. Innovative ideas can also be captured through financial incentives (e.g. innovation funds) as well as strategic processes such as spending reviews.

- **Developing proposals:** central budget agencies can play a role in developing common evidence-based frameworks and supporting tools to assess the financial viability and expected return on investment of project proposals. Budget arrangements which provide more predictable paths can allow agencies to make strategic investments to improve performance. Putting horizontal multi-year budget frameworks in place can support investments for large-scale innovations – such as shared services – which are beyond the scope of individual agencies and which take longer to reap benefits

- **Evaluating projects**: using rigorous methodologies for evaluation can help identify what works and target further experimentation where it is most needed. These initiatives can gain traction more rapidly when central leaders from the budget agencies or political leadership intervene to encourage their government-wide adoption.

- **Diffusing lessons**: Innovation funds can also be used to scale up and diffuse in other areas innovations once they have been successfully implemented in one place.

Other systemic elements of the budgeting process – such as performance management – also play an important role as an overarching framework sitting on top of the innovation lifecycle. Having a platform for dialogue between the central budget agency and line ministries on fiscal objectives and how to achieve them can strengthen the strategic view on where innovation can achieve the greatest impact.

The experiences of the countries studied also illustrate how strong political capital can be used to marshal support through the budget process to carry out innovations in service delivery and operations. The alignment of central budgets and management leadership can prove effective in lowering internal barriers as well as winning public support for more radical innovations.

The role of the central budget agency in promoting innovation

Traditionally, budgets would be the last place one would expect to nurture and champion management reform and innovation. Classically, budgeting is incremental in nature, favouring marginal changes in resource allocation from the baseline of the past. Such a stance has many advantages in promoting stability and reducing risks of the unknown. Budgeting is a creature of a demanding calendar of work and painful choices where the urgent often trumps the truly important. Longer-term policy issues and significant trade-offs that risk political stalemate and delays often fall victim to the drumbeat of this relentless process. The budgeting routine solves many problems for government, but it is most certainly not calculated to prompt policy innovation. Yet in recent years, in many countries, stark budget reductions and cuts have at times had significant effects on structures and systems, thus creating the conditions for radical innovation to occur to cope with and adapt to new realities.

In its role as guardian of the national treasury, the central budget agency can be expected to view agencies' claims for both resources and flexibility with some natural and, some would say, well-deserved suspicion. Indeed, the budget agency has traditionally brandished its role as what Allen Schick called "the central command and control post of government" (Schick, 2001), specifying items of expenditure, monitoring agency compliance and serving as a watchdog to the executive and the legislature for accountability over appropriated funds. Defining a new role for the central budget agency which is compatible with contemporary managerial concepts is a difficult task, for it entails balancing governments' critical need for financial discipline against managers' need for freedom to act.

However, the focus of budgeting and the role of the budget agency itself has been transformed in recent decades. The history of budgeting shows its evolution from a process focused on controlling public resources and preventing abuse to a system emphasising managerial efficiency and programmatic impact. Table 4.1 charts the history of budget reform in the United States, illustrating the shifting frameworks that have shaped budgeting over the past 100 years.

Table 4.1. The United States budget process since 1900: Evolving to meet the pressures of the day

Time	1900 to 1930s	1940 to 1950s	1960 To 2010s	2010 onwards
	Budget and Accounting Act of 1921	Budgeting and Accounting Act of 1950	GRPA 1993 Program Assessment Rating Tool (PART) 2004	Government Performance and Results (GPRA) Modernization Act of 2010
Focus	Dollars People Accounts	Transactions Activities Functions	Programmes Outputs Outcomes Impact	Whole-of-government Impact Evidence-based
Emphasis	Resources	Work	Purpose	Priorities

Source: Based on Schick, A. (1966), "The road to PPB: The stages of budget reform", updated with more current information.

Schick has noted that the changing orientation of the budgeting enterprise has reshaped the role of the central budget agency itself (Schick, 2001). As entitlements have taken a growing share of budgets, control over spending on line items has become a less effective strategy to control spending. As countries have sought to modernise their governance and management mechanisms, and given the impact of agencification (the process of creating new agencies or giving them more autonomy), many countries' budget agencies have jettisoned their traditional controls and championed reforms by integrating management reform with the budget process. Agencies have gained new flexibility over control of line items as budget agencies pursue government-wide influence by commanding broader fiscal, management and policy target setting and evaluation. The shifting locus of control from detailed transactions to broader goals and targets is one that befits a budget agency under pressure to help elected governments manage the economy and public expectations for performance, delivering on broader goals such as inclusiveness and productivity. Identifying broader goals and objectives, and aligning the budget and allocation process to these broad objectives, has also been identified as one of the ways to build governance for inclusive growth, following discussions held at the OECD Public Governance Ministerial meeting in Helsinki in November 2015.

These observations are reinforced by the OECD's survey of budgeting practices and procedures (OECD, 2014). The report found that OECD countries have increased line agencies' flexibility by reducing the number of line items, enhancing lump sum appropriations for operating costs, permitting executives to reallocate funding across line items after appropriations are received, and enabling carryovers for unused appropriations. While such flexibilities are often accompanied by reviews of the central budget agencies, they have been embraced across the OECD. For instance, 70% of OECD countries deploy lump sum appropriations for operating costs and nearly all countries allow ministries to reallocate funds within their jurisdiction with some restrictions (OECD, 2014). Challenges still remain to introducing innovations in the budget process itself, to foster allocation for multiple goals, or for interagency co-operation to address complex or cross-cutting issues.

The rest of this chapter looks at the role of central budget agencies in promoting, sustaining and expanding innovation through its lifecycle. In particular, it examines the following key central budget practices, rules and institutions, and their potential formative role in either promoting or inhibiting innovation in government:

- **Financial incentives**: central budget officials provide selected financial incentives linked to innovation which can play a vital role in identifying innovations and promoting interest in jump-starting innovation. Financial incentives also play an important role in scaling and diffusion innovations once they are proved successful.

- **Fiscal frameworks and targets**: in a fiscally-constrained environment, fiscal frameworks and targets are needed to keep a cap on overall expenditures. In this context, central budget officials can use fiscal frameworks and rules – e.g. top-down spending reviews, fiscal rules and other processes – as a catalyst for promoting innovation.

- **Flexibility**: line ministries and agencies often demand greater flexibility to pursue innovation within overall fiscal constraints and guidelines. Performance-driven approaches are supposed to give agencies more leeway in the way that they administer their resources to achieve stated objectives giving more scope for flexibility and innovation.

- **Strategic outcome goals**: the central budget agency and budget formulation process often play a major role in framing objectives and articulating the agenda for performance, setting targets and goals that can spur cross-cutting innovation by agencies to achieve them. **Performance and promoting useful evidence**: performance management and budget linkages can provide a platform for testing and scaling up innovations and management, including leveraging the power of "what works" approaches.

Financial incentives

There is an assumption that public servants are risk averse and not inclined to make the leaps necessary to achieve efficiency gains and innovation in service delivery. A rule- and process-based public sector is not considered to be naturally prone to innovation. While many consider this a questionable premise (see discussion in Chapter 2), it has driven countries to develop special incentives to identify and reward innovation. These programmes involve both special innovation funds set aside in the budget as well as routine efficiency dividends in agency budget allocations that may act as a spur to innovation.

Denmark stands out among the countries using innovation funds. Its Ministry of Finance allocated EUR 16 million to a public sector efficiency fund that was awarded on a competitive basis to promote the scaling up of innovation pilots. Projects included support for digitisation and information technology investments in regional and local government. While this was a one-time initiative, the Ministry of Finance continues to finance the use of private consultants to assess possible innovations in government efficiency. A new Centre for Public Innovation was established in 2014, with EUR 3.7 million in funding, to share best practice and collect successful innovations from across the regions.

In France, the institutional focus for innovation is the General Secretariat for the Modernisation of Public Action, founded in 2007. It has established a Future Investment Programme aimed at innovators within the public sector, and has invested a total of EUR 176 million so far. The goal is to stimulate innovative projects to act as prototypes that can be scaled up for broader implementation. It issues formal calls for proposals, which are reviewed by experts in the fields covered. Areas supported include the digitisation of public services, development of open data exchanges, streamlining the interface between agencies and their clientele, and strengthening capacity for experimentation (Box 4.1). One programme across a group of hospitals reduced collective waiting times at emergency departments by an average of 20% (McKinsey & Co., 2011: p.19).

Box 4.1. Using funds to strengthen innovation capacity in France

In France, the merger of regions in January 2016 has called for a rethink and adaptation of how state services operate at regional level to ensure more effective and innovative public action across the whole country. The vision is to develop the innovation capacity of state services at territorial level to deliver the modernisation and digitisation of public services.

On 16 March 2016, Jean-Vincent Place, Secretary of State for State Reform and Simplification, announced a call for projects dedicated to the territorial administration of the state in the Future Investment Programme (*Programme d'investissements d'avenir* - PIA). Two new calls for projects were launched officially on 8 April 2016 under the Digital Transition of the State and Modernisation of Public Action Fund. They focused for the first time on central government services delivered at local level with the aim of making the civil servant a key player in their transformation. The goals are to break down barriers between government departments, improve working conditions for civil servants, open up to the involvement of external partners, encourage sharing of experiences, promote local initiatives and develop a culture of innovation.

The first call for projects dedicated to "Territorial Professional Communities" aims to develop, adapt and diffuse new collaborative ways of working within local agencies of central government bodies on the basis of uses and digital tools. Projects supported under the PIA aim to strengthen collaboration among central government bodies at a local level and their innovation capacities.

Among those funded, the Territorial Innovation Laboratories programme aims to support the creation of innovation laboratories to enable the exchange of ideas and promote creative behavior among national civil servants operating at local level. The territorial innovation labs are expected to involve other stakeholders (such as operators, authorities, associations and users) and take full advantage of innovative digital solutions to strengthen the capabilities of national civil servants at local level.

Source: translated from SGAMP (2016), "L'action publique se transforme", www.modernisation.gouv.fr/la ction-publique-se-transforme/avec-les-administrations-et-les-operateurs-publics/investissements-davenir-deux-appels-a-projets-accompagner-transition-numerique-administration-territoriale.

Most of the countries reviewed reported applying some form of efficiency dividends to all departments in government. Originally pioneered by Australia, these mandated cuts in agency operating funds have also been applied by Denmark, France and the Netherlands. The premise behind them is that productivity grows in agencies every year and should be recaptured by the government either to reduce overall spending or to be reallocated within the agency or by the finance ministry. In most countries, efficiency dividends are a flat percentage of total operating funds available each year and, in effect, constitute an across-the-board cut in resources. Denmark applied a dividend of 2% each year and used the money for reallocation. On top of this, it imposed cuts of 2.5% and 5% in 2011 and 2012, as part of the country's fiscal consolidation. However, unlike an across-the-board cut, line ministries were required to submit implementation plans to a cabinet committee.

The record of efficiency dividends for innovation is mixed. In Australia, which has 25 years of experience of them, studies indicate that the dividend did promote greater efficiency among the agencies. However, in more recent years, the "low hanging fruits" of efficiency saving have disappeared, requiring agencies to institute cuts in services to meet these targets, particularly in smaller agencies. Other agencies have resorted to gamesmanship including building the dividend into the baseline of their budget requests and finding short-term savings with longer-term costs, such as deferred maintenance or hiring (Doggett, 2010).

Overall, innovation funds and efficiency dividends have provided agencies with incentives to innovate. However, officials indicate that the ability of these vehicles to encourage innovation relies on a several important factors. First, agencies need flexibility to use new resources or satisfy the dividend in areas that provide the greatest productivity yield to its programmes and clientele. Governments that have delegated greater powers over spending to agencies may be expected to reap more results from innovation funds and efficiency dividends than other countries. Second, excessive fragmentation may prevent strategic responses, such as reorganising or mutualising support services, and may lead to small agencies lagging behind and seeing their capacity to innovate severely reduced. Third, agencies are more likely to use awards and dividends to promote innovation if they believe they will have predictable budgets over several years. New delivery approaches and projects often require funding certainty over time and agencies will be reluctant to institute new arrangements if they do not know whether they will have stable funding going forward. In some cases, such as investments in rehabilitation in prisons, multi-year investments are needed before paybacks to the budget and the society can be realised.

Fiscal framework and targets

In times of fiscal constraints, the greatest influence the budget process has on innovation is perhaps through the allocation of limited resources. The OECD Principles on Budgetary Governance call for countries to articulate fiscal goals and expenditure ceilings for three- or four-year time periods. This provides more effective implementation of fiscal policy goals and also lengthens the time horizon of budgetary planning. If successfully implemented, medium-term frameworks can create a stable financial environment that can encourage agencies to consider innovation and prudent risk taking. Guaranteed base of funding over multiple years gives agencies the certainty they need to consider new programmes and innovations to achieve outcomes over the multi-year window.

The case study countries demonstrate what happens when such frameworks break down in periods of crisis and gridlock. When governments cannot pass appropriations due to political gridlock, provisions are made to enable government to work until new funding is passed. In Belgium, a caretaker government was in effect for 590 days pending the formation of a new coalition government. No new programmes or budgetary initiatives could be undertaken during this period, as agencies were funded every month based on one-twelfth of their previous budgets (Bouckaert and Brans, 2012). In the United States, the passage of full year appropriations has become a rarity, prompting Congress and the President to agree on a series of continuing resolutions, or interim appropriations, to forestall a government shutdown; often departments must cope with a series of several short-term continuing resolutions for a given year. During these periods, innovation stops as agencies are required to fund existing programmes based on a congressional formula anchored to the previous year's appropriation funding. A senior official at one major federal department said that these interim funding vehicles had prevented his department from instituting reforms and eliminating programmes and administrative units that could have achieved significant savings and reforms.

Budget crises punctuate the established fiscal equilibrium agencies face. Such interruptions can heighten the innovation imperative, prompting innovations that can both improve performance and reduce spending. However, it is by no means certain that budget crises will prompt innovation on their own. Rather, for innovation to take place, it needs to be supported by the following conditions:

- **Agencies have the capacity to plan and design the innovations needed**. For instance, the Netherlands Education Ministry suffered cuts in staff of over 30% over several years, which limited their ability to implement performance and evidence-based initiatives.

- **Agencies have the authority to reprioritise and reallocate limited funds**. If agencies have only incremental discretion, they may lose the ability to seize the impetus from cutbacks to achieve real innovation and performance gains.

- **Agencies are large enough to respond to budget cuts**. A 2008 report by the Australian National Audit Office (ANAO, 2008) alerted the government to the negative impact of the efficiency dividend on small agencies which do not have the capacity to adjust to productivity cuts and may experience significant reductions in their capacity to innovate.

- **Top-down fiscal reviews and targets go beyond incremental budgeting** to institute more fundamental zero-based reviews of major programme and policy areas. Innovation is not only about developing new programmes, but also about terminating less effective and relevant initiatives. Spending reviews have succeeded in pressing most OECD countries into instigating innovations and major reforms in services and strategic priorities. Box 4.2 discusses these initiatives in more depth.

Box 4.2. Spending reviews driving innovation

Spending reviews show much promise for incentivising and driving innovation across government. Reviews can promote innovation by focusing on cross-cutting goals and priorities that force line departments to rethink established management systems and routines in the service of government-wide goals and priorities. They can also prompt innovation when they spur efficiencies in achieving goals with fewer resources, prompting more targeting of programme beneficiaries, or new programme management strategies such as public-private partnerships or user fees. Reviews that call for more strategic reconsideration of priorities may also contribute by fostering additional fiscal space, replacing established programmes to make way for new policies. Nearly all of these strategies require the active engagement, planning and facilitation of the central budget agency, as they are the main actors in the system whose focus is both government-wide and fiscal in nature.

Spending reviews have led to decisions on innovative ways to achieve policy and programme outcomes. For instance, in the United Kingdom, senior budget officials attributed initiatives including the shift of higher education from grants to loans and changes to disability programmes to the spending review. The 2010 spending review endorsed the introduction of private financing under a social impact bond for rehabilitation of offenders and increase partnerships with private and voluntary sectors for counselling prisoners (National Audit Office, 2012).

Spending reviews also resulted in identifying efficiency practices that can be applied across organisations. In Denmark reviews resulted in shared services initiatives that have increased efficiency for back office management functions. Senior budget officials remarked that, notwithstanding the breadth of these proposals, most of the recommendations were accepted. The involvement of key stakeholders in the review process helped promote support across affected interest groups.

Source: OECD (2014) and interviews with senior officials.

Budgetary flexibility

In a fiscally constrained environment, greater budget flexibility in resource management – within the limits of established caps – can be instrumental in supporting innovation across its lifecycle.

The budget process influences innovation and efficiency in the way it balances accountability with flexibility. Under reforms embraced by many countries in the 1990s, governments sought to improve productivity and performance by granting line ministries greater flexibility over how they manage resources in exchange for heightened accountability over results. Borrowing concepts from private business models, this new public management also sought to incentivise innovation by introducing competition between the public and private sectors, and measuring feedback and satisfaction levels among "customers" of public services to introduce a focus on outcomes (Pollitt and Bouckaert, 2011).

Fiscal accountability is central to democratic control of spending. Legislatures face a principal agency problem in ensuring that a large and diverse executive bureaucracy will, in fact, carry out the legislative intent behind appropriations. Generally, appropriations are provided in specific budget accounts and often include other restrictions to ensure accountability. These restrictions can include:

- constraints on transferring or reallocating funds from original appropriations

- detailed restrictions on inputs such as personnel and contracts used to achieve the intended purposes of appropriations

- provisions limiting executive increases or decreases of spending following appropriations and budget approval by the legislature

- limitations on carrying over balances across fiscal years and borrowing from future year's appropriations.

While these provisions may be necessary for legislative accountability, they can handcuff agencies and serve to limit innovative programmes and managerial strategies to improve efficiency, effectiveness and responsiveness. In France, for instance, there are two related programmes targeted at homeless refugees. However, excess funds from one of these programmes cannot be reallocated to the other where the need is greater.

Line agencies in the United States face perhaps the greatest limits on fiscal flexibility, stemming from the presence of a powerful and independent Congress that asserts its own funding and management priorities that often differ from those of the president. Within each agency, there are often also many entities that have a range of independence in decision making ability for making and executing funding decisions. The US Department of Labor, for example, has nine bureaus, each with their own congressional appropriations for technology and information systems. Among other factors, appropriations restrictions curbed the ability of department leaders to consolidate IT systems and technology across these units.

Even in this context, the central budget authority can still play a formative role in fostering innovation at the agency level within existing financial boundaries. The Office of Management and Budget (OMB) M-12-14 memorandum encouraged agencies to submit funding requests for initiatives that demonstrate the use of evidence and evaluation in budget, management, and policy decisions. This shows how central budget authority can provide guidance that helps agencies move towards a model where experimentation is used to generate evidence without legal changes. This may indicate that agencies have in reality some flexibility in reallocating funds – such as small amounts for experimentation – without legal changes but do not always take advantage of it.

In contrast with the United States, with its politically separate legislature, most countries with parliamentary systems have a system under which government and parliament tend to work together to balance accountability with flexibility. Accordingly, it is not surprising that most OECD countries have relaxed input controls to provide greater flexibility and autonomy to line ministries and agencies to carry out performance objectives. Budget flexibility is a feature of all the countries reviewed for this study with the exception of the United States.

Several important provisions of budgeting and appropriations have a bearing on the flexibility that line ministries enjoy in the use of resources. Budget accounts themselves anchor the spending authority of agencies. These accounts have been consolidated to enable greater flexibility in the use of resources across many countries. Figure 4.2 illustrates the variation in the number of appropriations accounts across member countries, but also the impressive degree by which the totals have changed between 2007 and 2012 (OECD, 2014).

by the legislature. Increases generally require approval from the finance ministry or the legislature, while line ministries enjoy greater authority to institute reductions from enacted budgets without approval or review by central officials.

Another way budget rules influence the incentives to innovate (or to reveal innovations) is how savings are handled. According to line agencies, a key provision influencing incentives for innovation is how funds carried over from unused appropriations beyond the current fiscal year are handled. If savings from innovations are recaptured by central budget agencies at the end of the year, this may discourage line ministries from pursuing them. Moreover, such prohibitions may trigger a year-end spending spree on lower priority or wasteful items to tap unspent funds. However, central budget officials argue that permitting funds to be carried over locks in rigidities and prevents them from reallocating funds based on current priorities and potential innovation potential across government. They argue that unspent funds are a "canary in the mine" that signal that the original budget for that particular line ministry or programme was too high, relative to the needs elsewhere across government. Viewed through the prism of principal agent theory, central budget officials are principals with limited information on how the far-flung array of agencies are actually spending allocated budget funds; carryover provides a vital clue for these information-starved officials.

Across the OECD, most countries permit a portion of unused funds to be carried over across fiscal years, although most of these actions must be approved by central budget agencies (Figure 4.3).

Figure 4.3. Carryover provisions, 2012 (number of countries)

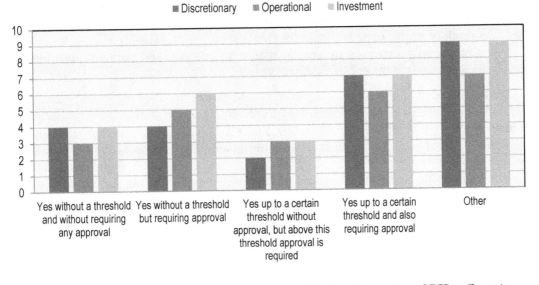

Source: OECD (2014), *Budgeting Practices and Procedures in OECD Countries*, http://dx.doi.org/10.1787/9789264059696-en.

However, even if agencies enjoy formal carryover authority, central budget agencies are free to use this information to reduce prospective funding for those activities and agencies in the next budget cycle. This in turn could create a disincentive for innovation by forcing agencies to spend money to avoid giving it back, while forestalling their ability to marshal resources over several years to support more timely and ambitious projects.

Among the countries studied, Denmark, the United Kingdom and Netherlands provided some limited carryover for line ministries:

- Denmark's agencies have DKK 15 billion (Danish kroner) in carryover out of a total budget of DKK 180 billion. Rather than being an incentive for innovation, some in the central budget agency view this pot as evidence of agencies retaining an accumulation of lower priority spending items, despite the potentially greater need for additional funds elsewhere in the budget. However, efforts to recapture these funds for reallocation have been thwarted by the pressures brought to bear by the spending ministries. Nonetheless, central budget officials take these funds into account when reviewing future budget requests from the ministries.

- In the United Kingdom, the new government elected in 2010 inherited a GBP 15 million (pounds sterling) carryover surplus, a tiny amount compared to the overall budget. As the new government implemented its fiscal austerity program in 2010, these funds were swept away by the Treasury to help offset cuts elsewhere in the budget. Following this, the Treasury has instituted a 2% limit on carryover by spending ministries.

- In Portugal, the overall fiscal crisis supported a rule prohibiting carryover for general revenue funding, with some exceptions.

- In the United States, agencies are prohibited from carrying over funds beyond their appropriated period, reflecting the strong congressional control of appropriations by agencies discussed above. However, a considerable portion of appropriations provided to agencies are multi-year in nature, and in some cases there is no limit on the period funds are available for. Grants to states often come with a three year appropriations, while funds for the acquisition of military aircraft or ships can be available for five years or longer. However, most funds for administrative expenses are only available for one year and agencies must return unspent funds at the end of the fiscal year.

In short, line ministries have enjoyed increased flexibility; over the years, with 70% of OECD countries deploying lump sum appropriations for operating costs and nearly all countries allowing ministries to reallocate funds within their jurisdiction with some restrictions (OECD, 2014). While this flexibility is important for innovation, it needs to be accompanied by a greater focus on performance goals and metrics. Without that focus, central budget officials and other central officials will lose confidence in the capacity of newly empowered frontline agencies to achieve national goals and accountability. Meanwhile, agency officials may lose track of how innovations improve their own ability to meet the needs of programme clients and the public.

Strategic outcome goals

The presence of compelling goals can foster successful innovation in public organisations. This is particularly true when the goals are put forward by high-level, strategic actors, such as budget agencies (Behn, 1999). Strategic goals help to frame objectives and focus on outcomes instead of processes. Especially when coupled with financial incentives, they can lead to the identification and spreading of innovation solutions to achieve them.

By setting up efficiency goals and targets linked with broad modernisation programmes, the budget agency can accelerate and support the identification of innovative solutions as well as their replication once they prove successful. In Denmark, the government has articulated broad modernisation plans with a goal of saving DDK 12 billion in public expenditure before 2020 for new initiatives (Danish Government, 2014: p.52). This amounts to an average annual efficiency requirement of 0.3%. The government plans a range of specific initiatives to support this overall target, including benchmarking and dissemination of best practice on policy interventions. The Ministry of Finance works in partnership with other government institutions to enhance the government's capacity to support these goals.

The United States offers an example of how the budget process can be enlisted to support the achievement of cross-sectoral goals and spread innovative solutions. Under the Government Performance and Results Modernization Act of 2010 initiative, selected policy and management initiatives that cut across line ministries are selected for OMB-led collaborations and reforms. Through the scheme, the OMB appropriates funds from agency budgets to fund cross-cutting initiatives while promoting collaboration and innovation across agencies (Box 4.3).

Box 4.3. Using a cross-cutting budget authority to implement government goals in the United States

In the United States, the central budget agency has been given budget authority to implement horizontal presidential management initiatives under the Federal Government Priority Goals (CAP Goals). Historically there has been no established means of funding the execution of these cross-agency efforts. Without such authority, CAP Goals leaders are constrained in their ability to implement effective solutions across agencies, leaving various federal programmes and activities to address shared issues in a siloed, ad hoc way. This scheme funds cross-cutting priority goals through transfers from agency budgets.

The programme goals were established by the Government Performance and Results (GPRA) Modernization Act (31 U.S.C. 1120) and are set at the beginning of each presidential term in consultation with Congress. The current Federal Government Priority Goals focus on areas critical to the country's economy and prosperity, including cybersecurity, insider threat and security clearance, job-creating investment, federal energy efficiency, science, technology, engineering and mathematics (STEM) education, service members' and veterans' mental health, and infrastructure permitting.

In the financial year of 2016, Congress provided USD 15 million in transfer authority for cross-agency implementation of the Federal Government Priority Goals. The amounts collected from agencies were set based on a formula derived from the budget authority. The OMB has responsibility for establishing and reviewing CAP Goals, and is responsible for making allocation decisions. It runs a mini-budget process asking each goal leader for requests and then makes final determinations based on what was received with approval from OMB leadership. For each CAP Goal, the OMB identifies goal leaders, regularly tracks performance throughout the year through a quarterly data-driven review, holds goal teams accountable for results, and publishes quarterly results on Performance.gov. The OMB, the Performance Improvement Council and agencies have worked to support progress on CAP Goals.

Source: Executive Office of the President (2016), *Congressional Budget Submission: Fiscal Year 2017*, https://obamawhitehouse.archives.gov/sites/default/files/docs/fy2017eopbudgetfinalelectronic.pdf

---

Central budget agencies could also play a role in better aligning strategic outcomes objectives with funding mechanisms and programmes. In 2013, the National Center for Chronic Disease Prevention and Health Promotion (NCCDPHP) in the United States, which manages federal grants to states, released a funding opportunity announcement (FOA) that brings together four previously standalone programmes: heart disease and stroke; nutrition, physical activity and obesity; school health; and diabetes. The FOA, entitled *State Public Health Actions to Prevent and Control Diabetes, Heart Disease, Obesity and Associated Risk Factors and Promote School Health*, aims to efficiently implement cross-cutting strategies in a variety of settings that improve multiple chronic diseases and conditions, while maintaining categorical appropriation funding levels and performance targets (State of Obesity, undated).

Overall, central budget agencies have shown how they can play diverse roles in stimulating, supporting and scaling up the innovation process, when coupling the budget process with well thought out sector objectives. Central budget agencies can and do play the role of stimulating and scaling up bottom- up innovations once they are identified and tested. But they are also well positioned to pursue their own top down innovations which gain significant traction across government thanks to powerful position of the central budget agency along with the resources that central budget agencies can prioritize to support these high level goals. These roles prompt budget agencies to play different roles than those of the controller and chief rationer. Rather central budget agencies can support innovation through the following actions:

- leveraging the resource allocation and rationing roles to support top management goals intervening in the innovation lifecycle with agencies

- establishing networks with other central actors for top-down initiatives and encouraging bottom-up engagement with agency allies

- being prepared to engage with external coalitions outside government to provide analytic resources and the legitimacy needed to support innovation and reform to achieve high-level policy objectives.

Performance and evidence

An enhanced focus on results and performance is critical to planning and monitoring the ultimate effectiveness of innovation projects. It can also be used as a tool to foster the diffusion of effective innovations once they have been tested so that they can be scaled up through the system. Government-wide performance management and evidence-based frameworks have become essential for underwriting the capacity of line agencies and ministries to design effective innovation. Moreover, performance accountability is essential if central controls over inputs are to be reduced in OECD countries. Over the past decades, performance management has become the way that governments in many countries hold themselves accountable. Nearly all OECD countries seek to integrate performance information and metrics into their management, accountability and budget processes (Curristine and Flynn, 2013).

Indeed, performance management has much potential to improve the output of government by encouraging leaders to make choices based on their relative consequences for outcomes and costs. Countries like the United States and United Kingdom have made performance information actionable by conducting performance reviews of individual programmes, articulating performance targets for line ministry officials and, lately, bringing to bear evidence-based approaches towards allocating resources based on their proven impact on outcomes.

Performance management has been now supplemented by a much-needed emphasis on using evidence to assess the impacts of public programmes on important outcomes.

While always important, evidence-based management and budgeting has grown in recent years to stimulate the design of new policy interventions calculated to improve prospects for impact. Central budget agencies can play a role in developing common frameworks and supporting tools to use evidence to assess proposed projects' financial viability and expected return on investment:

- In the United States, central budget and management agencies have been leading line ministries to develop innovations in service delivery based on evidence on policy impact (Box 4.4). The OMB has also led a new wave of evidence-based management and budgeting that seeks to institute new programme financing and delivery models based on findings from evaluation research. The OMB has pursued its evidence-based initiative in concert with the White House Agency of Science and Technology Policy and federal line agencies. With this initiative, the OMB played the role of both articulating a framework and providing investment to stimulate and fund agencies' evaluation and data management initiatives. It also supported selected pilots identified by line ministries as showing promise for improving programme impact based on evidence. This demonstrates the role that central budget authorities can play in linking the programme evaluation cycle to the production of useful evidence which can inform experimentation.

- In New Zealand, the Treasury have developed a set of tools to help improve the quality of the evidence to support more effective decision making. These include a cost benefit analysis tool, CBAx, which helps agencies monetise impacts and analyse returns on investment, and the Investor Confidence Rating, an assessment tool that indicates the level of confidence that ministers and the cabinet have in an agency's ability to realise a promised investment result if funding is committed.

Box 4.4. Using evidence and performance data for innovation in the United States

In the United States, the OMB has piloted initiatives with line ministries to test the efficacy of new approaches. These include:

- Social innovation bond funds, encouraging private investment in promising social interventions.

- Tiered evidence grant programmes, where funding for new projects in areas such as education and social services is proportional to their evidence base.

- Performance partnership grants for at-risk youth, consolidating funding for ten federal grant programmes across agencies for selected grantees whose application promised the highest social return. Notably, Congressional appropriators agreed to relax accountability for each programme in exchange for more rigorous focus on outcomes

- Additional resources for programme evaluation and data mining to generate more opportunities for evidenced-based policies.

Source: Author's interviews.

Countries are also beginning to use "pay for success" bonds to stimulate private investment in social programmes with high potential rates of return. The search for private finance can encourage public sector agencies to improve their programme design and delivery as well as their measurement and evaluation systems to increase investors' confidence. Yet it also requires sufficient flexibility and the capacity to adapt public finance rules and frameworks so that such financing can be used in an integrated way.

The innovation imperative combined with the use of innovative methods to achieve policy goals could strengthen the case for realigning performance measurement with budgeting decisions. By fostering better and improved measures of agency performance, central managers can generate the evidence needed to drive management decision and budget allocation.

Overall, the trade-off between performance and flexibility appears to be eroding as a basis for accountability in many OECD countries, and can have an impact on support for innovation. The innovation frameworks discussed in this section could prove useful to bring the spirit of performance back into performance budgeting, making it less of a compliance exercise and strengthening the better use of performance information at the agency level.

As discussed below, the financial crisis has prompted central leaders to rebalance authority for fiscal decisions and resource allocation. Countries such as the Netherlands have sought to recapture some of the authority given to agencies by limiting broad discretion over spending and rolling back accrual budgeting for those entities. Central leaders are also seeking to strengthen their leadership of whole-of-government problems that can fall between the cracks under an agency delegation strategy. Such recentralisation has strategic implications in terms of achieving the right scale to reap the benefits of innovation. In the Netherlands, as in other OECD countries, shared services have been implemented to achieve economies of scale for back office functions that can better be administered centrally rather than by individual agencies.

Fiscal austerity has prompted reassessment of the role and scope of budgeting

The fiscal austerity that has swept over much of the OECD in recent years has challenged budget and management throughout governments, with mixed consequences for innovation. While cuts can serve as a driver of invention, they can also sap the capacity of government to reach for innovative solutions and practices.

OECD countries face difficult choices when presented with daunting deficits. They can institute targeted cuts scaled and focused on specific "weak claims" or they can impose across-the-board cuts on all or most programmes and ministries. One study of European countries found that most had instituted a mixture of targeted and across-the-board cuts (Kickert et al., 2013). Interestingly, across-the-board cuts were implemented first in the hopes that the fiscal gaps would be temporary and not require fundamental changes to programmes and priorities. Figure 4.4 shows the patterns for nine European countries based on the perceptions of senior executives surveyed.

Figure 4.4. European governments' responses to austerity

Based on perceptions of European public sector executives

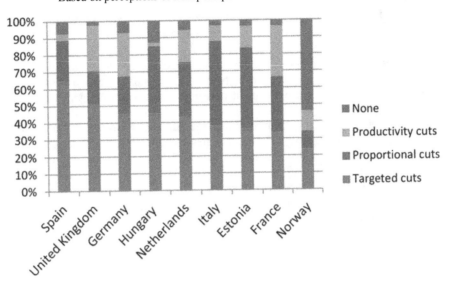

Source: Kickert et al.(2013), Fiscal Consolidation in Europe: A Comparative Analysis, COCOPS.

Targeted cuts are more likely to take into account the relative efficiency and effectiveness of programmes. As noted in the discussion of spending reviews, such strategies can be guided by performance and efficiency criteria, rewarding those initiatives with greater productivity while cutting back those with weaker implementation records. Recognising the inherent differences across programmes and agencies also enables budget officials to allocate fiscal cuts in ways that promote the government's broader strategic visions.

The significant cutbacks prompted considerable reform and innovation in service delivery across our case study countries. The 35% cut in resources for the Netherlands education ministry prompted a shift in the delivery of higher education assistance from grants to loans. This enabled reduced spending by distributing some of the financial burden from the general taxpayer to the beneficiary receiving the lifetime income enhancements provided by university education. Such changes reflect the disruptive effect of some of these cuts, which can also act as a powerful trigger for more radical innovation.

The combination of new technologies, fiscal pressures and strong leadership created the space to mount major innovations in health care delivery networks in Denmark (Box 4.5). Given the potential resistance from providers and others in the community, a strong partnership between the health community and the Ministry of Finance was essential to establish the strong policy and political foundation for these changes. This partnership demonstrates the role central budget agencies can play by using return on investment and business cases to identify innovative practices and technologies that could be scaled up through the budget process in order to introduce benefits throughout the system. According to interviews with senior health officials, the innovations came from the regions, illustrating that innovation can bubble up from any level in government.

Box 4.5. Telemedicine in Denmark: Capturing the fiscal benefits of technological innovation

Prompted by Denmark's continuing fiscal challenges, the Ministry of Health targeted innovations in the health care delivery networks as a promising way to both slow the rapid rise in health care costs and improve patient outcomes. Drawing from evidence-based research on innovative health delivery models, health officials targeted several interventions that promised the greatest return. First, they plan to reduce the number of hospitals by 50% and draw on the resulting savings to build new facilities. The new hospital network is designed to achieve more strategic locations in high demand areas, along with greater connectivity of facilities. Another reform was the launch in 2012 of Denmark's first nationwide telemedicine project: telemedical assessment of ulcers. This replaced traditional clinic-based consultations with consultations in the patients' homes, reducing the need for costly transportation and hospital space, saving EUR 40 million according to preliminary estimates.

Source: Based on interviews with government officials.

Surveys of senior managers in government found that managers perceived major improvements in costs, efficiency and innovation in government during this period of the fiscal consolidation. However most felt the public sector had become a less attractive employer and staff motivation had deteriorated (Costa et al., 2013).

As compelling as targeted cuts are as a means to spur innovation and performance improvement, across-the-board cuts offer the path of least political resistance. Spreading the sacrifice in equal proportions across all claimants in the budget process appears more equitable. It avoids the prisoner's dilemma phenomenon, where agencies singled out for targeted cutbacks put up an impassioned resistance, suspicious that their fiscal sacrifice will be exploited by other claimants in the budget process.

Although politically expedient, across-the-board cuts only give the appearance of equity. They can affect agencies and programmes in very different ways, depending on their past funding history, their potential slack and their capacity. Because the cuts apply to all claimants, regardless of how efficient or effective, they can end up retaining fat while cutting muscle: cutting effective programmes while leaving ineffective, outdated or lower-priority programmes in the base.

The United States relied extensively on across-the-board cuts to implement the demanding fiscal consolidation targets adopted in the 2011 Budget Control Act. These cuts were imposed during the middle of the fiscal year and averaged 5% for non-defence discretionary appropriations and 7.8% for defence. Agencies were required to apply these cuts uniformly to every programme activity in the budget (GAO, 2014). This formula left managers with limited flexibility.

Countries frequently resorted to across-the-board cuts affecting public employees – hiring freezes, layoffs, pay freezes and reforms to employee benefit programmes were among the primary strategies. Kickert and colleagues (2013) note that few countries instituted efficiency reforms, with most favouring across-the-board cuts in personnel and pay and chronic hiring freezes. The OECD's 2015 survey of human resource management (HRM) responses to the global crisis found that many of these cuts were instituted through new human resource management reforms driven by public sector downsizing (OECD, 2015).

Fiscal austerity did not only affect innovation through cutbacks. As discussed above, it also served to unwind the consensus on new public management that had anchored years of public management reform in OECD countries. Fiscal consolidation jeopardised both sides of the public management reform trade-off of greater flexibility in exchange for heightened performance accountability.

The need to make fiscal sacrifices has prompted the centralisation of authority within central budget agencies, as well as with elected political leaders (Ruadla et al., 2015). Fiscal austerity can be expected to increase conflicts between central budgetary principals and agents within line ministries, as natural differences in interests become exacerbated by the pressures brought about by having to make hard choices to reduce spending. The trust and deference that formerly characterised relationships between the centre and the periphery can be expected to fray during hard times.

Indeed, the case study countries have rolled back flexibilities over inputs formerly granted to line ministries. In the United Kingdom, steep budget cuts of over 20% in 2010 swept away carryover balances that had accumulated in ministerial accounts. The United Kingdom also prevented agencies from using depreciation as a source of additional spending in their budgets. The Netherlands reclaimed the budgetary discretion and authority independent agencies had previously enjoyed, rolling back accrual budgeting for capital investments among other reforms. It also placed greater central controls on hiring and contract authority for line ministries as well.

The OECD survey of budget flexibility similarly found that finance ministries took a more active role in requiring prior approval for agency reallocations in 2012 than in 2007, with nearly half of all countries requiring approval in 2012 compared with less than 20% in 2007 (OECD, 2014). Similarly, finance ministries were asserting greater control over the use of carryovers (Figure 4.5).

Figure 4.5. Carryover regimes, 2007 and 2012

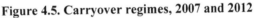

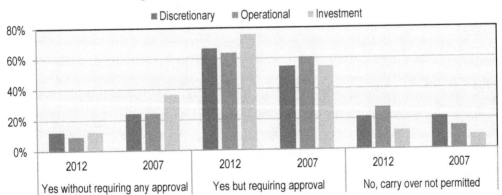

Note: Percentage of participating OECD countries (33 in 2012 and 33 in 2007).

Source: OECD (2014), *Budgeting Practices and Procedures in OECD Countries*, http://dx.doi.org/10.1787/9789264059696-en: p. 71.

Austerity has also led to the reconsideration of how performance management could be used in a more centralised way. Several budget officials interviewed expressed concerns that agencies used performance measures as a strategy to highlight the impact of cuts. The new government elected in 2010 abolished the United Kingdom's vaunted public service agreements between the centre and line ministries and the accompanying performance targets. Despite this, a survey of senior public sector executives in the United Kingdom in 2012 showed that the country's long-term emphasis on performance and outcomes has been sustained at the agency level, with 87% of UK civil servants believing that outcomes and results is one of the most important reforms in their areas (Andrews et al., 2013).

As austerity leads to greater centralisation of policy and budget decision making, performance management can also be viewed as a tool to enhance the centre's insight and control over line ministries and programmes. The French Finance Ministry sought to use the Loi Organique relative aux Lois de Finances (LOLF) reforms, which had introduced performance into the budget process ten years earlier, as a tool to rationalise cutbacks following the crisis. The United States updated its performance management framework in 2010 by both reducing the number of measures used to assess agencies' performance and instituting an annual assessment of agencies' progress in implementing their strategic plan objectives.

Fiscal austerity has thus rationalised and downsized performance management frameworks across many countries. However, senior managers nonetheless felt that performance information actually increased in importance. One insightful study based on the COCOPS survey found that senior managers across the 19 European countries studied perceived that the relevance of performance information increased following the crisis (Douglas et al., 2015). As Table 4.2 shows, decidedly more managers report that performance information and the power of the Ministry of Finance increased as a result of the crisis.

Table 4.2. Responses to the COCOPS survey on performance and power

	1 Strongly disagree	2	3	4	5	6	7 Strongly agree	Number of responses	Mean
Increased relevance of performance information	7.1%	10.1%	9.9%	18.8%	23.3%	20.5%	10.4%	5 352	4.44
Increased power for ministry of finance	3.6%	4.4%	4.6%	13.7%	18.5%	24.7%	30.6%	5 407	5.36

Source: Douglas et al. (2015), "Responses to fiscal crisis: The impact of greater centralization on the relevance of performance information in European governments", paper presented at IIAS International Conference, June 22-26, 2015, Rio de Janeiro.

Overall, fiscal austerity accentuates the urgency of innovation within government. As fiscal rules and budget discipline shrink budget envelopes, it becomes ever more important for line and central budget agencies alike to redouble the emphasis on performance and on incentives and capacity for innovation. Chronic fiscal austerity can serve in this respect as a double-edged sword. On the one hand, fiscal crises can promote innovation if performance regimes remain strong and agencies retain the flexibility to use resources in the most effective ways. However, chronic constraints on hiring and more centralised control over more limited resources may serve to undermine the innovation impulse just as it is most needed. It is important that budget austerity does not squeeze out spaces for innovative thinking, but the centralisation of the budget process can help to support greater focus on desired outcomes and how to achieve them, create more pressure for evaluation of programmes and provide mechanisms for scaling up effective interventions in order to achieve the benefits of innovation across the system.

The OECD's recently launched report, Engaging Employees for a High Performance Civil Service (OECD, 2016) takes stock of austerity-driven HRM measures implemented in the wake of the 2008 financial crisis and their impacts on employee trust and motivation. It shows that during the period 2008-13 many OECD countries implemented cost-control measures, including workforce downsizing, hiring freezes, pay reductions/freezes and cuts to training and development. As a result, over 50% of countries reported measurable decreases of trust within public organisations, and many reported declines to motivation and commitment. If trust and commitment are important ingredients of an innovation-oriented climate, one can assume that such measures had a negative impact on innovation. Additionally, increases in work intensity and workplace related stress emerge as a trend across OECD civil services, and could signal reductions in time and opportunities available for innovation-oriented activities.

The COCOPS survey of senior government managers in European countries provides a scorecard of the impacts of fiscal actions on public management reform and innovation. Overall, about an equal share of managers report that public administration have improved or worsened over during the period following the financial crisis. Consolidation appeared to enhance innovation and efficiency, as respondents noted that cost efficiency, service quality and innovation were the three areas with the greatest improvement. However, they also noted that actions taken since the crisis had had negative impacts on staff motivation, the attractiveness of public sector as an employer and citizens' trust in government.

Conclusions

A robust innovation process is critical not only for public sector managers and clients, but also for the fiscal future of OECD countries. As countries recover from the financial crisis, they must adapt and innovate in the face of major demographic shifts whose effects on pensions, health care and economic growth portend unsustainable finances well into the next several decades.

Budgeting can have a range of impacts on the incentives and capacity to innovate which can be categorised as follows:

- **Restrictive:** detailed public finance rules and controls prevent effective innovative practices to take place.

- **Stimulative:** active measures provide incentives for and promote innovation, such as innovation funds.

- **Accommodative:** greater budget flexibility enables line ministries and agencies to innovate, such as consolidation of budget accounts

- **Unresponsive:** new information and reforms arising from innovations are ignored.

- **Sceptical:** actively working to thwart or overturn flexibility and other rules designed to encourage innovation, such as not allowing agencies to carry over funds.

This chapter has illustrated how the budget process can play a formative role in determining whether and how specific countries undertake public sector innovation. The budget process has evolved to become more relevant to policy and management innovation. This is not to say that budget processes always stimulate innovation; in some cases budgeting serves to dampen flexibility and impose mandates that potentially constrain innovation. However, in a number of cases, budgetary targets, allocation rules and value-for-money routines have worked to stimulate and institutionalise both policy and management innovation. As countries become more preoccupied with fiscal consolidation, the role of central budget agencies has been strengthened.

Budget agencies wishing to promote innovation should carefully consider which of the following strategies are appropriate to stimulate particular innovations, taking into account the particular level and stages of the innovation process they are targeting:

- **nurturing innovation** in line ministries and agencies through judicious and evidence-based pilot programmes

- **promoting greater flexibility** for line ministries and agencies to encourage innovation within overall fiscal constraints and guidelines

- **scaling up** proven and tested innovation initiatives through the use of management and evidence-based approaches

- **stimulating the adoption of innovative reforms** through resource allocation processes, such as spending reviews

- **championing forward-looking management** and policy goals that can most effectively be pursued on a whole-of-government basis by the centre, while ensuring that implementation benefits from collaboration with key line agencies and other officials to ensure consistency and co-ordination.

Promoting innovation throughout government requires budget agencies to strike an appropriate balance between enhancing the capacity and flexibility of line agencies and ministries to pursue much-needed innovation, while retaining a focus on achieving central strategic performance goals and reforms. These tensions between the centre and the periphery become more daunting during times of fiscal austerity where trade-offs among competing interests become more challenging.

Finding this balance requires substantial innovations in the budget process itself. The budget agencies that were most likely to influence innovation through measures such as the articulation of government-wide management priorities, adopting performance-based models and using comprehensive spending reviews had to undergo transformations in their own internal organisational structures, staffing and roles and responsibilities in recent years.

Budget agencies wishing to promote innovation should consider the following measures:

- Adopting or strengthening the integration of budgeting with strategic planning. The annual budget formulation process should be anchored in a longer-term strategic outlook that identifies the goals and future trends that budgeting has to anticipate and steer.

- Striving to allocate resources based on how annual decisions contribute to the broader public policy goals articulated by the government in strategic plans and other forums. Like spending reviews, such processes should be comprehensive and inclusive of all relevant government tools deployed to achieve government objectives in a policy area.

- Enhancing foresight capacity to model the future fiscal implications of major budgetary commitments on both the tax and spending sides of the budget. This should prepare budget officials to understand the probabilities of risks and shocks to the budget stemming from a range of future demographic, economic and environmental changes.

- Periodically integrating government-wide management policies with the budget. While the actual implementation of those management regimes may sit outside the budget agency, these policies should nonetheless be considered in the budget process to ensure that resource allocation and management policies mutually support each other.

- Increasing the capacity of budget agencies, line ministries, auditors general and other institutions to gather and use evidence on innovations to promote greater fact-based deliberation about the scalability of these initiatives across government.

- Providing more incentives and flexibility to line agencies to undertake the experiments so necessary in seeding the innovation process. This can be done through centrally managed innovation funds reviewed using established performance criteria.

Ultimately, the innovation agenda poses delicate trade-offs for OECD countries. Ideally the central budget agency and line ministries work together as partners to promote a climate conducive to experimentation and innovation. The budget agency would trust line and programme managers with the flexibility they need to foster new ways of managing service delivery at the level where government programmes must deliver services and interventions that make a difference. These innovations would be assessed through social science research to ascertain which were appropriate to scale up and expand.

However, inherent differences between central budget principals and line agencies and programme officials are built into the landscape of governance. They may have different ideas about even how to define innovations worth implementing. Some elements of the innovation process, such as managerial flexibility and experimentation, will conflict with other values, such as accountability over government-wide norms and laws and the desire to assure fair and consistent treatment of all programmes and claimants. As fiscal austerity continues to dominate agendas throughout the OECD, conflicts between the centre and the periphery in governments will intensify.

At a time when fiscal limits loom for as far as the eye can see over ageing OECD countries, budgeting is destined for even more difficult times as leaders stretch increasingly limited resources to meet more expansive claims. A focus on performance and innovation will become even more necessary as countries seek to stretch limited resources to cover greater demands for public services. Central budget officials will have to become ever more strategic and agile if they want to achieve pressing national goals while building agencies' capacity to innovate to achieve more effective public services.

Note

1   This chapter has been prepared by Paul Posner and Tim Higashi, George Mason University.

References

ANAO (2008), Submission to the Joint Committee of Public Accounts and Audit, Inquiry into the effects of the ongoing efficiency dividend on smaller public sector agencies

Andews, R., J. Downe and V. Guarneros-Meza (2013), Public Sector Reform in the UK: Views and Experiences from Senior Executives, Country Report as part of the COCOPS Research Project, Coordination for Cohesion in the Public Sector of the Future.

Behn, R.D. (1999), "Do goals help create innovative organizations?" in H. George Frederickson and Jocelyn M. Johnston (eds.), Public Management Reform and Innovation: Research, Theory and Applications, University of Alabama Press, Tuscaloosa, pp 70-88.

Bezes, P. (2010), "Path-dependent and path-breaking changes in the French administrative system: The weight of legacy explanations" in M. Painter and B.G. Peters (eds.), Tradition and Public Administration, Palgrave Macmillan, New York, pp. 158-173.

Bouckaert, G. and M. Brans (2012), "Governing without government: Lessons from Belgium's caretaker government", Governance; An International Journal of Policy, Administration and Institutions, Vol. 25/2, pp 173-176.

Costa, Carla Guapo, Luis Motal and Marie Engracio Cardim (2013), "The impact of the financial crisis in the public sector", unpublished paper for COCOPS project.

Curristine, T. and S. Flynn (2013), "In search of results: Strengthening public sector performance" in M. Cangiano, T. Curristine and M. Lazare (eds.), Public Financial Management and Its Emerging Architecture, IMF, Washington, DC pp. 225-255.

Danish Government (2014), The National Reform Programme: Denmark 2014, Danish Government, http://ec.europa.eu/europe2020/pdf/csr2014/nrp2014_denmark_en.pdf.

Doggett, J. (2010), "Beyond the blunt instrument: The efficiency dividend and its alternatives", Occasional Paper, No. 11, Centre for Policy Development.

Douglas, J.W., R. Ruadla, R. Savi and T. Randma-Liiv (2015), "Responses to fiscal crisis: The impact of greater centralization on the relevance of performance information in European governments", paper presented at IIAS International Conference, 22-26 June 2015, Rio de Janeiro.

Executive Office of the President (2016), Congressional Budget Submission: Fiscal Year 2017, Executive Office of the President of the United States, www.whiteh ouse.gov/sites/default/files/docs/fy2017eopbudgetfinalelectronic.pdf.

GAO (2014), 2013 Sequestration: Selected Federal Agencies Reduced Some Services and Investments While Taking Short Term Actions to Mitigate the Effects, GAO-14-452, United States Government Accountability Office.

GAO (2004), Performance Budgeting: Observations on the Use of OMB's Program Assessment Rating Tool for Fiscal Year 2004 Budget, GAO-04-174, United States Government Accountability Office.

Hague Governance Quarterly (2014), "Decentralization in the Netherlands: From blueprints to tailored services?, The Hague Governance Quarterly, Vol. 2, www.governancequarterly.org/issue2-main-en.html.

Huerta Melchor, O. (2008), "Managing change in OECD governments; An introductory framework", OECD Working Papers on Public Governance, No. 12, OECD Publishing, Paris, http://dx.doi.org/10.1787/227141782188.

Kickert, W.J.M., T. Randma-Liiv and R. Savi (2013), Politics of Fiscal Consolidation in Europe: A Comparative Analysis, COCOPS.

McKinsey & Co. (2011), Better for Less: Improving Public Sector Performance on a Tight Budget, McKinsey & Co.

Magone, J.M. (2011) "The difficult transformation of state and public administration in Portugal: Europeanization and the persistence of neo-patrinomialism", Public Administration, Vol. 89/3, pp. 756-782.

National Audit Office (2012), Restructuring of the National Offender Management Service, the Stationery Office, London.

OECD (2016), Engaging Public Employees for a High-Performing Civil Service, OECD Public Governance Reviews, OECD Publishing, Paris, http://dx.doi.org/10.1787/9789264267190-en.

OECD (2015), "State of public finances 2015", draft report prepared for the 36th Annual Meeting of Senior Budget Officials, 11-12 June, Rome.

OECD (2014), Budgeting Practices and Procedures in OECD Countries, OECD Publishing, Paris, http://dx.doi.org/10.1787/9789264059696-en.

OECD (2014), Spending Reviews, article by Marc Robinson in the OECD Budgeting Journal, No. 9, Volume: 13, Issue: 2, Pages: 81–122

OECD (2005), Reallocation: The Role of Budget Institutions, OECD Publishing, Paris, http://dx.doi.org/10.1787/9789264015760-en.

OMB (undated), "The mission and structure of the Office of Management and Budget", White House website, https://obamawhitehouse.archives.gov/omb/organization_mission

Pollitt, C. and G. Bouckaert (2011), Public Management Reform: A Comparative Analysis – New Public Management, Governance, and the Neo-Weberian State, Oxford University Press, New York.

Portuguese Ministry of Finance (2014), Economic Adjustment Programme.

Robinson, M. (2015), "Budget reform before and after the global financial crisis", GOV/PGC/SBO(2015)7, report prepared for the 36th Annual Meeting of Senior Budget Officials, 11-12 June, Rome.

Robinson, M. (2013), "Spending reviews", GOV/PGC/SBO(2013)6, Report prepared for the 34th Annual Meeting of OECD Senior Budget Officials, 3-4 June, Paris.

Ruadla, R., J.W. Douglas, T. Randma-Liiv and R. Savi (2015), "The impact of fiscal crisis on decision-making processes in European governments: Dynamics of a centralization cascade", Public Administration Review, Vol.75/6, pp. 842-852.

Schick, A. (2007), "Performance budgeting and accrual budgeting: Decision rules or analytic tools", OECD Journal on Budgeting, Vol. 7/2.

Schick, A. (2001), "The changing role of the central budget office", OECD Journal of Budgeting, Vol. 1/1.

Schick, A. (1966), "The road to PPB: The stages of budget reform", Public Administration Review, Vol. 26/4, pp. 243-258.

SGAMP (2016), "L'action publique se transforme", Secrétariat General pour la Modernisation de l'Action Publique website, http://www.modernisation.gouv.fr/laction-publique-se-transforme/avec-les-administrations-et-les-operateurs-publics/investissements-davenir-deux-appels-a-projets-accompagner-transition-numerique-administration-territoriale

State of Obesity (undated), "Federal funding for obesity prevention", State of Obesity website, http://stateofobesity.org/federal-funding-obesity-prevention/.

Tomkin, S.L. (1998), Inside OMB: Politics and Process in the President's Budget Office, M.E. Sharpe, Armonk, New York.

Chapter 5.

Organisations supporting innovation[1]

In recent years, there has been significant growth in the number of organisations dedicated to supporting innovation by addressing some of the barriers to it in the public sector. Based on a survey of more than 70 innovation teams across OECD countries, this chapter examines their role in creating a culture of innovation and spreading the use of innovation processes and methods. It categorises them according to their activities, from units supporting and co-ordinating the development of innovative solutions to innovation labs providing space for experimentation, performance teams supporting service delivery, including through innovative methods, innovation funds, and organisations providing capacity building and networking support. The chapter considers the implications of where innovation organisations sit in government, whether centrally or independent from the executive and how that affects their work. It examines when innovation teams were formed and how they are beginning to measure their impact. It discusses the considerations governments might take into account when deciding whether to set up an innovation organisation and what kind to create, and concludes with some questions for further research.

"This chapter was initially authored in 2014 by Jo Casebourne and Ruth Puttick of Nesta, and has been updated by the OECD to reflect more recent developments."

Introduction

While individual innovation can be spontaneous, the ability of institutions to foster, identify and capture this innovation may not come so naturally. Even worse, traditional institutional structures tend to work against the collaboration of individuals across organisations to bring their knowledge and insights to bear on common problems. In response to this, in recent years there has been a significant growth in the number of public sector teams, units, labs and institutions to support innovation in the public sector across OECD countries and beyond. These draw from the pioneering experiences of policy laboratories and delivery units in the early 1990s, while acknowledging that achieving innovation can be difficult and that it may require additional targeted support and resources.

Dedicated innovation units can help address some of the barriers to public sector innovation. They can compensate for the lack of innovative leaders and champions (Bason, 2010; European Commission, 2013) and help overcome rigidities in the reward and incentive systems which can often hinder innovative performance (Kohli and Mulgan, 2010). Innovation units can foster organisational knowledge about how to apply innovation processes and methods (European Commission, 2013), and support more collaborative and "joined up" approaches in problem solving to counter departmental silos (Carstensen and Bason, 2012; Queensland Public Service Commission, 2009). They can also provide safe environments for risk taking and experimentation (Hambleton and Howard, 2012; Townsend, 2013).

Innovation units and teams can also be seen as a structural response to the nature of innovation projects, which are often cross-cutting and interdisciplinary, and to the tensions involved in continuing business-as-usual work at the same time as experimenting and introducing new approaches. Innovation units can bring together different or new tools, methods and skills, as well as facilitating different conversations and different connections and thus introducing new insights.

Innovation units and teams contribute to the innovation process in a number of ways (Figure 5.1).

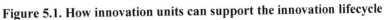

Figure 5.1. How innovation units can support the innovation lifecycle

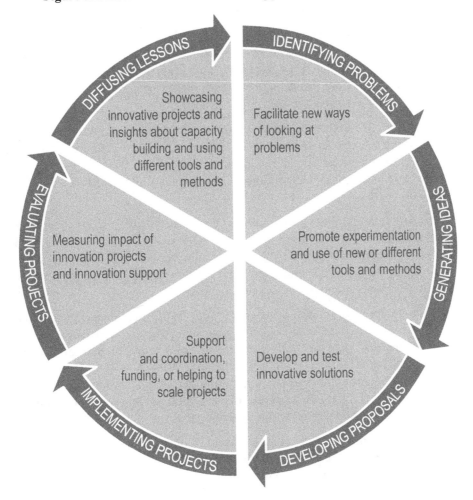

- **Identifying problems**: innovation teams can support the identification and understanding of problems requiring an innovative response in a number of ways. They can be tasked with discovering and investigating specific problems using different approaches – including through direct contact with users as part of co-production processes – or they can assist in connecting areas with new tools, advice, or other support that allows them to better understand where and how innovation might be needed.

- **Generating ideas:** innovation teams can help with the generation of innovative ideas by contributing to creating a culture of innovation and safe spaces where public sector employees feel more able to take creative risks and put forward their ideas. Innovation units can also assist by spreading the use of innovation processes and methods and equipping people with the skills and competencies they might need to best understand the problem and what would make for a corresponding good idea. Innovation units may also be tasked with coming up with ideas as part of their investigation of a specific issue.

- **Developing proposals:** some innovation units will develop and test proposals that can be implemented as part of their investigation of a specific issue. Other innovation teams may assist the development of innovative proposals and business cases by providing advice about the innovation process, sharing lessons, or suggesting specific tools and methods to aid the development process.

- **Implementing projects**: innovation units may sometimes be involved in the implementation of an innovative project, though they will be more likely to support implementation through other means such as support and co-ordination or even through funding projects. Sometimes teams may also play a role in helping to scale up innovation projects.

- **Evaluating projects**: innovation units attempt to measure, in some form, their impact and the impact of innovative projects. This is a difficult area and many teams start out measuring outputs rather than outcomes. This may evolve as a more sophisticated understanding of the work of dedicated innovation units evolves.

- **Diffusing lessons:** innovation unites can work to diffuse lessons from innovation projects and the innovation process more generally through promoting innovation across government, capacity building and networking support, showcasing innovation projects and innovators, and by sharing insights about how different innovation tools and methods can best be used.

Reflecting the relative newness of innovation units, the landscape is constantly changing and evolving, with new organisations emerging and others developing and maturing. Despite this state of flux, establishing an overall picture of the types of organisations that countries are creating, what they do and how they function provides insight into how countries are supporting public sector innovation. This will enable countries to map and compare themselves, identify what models work best and in which organisational context, and learn from others' experiences.

This chapter is based on data on more than 70 innovation teams, units and funds established by governments to support public sector innovation from across the OECD. It categorises these organisations by their different activities and methods they use. Drawing on a survey of 34 countries by the OECD and Nesta in the period 2014-16 (the OECD survey of institutional arrangements supporting innovation), and other sources,[2] it gives a first-hand account of how innovation units operate in different countries and levels of government. It ends by trying to contextualise the development of innovation units into the broader trajectory of delivery on specific priorities in the public administration, and looks to the future of innovation teams. Its collection of innovation units is by no means exhaustive and there are many organisation supporting public sector innovation across governments in both OECD and non-OECD countries which have not been included.

The role of innovation teams, units and organisations

Innovation teams, units and organisations tackle many of the barriers to innovation in the public sector head on. They are led by champions of innovation, have money allocated to innovation and bring together people with a diversity of skills from different silos of government, creating opportunities for collaboration. They also play key roles in creating a culture of innovation to tackle risk aversion and promote experimentation, and in spreading the knowledge and use of innovation processes and methods.

Creating a culture of innovation

Innovation organisations, units, teams, programmes and funds can help to create a culture of public sector innovation, by putting experimentation at its heart (European Commission, 2013; Christiansen and Bunt, 2012). Part of this may involve "unfreezing" embedded practices in organisations, operating as neutral spaces dedicated to problem solving in a highly experimental environment.

Dedicated innovation teams and units can help change attitudes to risk in the public sector. As Chapter 2 explored, there are good reasons why the public sector often has a cautious attitude towards risk and failure – public sector innovators face political consequences when things go awry, with "loss aversion" meaning that the personal cost of being associated with failure can be more severe than being associated with success. This can make it safer to stick with the status quo than to try anything new. It is also harder to know in the public sector if a risk is actually paying off, as it is harder to find quantitative metrics, unlike in the private sector where organisations can just look at profit (although there are increasing numbers of examples of impact metrics being developed by governments) (Townsend, 2013).

Recent research has shown a number of different forms of fear arising from perceptions of risk in the public sector (Hambleton and Howard, 2012: p.39):

- fear of failure – of what happens if things go "wrong"

- fear of departing from the norm – "best practice" can discourage fresh thinking

- fear of freedom – becoming too dependent on rules and procedures, and losing confidence in your own judgement

- fear of the new – of not being able to cope in this situation

- fear of friction with colleagues – that not everyone else is "up for this"

- fear of "the other" – being used to working with colleagues like oneself (such as other local authority professionals).

Challenging perceptions of risk is a key element of an innovative public sector (Mulgan, 2009) and a key element of institutional structures for innovation. Research has shown (Potts and Kastelle, 2010; Queensland Public Service Commission, 2009; Townsend, 2013) that perceptions can be changed by leaders taking responsibility for failure, meaning employees feel safe to experiment and take risks; ensuring reward structures are aligned with the potential benefit of innovation; recognising staff successes and protecting them when things go wrong; building narratives about successful risk taking; and training staff in risk management rather than risk avoidance.

Spreading the use of innovation processes and methods

Innovation organisations, units, teams, programmes and funds play a key role in spreading the use of innovation methods such as prizes, design, ethnography, co-creation and rapid prototyping. They can share evidence and support the adoption and diffusion of innovation within the wider public sector (Bellefontaine, 2012; Cartensen and Bason, 2012; Puttick et al., 2014; Torjman, 2012).

One important function of such structures is to generate new ways of designing and delivering services. There is a growing recognition of the importance of involving service users in the co-design and co-creation of services, as the relationship between the citizen and the state changes from one where things are done to people to one involving the people themselves in how services are produced (Christiansen and Bunt, 2012; European Commission, 2013; Mulgan, 2012).

Design methods are a key way of engaging people in coming up with new ideas. The Design Commission (2013) has highlighted how good design starts from the point of view of how people really experience those services, and how those experiences might be made better, quicker and cheaper. Innovation teams often use design methods such as customer journey mapping, observation and profile building as ways of understanding a problem or service from the user's perspective. Design as a discipline is comfortable with complexity and uncertainty (Christiansen and Bunt, 2012) and it is possible to prototype services in an iterative process (Design Commission, 2013).

Once new ideas have been prototyped, innovation teams can also run formal experiments to test whether new models actually work. They can also help governments understand what constitutes good evidence and how to balance the need for good evidence with the need for innovation. One approach is to use "standards of evidence" to ensure that the evidence is appropriate to the stage of development of an innovation (Puttick and Ludlow, 2013).

Once evidence has been collected about innovations that work, innovation teams, units and funds have a role to play in helping spread the innovation across the wider system. New ideas, products and processes only have an impact if they are taken up. Making sure this happens, and happens fast, is a key challenge in the public sector. The adoption of innovations can be extremely variable, as shown by a recent study of the adoption of innovation in health in England (Stokes et al., 2014). This research found that family doctors in England rely on a broad range of sources to identify new innovations, including informal local networks and more centralised guidance and information systems. Helping those working in the public sector find out about and take up innovation is a key role for structures promoting innovation.

Innovation teams in perspective

Creating teams, units or funds dedicated to supporting innovation in the public sector is by no means the only solution that governments could, or indeed have, developed. The development of innovation teams and the history of organisations dedicated to solving specific challenges in the public sector may help to shed light on why governments have developed an organisational response to the challenge of innovation, and how innovation teams might develop in the coming years.

While there is wide variation in how the innovation teams and units looked at in this chapter operate, some common organisational attributes frequently occur:

- **Central position:** operating in a cross-cutting way from a central department or agency, whether at central government or subnational level.

- **Focus on outcomes:** moving away from a focus on measuring outputs and more towards defining and achieving outcomes.

- **Project-based working:** working on discreet projects for a defined period of time, rather than having a continual standing policy function.

These characteristics have much in common with other problem-oriented teams and units created in previous decades. In 1997 the British government created the Social

Exclusion Unit in the centrally located Cabinet Office to reduce social exclusion by "producing joined-up solutions to joined-up problems". It worked mainly on specific projects chosen following consultation with line ministries (Office of the Deputy Prime Minister, 2004). It also involved external actors, used rapid prototyping, had a strong emphasis on data, holistic solutions, and achieved impressive results, such as dramatic declines in street homelessness (Puttick et al., 2014). The Social Exclusion Unit prompted the creation of the Performance and Innovation Unit in 1998, which evolved into the Strategy Unit.

In addition to the creating task forces to solve specific public sector challenges, governments have also created a wave of delivery units (see also discussion in chapter 2). The first of these was the Prime Minister's Delivery Unit (PMDU) created in 2001 in the United Kingdom. It was charged with providing support and scrutiny to a number of government's performance indicators in high priority areas across four key public services, education, health, crime and transport (Panchamia and Thomas, 2014). The PMDU evolved to take on four clear roles: 1) measuring progress in the improvement of public services; 2) developing and embedding the skills and competencies to support delivery across government; 3) monitoring performance to generate, track and fully exploit data to understand how government is performing; and 4) tackling projects focused on particular priority issues or problem areas. Another important aspect of the PMDU's approach was its collaborative way of working with departments to analyse and develop solutions together. The PMDU inspired similar models in other countries. Australia created the Cabinet Implementation Unit in 2003; Malaysia created its Performance Management and Delivery Unit in 2009; and Chile created a Presidential Delivery Unit in 2010 to name a few (OECD survey of institutional arrangements supporting innovation).

Against this background there has been a growing interest in the pursuit of innovation in the public sector. It is increasingly acknowledged that the creativity, flexibility, risk and culture change that innovation by its very nature requires can be difficult to achieve in long-standing government structures with a statutory obligation to ensure the continuity and quality of public services. It is in this context that innovation teams have emerged, offering an organisational model which draws strongly on earlier approaches to problem solving and results delivery, but which uses new methods to achieve its desired results.

It might be worth also considering the lifecycle of other organisational units in government and what this might mean for the future of innovation teams. In general, task forces and dedicated government units do not tend to remain in existence forever. They evolve, merge or are disbanded as social and government priorities change. For example the PMDU was disbanded in 2010 when the new Conservative-Liberal Democrat coalition government came to power. However, although some of these units' specific activities may disappear with them, arguably their functions often continue in another form. In fact, dedicated units may disappear because the skills, practices and behaviour that they sought to cultivate have become embedded in government, reducing the need for a dedicated team or unit leading from the centre of government. In the case of the United Kingdom, for example, the Cabinet Office's Implementation Unit has taken on many of the functions, and even the staff, from the previous PMDU (Panchamia and Thomas, 2014).

In a similar vein, the current creation of innovation teams may reflect the impetus that public sector innovation requires today, as governments begin to see innovation as a defined activity and adopt a concerted effort to promote it. Over the longer term, as innovation and the capacity to support it grows across government as a whole, and supporting innovation becomes more embedded throughout the public sector, the need for dedicated innovation teams will be reduced, moving towards a model where innovation is supported and thrives across the public administration.

Organisations for innovation: The current landscape

A wide range of innovation units, teams and funds operate at different levels of government and sectors across the OECD (Table 5.2). A few innovation units focus on individual policy areas, most notably health and education, such as Kennisnet in the Netherlands which focuses exclusively on education, or the Department of Health and Human Services (HHS) Idea Lab in the United States, which concentrates on healthcare and human services. However, most organisations tend to work on encouraging innovation generally across government, suggesting that they intervene across policy areas as required. This probably reflects the fact that this report drew on generalist and non-policy specific information sources; research on innovation organisations in the health sector, for example, would inevitably produce different results.

Despite this caveat, it is fair to say that the vast majority of organisations supporting innovation are operating across the public sector as a whole and acting as a resource for many departments and agencies. For instance, the Canadian Central Innovation Hub works across government to provide expertise and advice on new innovation methods and techniques, such as behavioural economics, big data or social innovation. Similarly the Australian Innovation and Policy Coordination Team attempts to ensure innovation efforts are joined up across central government. The wealth of organisations operating at this level suggests that the skills and activities required to support innovation are broadly similar across different policy areas.

What do innovation organisations do?

Looking at the organisations created to support innovation it is clear that they are not all the same. In fact, there are distinct differences in how they operate and the activities they pursue (Figure 5.2). Based on their main activities, they can be divided into five main categories:

- support and co-ordination for innovative solutions
- experimentation
- supporting service delivery
- investment and funding
- networking support.

Figure 5.2. Innovation organisations: Breakdown of activities

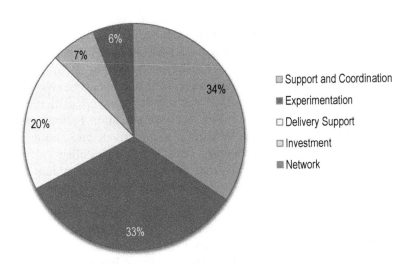

Sources: OECD survey on institutional arrangements supporting innovation; Puttick et al. (2014), *I-teams: The Teams and Funds Making Innovation Happen in Governments Around the World*, www.nesta.org.uk/sites/default/files/i-teams_june_2014.pdf; Nesta (2015), "World of labs", www.nesta.org.uk/blog/world-labs.

It should be noted that many organisations combine activities across more than one area. For instance, Mindlab in Denmark has three strategic objectives – supporting public sector innovation, building capacity on new approaches to public problems and supporting the visibility and legitimacy of the public sector innovation agenda. As such, it straddles the categories of promoting experimentation and supporting and co-ordinating innovation (Puttick et al., 2014). The Laboratorio de Gobierno in Chile combines developing innovative projects for public services in high demand with mobilising civil servants and their organisations to develop innovation capabilities and investing in solutions and prototypes to meet the demands on public services. Its activities cover experimentation, support and co-ordination, and investment and funding.

Organisations providing support and co-ordination for innovative solutions

One-third (34%) of the organisations analysed provide support and co-ordination for innovation in the public sector. These types of organisations track innovation practices across a wider organisation, policy area or administration; report on progress; identify weaknesses; provide support and help other organisations to build staff capacity for innovation. The mandate of these organisations may include support for the implementation of a policy or strategy for innovation across government.

In Australia the **Innovation and Policy Coordination team** (IPC) in the central government Department of Industry provides guidance to government agencies to develop their innovation capability, supports individual public services to understand and use innovation to improve outcomes, showcases and highlights examples of public sector innovation by hosting events, and co-ordinates innovation efforts across the public sector to share lessons and experiences. The team organises an annual Innovation Month (Box 5.1) to help build an understanding of innovation, involving events, workshops and training. Another strand of work is their Public Sector Innovation Toolkit (see below).

In the United States the **Office of Citizen Services and Technologies** (OCSIT) was established to champion innovation throughout government and to leverage citizen engagement, providing tools and capabilities to federal agencies to accelerate the adoption of cloud computing, digital services and other means to foster open government. Based within central government with a budget of USD 50 million, it provides shared services and solutions for innovative technology and citizen services, including providing tools, models, and lean and agile software development that agencies across government can learn from to enhance their ability to innovate and deliver services that engage the public. One of OCSIT's programmes is the Presidential Innovation Fellows programme which attempts to bridge the gap between innovation in the private and public sectors by bringing in talented innovators into government. These innovators collaborate to rapidly solve challenges of national importance, which currently include making digital the default in government, data innovation, and crowdsourcing to improve government.

Organisations that support and co-ordinate innovation use a variety of methods depending on their specific context and the activity that they are working on. These include the development of toolkits to accompany the development of ideas through the policy making process or to guide the actual implementation of innovative practices along their lifecycle (from design to diffusion). These toolkits are usually directed at policy makers in line ministries and subnational levels of government. In Australia, the IPC team has developed an Innovation Toolkit, including a showcase of examples of innovation and a blog reporting on developments in the innovation field. The Toolkit is an ongoing project, with resources being added over time and with guidance reviewed to ensure its relevance and value to public servants.

Organisations also use specific events such as workshops, hackathons, and innovation competitions to raise awareness of innovation across government. They are sometimes combined with prizes or awards for innovation to draw attention to particular practices, demonstrate that innovation is occurring and motivate staff to innovate. Events also provide the context for motivated "innovators" across government to come together, share experiences and support each other. Some organisations also use events and networking in an international context to learn about what other countries are doing to support innovation and share experiences.

Box 5.1. Innovation Month, Australia

The IPC team co-ordinates an annual series of activities and events designed to build engagement and understanding with the innovation agenda under the banner of Innovation Month. In 2014, Innovation Month ran from 7 July to 1 August around the theme Empower, Collaborate, Transform and involved a number of events including the launch of a video of eight examples of innovation from across the Australian Public Service, senior leadership discussing matters relating to innovation, workshops on disruptive innovation, ideas management systems, and collaboration and training around risk and design thinking.

Innovation Month serves as a useful platform for ensuring that agencies give consideration to their innovation efforts and share and disseminate ideas, experiences and insights about the innovation process. It generally results in an increased level of interest, in part demonstrated by increased membership of the Public Sector Innovation Network.

Source: OECD survey on institutional arrangements supporting innovation.

Some of the organisations included in the survey perform a monitoring and co-ordination role, where a central institution has a cross-cutting perspective on a particular policy area, monitoring progress towards specified goals or objectives across line ministries and government agencies. This role may also include developing performance or outcome indicators, providing regular reporting and addressing blockages. Ongoing monitoring allows governments to track whether progress is being achieved and if not to identify solutions. In New Zealand, the Better Public Services Results Programme uses innovative service delivery approaches and a target monitoring regime, identifying and monitoring results across government in five key priority areas that matter to citizens (Box 5.2).

Box 5.2. Monitoring target results: Better Results Programme, New Zealand

The public management system incentivises ministers and agencies to deliver on their own individual objectives, but many of the most intractable issues require collective action by government and non-government agencies. Addressing these difficult issues requires new approaches to service design, so that the service is fit for purpose in particular contexts. These issues need to become priorities so that more resource and effort can be concentrated on achieving better outcomes.

The "Better Results Programme" specifies government priorities in areas that matter to citizens: welfare dependence; better health, education and welfare services for vulnerable children; boosting skills and employment; reducing crime and re-offending; and making government interaction with business and citizens easier, particularly online services.

Governance arrangements were established for each result area, supported by a result team located in the lead agency. The first deliverable for these teams was a Result Action Plan which, in addition to outlining the actions that would be taken and how they would be resourced, provided the intervention logic for achieving the result, how progress would be measured, and how agencies would be organised to achieve the result. To strengthen their mandate, the Result Action Plans were agreed by Cabinet.

Central agencies were tasked with changing the way they worked together to support the agencies responsible for achieving the results. A result lead was appointed for each result area and charged with co-ordinating central agency advice, support and oversight. Central agency teams meet regularly with their counterparts in agencies, and also play a part in governance groups set up to support each result lead chief executive. Central agencies support the responsible agencies as they design collaborative approaches to joint policy development and planning, establish joint workstreams, fund across agency and vote boundaries, design multi-agency governance approaches, and lead system transformation.

As the results approach demanded a new way of working for all concerned, forums were established where agencies could share what they were learning and apply solutions found in one result area to other result areas. Central agencies established Better Results Programme Results Community of Practice workshops on topics such as cross-agency funding, innovation in service delivery and working with non-government agencies. These workshops were also used as opportunities to celebrate success.

Source: OECD survey on institutional arrangements supporting innovation.

A number of organisations provide services to develop the skills and competencies of staff to innovate. This may come in the form of specific skills-based training for technical skills such as data analysis, project management and the application of human-centred design, or it may be more competency-based training such as developing creativity and inspirational leadership. Coaching may provide more sustained support to innovators, innovative organisations or innovative projects.

One example of this is the creation of 16 expert teams across the Polish government, who work with government units on projects related to their areas of expertise. The expert teams use a co-operative model, in partnership with the central administration, local authorities and civil society. Within a broader remit, the innovation teams deployed in the United States with the support of Bloomberg Philanthropies apply the Innovation Delivery Approach which not only generates innovative new approaches but combines this with project management techniques to ensure that the results are delivered. For example, in New Orleans the Innovation Delivery Team (see also Chapter 2) is based in the mayor's office and is tasked with solving mayoral challenges. Their public safety efforts led to a 19% reduction in the number of murders in 2013 compared to the previous year.

Organisations promoting experimentation

Organisations in this category are engaged in experimenting and testing different approaches for the design, development and delivery of public services. These organisations tend to more typically use the language of public sector innovation today – describing themselves as organisations that conduct prototyping, human-centred design and ethnography.

Not only do the organisations in this category conduct experiments to find the most effective solutions, they also experiment with different disciplines and methodologies to explore and address public policy issues. Many of the teams also draw heavily on data, and the stories that data analysis can reveal.

Many of the organisations in this category work across the whole of government in different policy areas as needed. They work on defined projects, applying their innovative approaches, and also in many circumstances use those projects to build expertise in specific methods in the relevant policy area to create long-term capacity for innovation across government. To that end, a number of them also provide coaching and support to policy makers beyond individual projects.

Innovation labs are one kind of organisation typically engaged in this type of activity, although the term "innovation lab" is not always synonymous with experimentation (Box 5.3).

Box 5.3. Innovation labs: Examples from Chile, Denmark and France

Denmark's MindLab, based in the central Danish government, uses human-centred design as a way to identify problems and develop policy recommendations.

Similarly, Chile's Laboratorio de Gobierno (Laboratory of Government, https://lab.gob.ci/) aims to develop, support and promote innovation processes to create better people-centered public services, with the aim of helping to create a new relationship between government and society. To support this mission, it has three streams of action: 1) innovation projects for public services in high demand; 2) improving innovation capabilities for civil servants and public institutions; and 3) opening public challenges to the private sector through challenge prizes and grants to invest in solutions and prototypes that could meet the needs of public services.

> **Box 5.3. Innovation labs: Examples from Chile, Denmark and France** *(cont.)*
>
> Based within central government in the Office of the Prime Minister in France, Futurs Public (www.modernisation.gouv.fr/mots-cle/futurs-publics) is testing new solutions for public sector challenges on a small scale to help create an "ecosystem" that supports innovation. This "lab" works with non-governmental organisation (NGOs) and social entrepreneurs to bring expertise into service design, such as agile software development. Futurs Public also works with external research labs to draw in specialist skills on digital technology or ethnography. It is also developing partnerships with universities and higher education establishments to help engage students in finding innovative solutions to address issues in government. Example projects include changing how people apply for social benefits, trailing more personalised approaches for disability benefits, and reorganising public services in rural areas.
>
> *Source*: OECD survey on institutional arrangements supporting innovation.

There has been a significant growth in the number of innovation labs across the public sector landscape in recent years. This has occurred partly in response to the increased complexity of public policy issues, requiring new approaches and new ways of working. Labs provide a place to help the public sector frame issues in new ways and redesign service delivery systems by focusing on outcomes and drawing on a broad range of perspectives from across the public, private and civil society sectors. Labs help institutionalise co-creation by actively involving the users of public services at all stages of policy and service development and by using different disciplines, from design and ethnography to psychology and sociology. At their best, innovation labs are about the public sector working in new and often challenging ways to yield results which accurately address service users', and society's needs to improve outcomes.

The term "laboratory" is borrowed from science and refers to the practice of experimenting – investigating a situation, exploring how it occurs and testing solutions in a safe and controlled environment. On occasion, governments around the world have invested time, money and social capital in large-scale policies and programmes which have failed to achieve the results expected. Public-sector labs can provide something of an antidote to this. They are dedicated spaces for investigating and experimenting through trial and error to understand better what works in public service design and delivery.

Innovation labs are still in their infancy, so understanding about the different models that exist globally, how they function and their impact is still developing. While there are few frameworks available to assess how labs are functioning, some common findings are emerging from the labs' experiences which may provide a useful starting point to understanding their role and impact. Based on its own long-standing work, Mindlab, one of the oldest and most renowned public sector innovation labs, has proposed four dimensions which are especially relevant to consider when establishing a lab: 1) governance structure; 2) activities; 3) impact and measurement; and 4) skills and competencies (Mindlab, 2014). Nesta has equally set out 10 pieces of advice for innovation teams and labs (Puttick et al., 2014). Drawing on this work and from conversations with lab practitioners, five dimensions have been identified as playing a role in the development and success of a lab (Figure 5.3).

Figure 5.3. Innovation labs: Elements for success

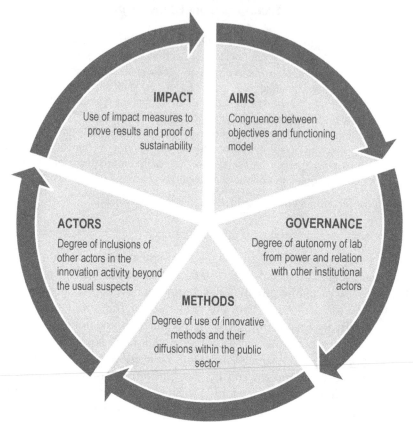

These dimensions have not yet been consistently explored by research nor have they been applied to a comparative analysis of labs. However, initial evidence seems to indicate the usefulness of using these dimensions to better understand the past trajectory and future development of labs within the wider public sector system and how they can be used to compare experiences at international scale (Box 5.4).

Box 5.4. Drawing on international experience: Northern Ireland's Innovation Lab

In 2014 Northern Ireland created an innovation lab to modernise and reform its public services. True to the experimental philosophy of innovation labs, Northern Ireland's lab has been developed progressively, drawing on other international experiences, testing and adapting as it evolves. To date the Lab has hosted 12 projects. One of the lab's most recent projects on dementia reflects an important turning point in its development by bringing the sufferers of dementia and their families into the project itself.

The experience of innovation labs in other contexts has underscored how powerful involving service users in the labs themselves can be, for both the civil servants and the service users involved and Northern Ireland's experience reiterates this. It was revelatory for the civil servants to personally hear the voice of users – as one of them reflected, the public administration traditionally develops services for lives that it does not live. Interviewees reflected that the dementia lab provided an opportunity for public servants to actually hear the voice of users.

Source: OECD (2016), *Northern Ireland (United Kingdom): Implementing Joined-up Governance for a Common Purpose*, http://dx.doi.org/10.1787/9789264260016-en.

Organisations supporting broad service improvements

Developing and supporting innovative solutions is often part of the mandate of public sector organisations delivering tasked with overall service improvement, whether across multiple service areas, or implementing a specific agenda such as open government data, transparency or digitisation.

New Zealand has created a **Performance Hub** across two central government agencies, the State Services Commission and the Treasury, to improve analytical capacity and cross-fertilisation between them. Within the Hub, the **Performance Improvement Group** works to ensure that there is "continuous improvement" in state services, with a vision that these will be centred around improving customer value, that decisions are supported by data and metrics, that service leaders enable incremental improvements, and that the wider systems and culture foster contributions from people at all levels. To achieve this vision, a team of ten has undertaken the training, coaching and development of leaders and staff to operate effectively in a culture of continuous learning. Individual agencies are engaged using an "internal consulting" model. This approach is currently being tested and evaluated in three public agencies: Land Information, Customs, and the Ministry for Environment. The group's work with the customs agency was awarded the 2014 Auckland International Airport Service award for "improvements and initiatives, including a successful project to improve the international departure processes".

In Denmark, the **Agency for Digitisation** in the Ministry of Finance is responsible for developing innovative digital solutions across government as part of its mandate to enhance digital communication and accelerate the use of information and communications technology (ICT) in frontline public services. It includes a plan for testing promising technologies quickly to determine whether it would be advantageous to use them throughout Denmark. In Germany, the **Open Government team** in the German Federal Ministry of the Interior focuses on linking existing projects and initiatives in federal, state and local government to make it as easy as possible for citizens to access government data as part of its agenda to increase transparency, participation and co-operation between government and citizens. Similarly, in Mexico, the Open Mexico unit within the **National Digital Strategy team** works exclusively on citizen engagement to identify solutions to open up public information and develop better public services with citizens. Open Mexico's "Data Squads" have been created to help ministries and agencies open up government data. Individual members of staff are seconded as "Change Makers" to drive change in specific ministries or agencies.

Organisations funding innovation

Organisations engaged in funding innovation provide funding to invest in programmes or activities that advance or support public sector innovation. Sometimes this occurs alongside research and development (R&D) investments to support innovation in the private sector. Sweden's innovation agency **Vinnova** provides R&D funding to range of public innovation projects, including projects exploring ways to use procurement as a driver for innovation and processes for scaling health care innovations.

Given the constraints on resources and the high level of risk aversion in the public sector, providing funding directly to support pilot projects may give innovative ideas and nascent practices much needed space and protection to grow and be nurtured. For example, Vinnova has created Innovation Centres and Test Beds in health services to support ideas for needs-driven innovations across local government. Similarly in France the **Experimentation Fund for Youth** (*Fonds d'experimentation pour la jeunesse*) has supported over 554 projects and experiments, serving around 498 000 young people. Another example is **Sitra**, Finland's innovation agency, which uses its endowment of EUR 535 million to drive innovation within areas such as healthcare and sustainability. It is estimated that Sitra's work on sustainable energy has led to around EUR 1 billion in savings for the Finnish government.

Organisations providing capacity building and networking support

Finally, some of the organisations looked at aim to help other organisations to build innovative capabilities through training and coaching and develop networks of innovators, providing a platform for them to come together to share ideas and create a cohesive network. What makes these organisations different from traditional approaches to capacity building is that they use a wide range of tools for building capacity, such as learning-by-doing experiences, human-centred design, and prototyping.

In France, **La 27e Région** (27th Region) works to help subnational governments to explore new ways of designing and developing public policies. So far it has helped design more than 20 social innovation pilots across 9 French regional governments. In Chile, the **Laboratorio de Gobierno** (Government Laboratory) acts as a learning-by-doing area for civil servants and provides a controlled environment that permits risk taking and connects a diversity of actors related to public services to co-create and test solutions (Box 5.5).

Box 5.5. Building innovation capabilities in the public sector: The case of the Laboratorio de Gobierno (Chile)

The Laboratorio de Gobierno is a multidisciplinary institution of the Government of Chile which was set up in 2014 to implement the President's mandate on public sector innovation. It has the mission of developing, facilitating and promoting human-centred innovation processes within public sector institutions. The Laboratorio de Gobierno represents the Chilean Government's new approach to solving public challenges which put the citizens right in the centre of public action and transformation processes.

In addition to activities aimed supporting public sector institutions to seek innovative solutions that improve the services the state, the Laboratorio engages in developing innovation capabilities. This includes actions focused on developing the capabilities of civil servants to initiate and carry out innovation processes within public sector institutions through learning-by-doing experiences. Projects include *Experimenta* (an experiential programme for civil servants) and managing networks of innovations such as the *Innovadores Públicos*, the Public Innovators Network.

In carrying out its programme and activities, the Laboratorio uses a wide range of innovative methods from human-centred design to prototyping, from the use of experiments to co-creation, and from engaging individual institutions to calls for open innovation. Through their skills and capability building streams of activity, the *Laboratorio* is engaging with employees of public institutions to teach innovative methods and build their capabilities to innovate.

The Laboratorio is administratively part of CORFO, the Chilean Economic Development Agency (under the auspices of the Ministry of Economy), and has a governing board composed of five ministries (including the Ministry of the Economy, the General Secretariat of the Presidency, the Ministry of Finance, the Ministry of Social Development, and the Ministry of Interior and Public Security), CORFO, the National Civil Service Directorate, and three members of civil society.

Source: OECD (2017), *Innovation skills in the public sector: building capabilities in Chile*, https://www.oecd.org/publications/innovation-skills-in-the-public-sector-9789264273283-en.htm

---

In the Netherlands, the Ministry of the Interior manages the **Slimmer Network (Smarter Network)**, a network of around 4 000 innovative officials and advisors within the government, provinces, municipalities, water authority and police. The networks help promote and support innovative initiatives underway. In Finland, the Ministry of Finance operates the **Change Agents / Change Makers Network** (discussed in Chapter 2), a loose network of civil servants from different line ministries who all share a common desire to enhance new, modern, exploratory ways of working within government. The network aims to support the development of a new working culture in the Finnish administration through discussion, supporting new initiatives, launching new experiments and supporting innovative initiatives. Examples of projects supported by the network include influencing the creation of a new service support function for the whole of government, enabling new ways of working and thinking within government, and designing and arranging common working facilities that support experimental policy development.

Where are innovation organisations located?

The location of innovation teams within government is a useful way to assess their capacity to exert influence over other organisations and their ability to achieve results within a given administrative structure and context.

Many innovation teams, units and funds are centrally based, reflecting the cross-cutting nature of innovation as an activity, but also the leadership and support they enjoy to carry out their actions; organisations close to executive power might thus be the most effective at delivering results. In some countries this may also reflect the linking of innovation with a longer history of government teams and units dedicated to supporting particular government activities (e.g. delivery units in the United Kingdom).

On the other hand, independence and distance from the executive power might provide innovation teams with greater freedom and organisational flexibility but their voice might not be heard: while removal from executive power might enable them to be more creative and radical, they could face greater challenges in demonstrating their impact. Organisations which are co-owned across multiple ministries and agencies may be able to gain greater traction across the organisations which own them but can also suffer from multiple and perhaps confusing goals and priorities; they might be more collaborative and consensual but they may also find it harder to reach agreement and change direction.

Previous research has found that proximity to government and executive leadership affects innovation teams' mission and mandate (Puttick et al., 2014). This research analysed innovation teams' proximity to executive power, ranging from being closely aligned with a political sponsor through to being an entirely independent entity. Some of the innovation teams studied are physically based in the mayor's or president's office, such as the Mayor's Office of New Urban Mechanics in Boston, United States, with their agenda directly set by their executive leader. Although their remit may not be of radical innovation, their work is radical compared to the rest of government. At the other end of the spectrum are organisations like Sitra, which are independent of government and free to set their own agenda, fostering a more radical innovation agenda (Puttick et al., 2014).

Recent OECD work complementing this data has highlighted the frequent role played by the centre of government (CoG), with many teams and units being located here (see Table 5.1 for a selection). Innovation teams and units are also frequently located in public spending, finance and economics ministries. This reflects the fact that many cross-government activities are often jointly executed by the CoG and finance ministries. While CoG bodies may have strong political capital in a given area, finance ministries ultimately control the purse strings, with the ability to set line ministries' budgets, and work with line ministries to enhance the efficiency, effectiveness and value for money of public spending programmes. They also support the implementation of the government's goals and priorities, which are reflected in budgetary allocations across government.

Table 5.1. Where are innovation teams located in government? Selected examples

Executive office*	Finance and centre of government** ministries	Responsible line ministry	Co-owned across multiple ministries and agencies	Independent; agenda and funding provided by government	Independent; sets own agenda, funding provided by government
Innovation Service, General Directorate for State Modernisation, Secretariat-General for Government Organisation, France **Seoul Innovation Department, Metropolitan Govt, Korea** **Innovation Delivery Teams, United States**	Central Innovation Hub, Canada General Services Administration Office of Citizen Services and Innovative Technologies, United States Northern Ireland Innovation Lab, United Kingdom Change Agents / Change Makers, Finland Open-Government/Open Data Team, Germany Citizen and Information Policy Department, Netherlands State Sector Performance Hub, New Zealand	Innovation and Policy Coordination team, Portfolio Strategic Policy Division, Australia Social Innovation Division, Dept of Employment and Social Development, Canada Rijksinnovatielab (Central Government Innovation Lab), Netherlands	Laboratorio de Gobierno, Chile Mindlab, Denmark Behavioural Insights Team, UK	La 27e Region, France	Sitra, Finland

*The executive office is a unit that is shared by virtually all CoGs. It is the unit that serves specifically the head of the government, but not the CoG collectively. It has a variety of names, such as the Cabinet of the Prime Minister or the private office (OECD, 2015b).

** The centre of government refers to the administrative structure that serves the executive (president or prime minister and the cabinet collectively). It has various names in different countries, such as General Secretariat, Cabinet Office, Chancellery, Office/Ministry of the Presidency, Council of Ministers, etc. (OECD, 2015b).

Source: OECD survey on institutional arrangements supporting innovation; Puttick et al 2014; Nesta 2014.

Future work might usefully try to evaluate the extent to which the location of innovation teams within government shapes and influences their capacity to deliver on their agenda.

When were innovation organisations created?

The majority of the institutions identified in the Nesta and OECD survey were established since 2010, with a significant number created very recently in 2013-14 (Figure 5.4). This recent emergence of innovation teams may reflect the increasing interest in public sector innovation as a concept in recent years, and as an activity that governments would like to develop and encourage.

Figure 5.4. A timeline of selected innovation teams and units

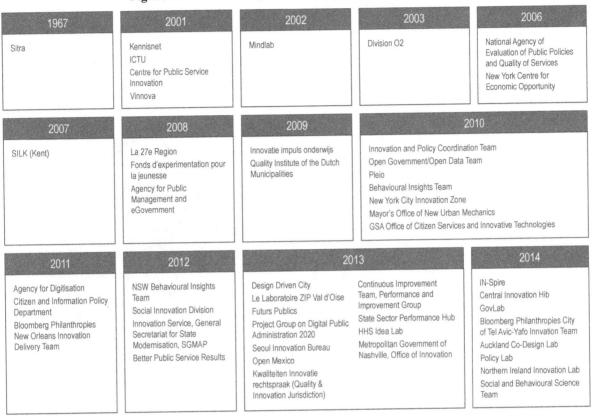

Source: OECD survey on institutional arrangements supporting innovation.

How do innovation organisations measure impact?

It is important to be able to demonstrate the impact of all government activities, both from the simple democratic perspective of measuring the effectiveness of government actions or to ensure value for taxpayers' money, and to ensure the viability of the organisations themselves. Measuring impact is a challenge for government as a whole; even more so when it comes to innovation. Results may take many years to materialise, and may be diffused across a wide range of policy areas. Effects are often qualitative and subjective, and causality is difficult to establish. Public sector data are notoriously weak, being difficult to obtain, compare and share. In a context where only a few countries report and account for almost all direct financial benefits realised through ICT projects, it seems overly demanding to expect that innovation projects should be able to demonstrate the impact of their support given they operate in an infinitely more diffuse and qualitative setting (see OECD, 2015b).

Many of the innovation organisations in the survey acknowledge that measuring impact is very difficult. Figure 5.5 demonstrates the range of different, complementary efforts they deploy to measure impact. These range from the very simple, qualitative judgements that would normally apply to all types of policy making, such as the quality of advice provided to ministers and senior staff (cited by Canada's Social Innovation Division in the Department of Employment and Social Development) to advanced performance measurement regimes that include outcome indicators for the organisation's activities (e.g. building staff capacity) as well as the impact of its work (e.g. reducing youth unemployment). The Mayor's Office of New Urban Mechanics in the United States is the organisations that perhaps comes closest to this, with one specific set of categories to measure the impact of the team overall, and a second set specific to each project.

Figure 5.5. Graduated approaches to impact measurement for innovation organisations

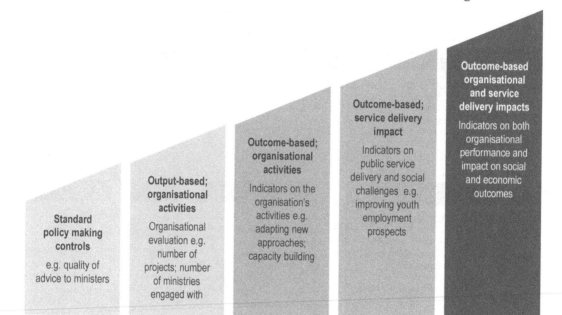

Reflecting the difficulty of measuring impact, many of innovation organisations try use simple output indicators to measure their activity (such as the number of projects that they conduct) as a proxy. In the future, organisations might consider complementing this approach with outcome-based indicators.[3] This would mean considering how innovation organisations change how government works (for an example of how one Canadian organisation is approaching this challenge, see Box 5.6). Beyond this, innovation organisations should consider not only how they can measure the impact of their organisation on government, but also on the broader policy goals that they are trying to influence in society. New Zealand's Better Public Services Results Programme provides an inspiring example of how data and impact can be transformed into a story for citizens about the changes that are being achieved in service delivery – for each indicator (result) in the programme a "data story" is published which explains the indicator's data and what its rating says about the progress being made towards the target.

Box 5.6. Measuring impact, IN·Spire, Canada

As a new innovation team, IN·Spire is in the process of establishing a performance measurement framework to demonstrate influence and impacts. IN·Spire works with partners to (1) build capacity for change which will support (2) the design of solutions and improvements that can be (3) scaled up and sustained over time (when and where applicable). Taken together, the value propositions are the foundation of a performance framework that can be applied to assess and report IN·Spire's cumulative impact and by individual project.

The table below is a selection of quantitative and qualitative indicators that will be tracked to measure progress and impacts over time. As an 18-month pilot, IN·Spire will focus on its immediate outcomes.

Value proposition **Building awareness and capacity for change** (T1)	Value proposition **Leading and supporting solutions and improvements** (T2)	Value proposition **Driving and sustaining change** (T3+)
Key outputs	Key outputs	Key outputs
Learning labs on new ways of working (e.g. systems thinking, design methods, collaborative on-line tools, video blogging and crowdsourcing). Innovation toolkit and internal web content.	Solution or improvement design process and workshops. Knowledge products (e.g. problem scoping, research, reports).	Open reporting of pilot results and opportunities to scale. Governance committee engagement. Policy and operational changes.
Key outcomes	Key outcomes	Key outcomes
NRCan employees and senior management are aware of new ways of working to solve problems and/or continuously improve. Indicators: user feedback via surveys, number of requests for IN·Spire services, internal website analytics.	Partner(s) pilot co-created solution or improvement, e.g. micro-assignments open badges social and policy innovation upward feedback pilot. Indicators: % of solutions and improvements that are piloted by partners.	Partner(s) adopt co-created solution or improvement based on results of pilot. Policy and operational changes enable innovation. Indicators: % of solutions scaled up across the department.
Key impacts	Key impacts	Key impacts
Demonstrated use of new ways of working in learning labs and IN·Spire led or supported events. Indicators: % of NRCan employees participating in learning labs and IN·Spire led or supported events.	Impacts of solution pilot(s) and improvements to be tracked by individual project. Indicators: to be tracked by individual project, e.g. # employees and managers using micro-assignments; % of micro-assignments identified as positive experiences by employees and managers in follow-up evaluations.	Solutions and improvements are scaled up across NRCan (and possibly the federal public service), where applicable. Indicators: to be tracked by scaled solution and policy or operational change.

Source: OECD survey on institutional arrangements supporting innovation.

Establishing an innovation unit: Considerations for organisations

As discussed above, innovation units can provide "room" within an organisation's structure for new ideas, new tools and new ways of doing things. In establishing an innovation unit, organisations should identify what is being sought from the new team, as different functions may be supported in different ways. Innovation units may do some or all of the functions described in the case studies above. Given their relative newness, there may also be additional activities where an innovation unit can provide value.

Given this wide variation in the forms and functions of innovation support organisations, how can public sector leaders decide which kind is appropriate for their own context and needs? Table 5.2 takes an objectives-oriented approach, considering the objectives that policy makers want to achieve and matching them with the activities, types of organisations, and methods and skills that other countries are using to support those aims. This is not intended to be exhaustive or scientific; it is not yet possible to link the types of organisations and their methods with measurable outcomes. However, it is hoped that this can be a useful tool for policy makers at all levels of government when deciding if and how they want to support innovation using an organisational approach.

Table 5.2. Organisations for innovation: A typology and selected examples

Objective?	Core activity					What type of organisation?	Methods used	Examples
Promote innovation across government	**Support and co-ordination**	Support in specific area or function	Experimentation	Investment and funding	Capacity building and networking	- central government innovation units	-tools and guidance -monitoring and co-ordination -training and coaching -events	-Innovation and Policy Coordination, Australia -Central Innovation Hub, Canada -Better Public Services Results Programme, New Zealand
Promote service improvement in functional areas	Support and co-ordination	**Support in specific area or function**	Experimentation	Investment and funding	Capacity building and networking	- dedicated teams and units for functional policy areas (e.g. digital or open government)	- project implementation support - dedicated squads /change teams	-Open Government Team, Germany -Open Mexico, Mexico -Laboratorio de Gobierno, Chile
Develop and test innovative solutions	Support and co-ordination	Support in specific area or function	**Experimentation**	Investment and funding	Capacity building and networking	-innovation labs -behavioural insights units -innovation units -delivery teams	- prototyping - human-centred design - randomised controlled trials - project-based working - data analysis	-Futurs Public, France -Mindlab, Denmark -Laboratorio de Gobierno, Chile -Behavioural Insights Unit, United Kingdom
Fund innovation	Support and co-ordination	Support in specific area or function	Experimentation	**Investment and funding**	Capacity building and networking	-funds	- piloting - grant funding - competitions and awards	-Vinnova, Sweden -NYC Innovation Zone (iZone), United States
Develop capacity for innovation and networking	Support and co-ordination	Support in specific area or function	Experimentation	Investment and funding	**Capacity building and networking**	-central government -innovation units -innovation labs -formal and informal networks across government	- project shadowing - training and coaching - tools and guidance - events - regular meetings - network communications	-Mindlab, Denmark -Laboratorio de Gobierno, Chile -Slimmer Network (Smarter Network), Netherlands -Change Agents / Change Makers, Finland

Note: Organisations are categorised for illustrative purposes although many organisations conduct activities across multiple categories.

When creating an innovation unit, an organisation may first need to consider the signal it sends to the rest of the organisation. If poorly implemented, innovation teams can actually become an impediment to innovation, rather than an enabler. One way to mitigate this is to involve people both from outside and within the public sector in a way to combine new skills with existing system intelligence (see Chapter 6).

Attention should also be paid to striking a balance between being prescriptive about the function and leaving room for evolution and experimentation. As a new function, there may need to be adjustments as the team learns what works and what it is capable of. On the other hand, if the remit of the team is too loose, the team may not be regarded as legitimate by others within the organisation.

The expectations for the unit should also guide its location within the organisation. If the team is close to the centre it will have more authority and be able to better diffuse innovative practices and projects, but it may be limited in its ability to experiment because of its links with current practice. A team that is located more on the edge (or even outside of the organisation) will be open to much more experimentation and potentially radical innovation, but its ability to feed insight back into the organisation will be much reduced because it will be less visible and connected with core business.

If an organisation chooses not to have a dedicated innovation unit, but regards innovation as important, it will need to give thought to how it will support:

- a culture of innovation where there is an openness to new ideas and projects

- the spreading and adoption of new ideas and methods

- innovative projects that do not fit with existing business

- the provision of guidance, advice and support for those wishing to undertake innovative projects

- experimentation outside identified projects

- promising innovations that require additional resources to come to fruition

- identification of opportunities for innovation, assessment of the organisation's innovation portfolio, and evaluation of the outcomes of innovation projects to guide future decision making.

Conclusions

OECD countries demonstrate an impressive range of different types of organisations supporting innovation, operating at different levels of government and supporting innovation in different ways. Some organisations are focused on the technical process of innovation, drawing on science to experiment by investigating issues and testing different solutions. Some organisations take a more policy-oriented approach by co-ordinating and supporting innovation across government, while others are thinking about the specific resources that innovation requires by providing competitive grants to nurture innovative ideas.

No one size fits all, and in fact many countries are combining different approaches and activities to provide more holistic support to innovation. As governments look to establish new innovation teams or units, or to re-evaluate and modify their existing approach, an outcomes-oriented approach is a good place to start. Governments should think about the final outcomes that they want to achieve for public sector innovation and what kinds of objectives these translate. This chapter has matched government objectives with activities, methods and organisational types to help support governments identify which type of organisation might be appropriate for their specific needs.

Despite the wide variety of innovation organisations, some commonalities have emerged. Government organisations for innovation often operate at central government level, are outcome-oriented and their work is project based. These are useful characteristics to drive the public sector as it seeks to create other teams and units that support innovation. Another notable common feature is their similarity with previous organisations that government has created to solve specific issues, such as task forces or delivery units. If organisations for innovation follow a similar trajectory, then, as innovation and the support system that encourages it grows and becomes embedded across government, the dedicated innovation organisations themselves may no longer be required. While measuring the impact of innovation organisations is inherently difficult, the ultimate impact indicator of an innovation organisation might then be that it has become obsolete because innovation is being nurtured and thriving across the whole of government.

While this chapter begins to draw some conclusions about innovation organisations it is by no means exhaustive and there remain many unanswered questions. Further research to explore the role of innovation organisation in OECD countries might focus on:

- **Effectiveness:** are innovation teams, units and funds actually being effective in supporting innovation? What characteristics make them more or less effective?

- **Operating in an ecosystem:** innovation teams and units are one aspect of a government's approach to supporting innovation – how do these entities complement the action of other enablers such as human resources, financial and information management?

- **Sustainability:** how can innovation teams and funds function to best build long term capacity for innovation across the public sector so that innovation becomes a sustained activity (and not a one-off activity confined to an innovation team or unit)?

Notes

1. This chapter was initially authored in 2014 by Jo Casebourne and Ruth Puttick of Nesta, and has been edited and updated by the OECD to reflect more recent developments

2. The OECD-Nesta research was conducted in 2014 and the data were updated in 2016. The survey asked representatives from 34 central governments in OECD countries to identify the teams, units and agencies within their public administration that have objectives aligned to innovation in government, defined as "Innovation that occurs in how the government delivers public services to citizens and how the public administration functions and operates itself". These teams, units and agencies could include those that were creating better public services, improving outcomes, improving efficiency or making better policies, and were invited from across central, regional and local levels of government. Some countries may also have less formal co-ordinating mechanisms, such as cross-government working groups, to steer and promote innovation. These were not, however, the focus of this research. In addition to the OECD-Nesta resource, the chapter also draws on Nesta 2014 i-teams report (Puttick et al., 2014) and the 2015 "World of Labs" searchable map (Nesta, 2015) which captures innovation labs in government at different levels of government. These sources have also been complemented by desk research.

3. Outputs measure the quantity of an activity performed whereas outcomes measure the difference that the activity achieves.

References

Bason, C. (2010), Leading Public Sector Innovation: Co-creating for a Better Society, Policy Press, Bristol and Portland, OR.

Bellefontaine, T. (2012), Innovation Labs: Bridging Think Tanks and Do Tanks, Policy Horizons, Government of Canada.

Carstensen, H.V. and C. Bason (2012), "Powering collaborative policy innovation: Can innovation labs help?", The Innovation Journal: The Public Sector Innovation Journal, Vol. 17/1, article 4.

Christiansen, J. and L. Bunt (2012), Innovation in Policy: Allowing for Creativity, Social Complexity and Uncertainty in Public Governance, Nesta and MindLab, www.nesta.org.uk/sites/default/files/innovation_in_policy.pdf.

Cunningham, P and A. Karakasidou (2009), "Innovation in the public sector", Policy Brief, No. 2, Manchester Institute of Innovation Research, University of Manchester.

Design Commission (2013) "Design and public services", Restarting Britain, 2, Design Commission, www.policyconnect.org.uk/apdig/sites/site_apdig/files/report/164/fieldre portdownload/designcommissionreport-restartingbritain2-designpublicservices.pdf.

Economist (28 March 2015), "Improving government: Delivery man", The Economist, www.economist.com/news/books-and-arts/21647263-tony-blairs-deliverology-expert-explains-how-reform-public-services-delivery-man.

European Commission (2013) Powering European Public Sector Innovation: Towards A New Architecture, Report of the Expert Group on Public Sector Innovation, European Commission, Brussels, https://ec.europa.eu/research/innovation-union/pdf/psi_eg.pdf.

Fernandez, S and T. Moldogaziev (2012), "Using employee empowerment to encourage innovative behaviour in the public sector", Journal of Public Administration Research and Theory, Vol. 23/1, pp. 155-187.

Farrell, D. and A. Goodman (2013) 'Government by design: Four principles for a better public sector', McKinsey & Company website, www.mckinsey.com/insights/public_s ector/government_by_design_four_principles_for_a_better_public_sector.

Hambleton, R. and J. Howard (2012), Public Sector Innovation and Local Leadership in the UK and the Netherlands, Joseph Rowntree Foundation.

Kohli, J. and G. Mulgan (2010), Capital Ideas: How to Generate Innovation in the Public Sector, Center for American Progress and The Young Foundation, http://cdn.amer icanprogress.org/wp-content/uploads/issues/2010/07/pdf/dww_capitalideas.pdf .

Mindlab (2014), "Innovation labs", Presentation to the OECD conference Innovating the Public Sector: from Ideas to Impact, 12-13 November 2014, http://fr.slideshare.net/O ECD-GOV/presentation-by-mindlab-on-educational-use-of-digital-technologies-in-schools-made-at-the-oecd-conference-on-innovating-the-public-sector-from-ideas-to-impact-1213-november-2014.

Mulgan, G (2012), "Government with the people: The outlines of a relational state", in G. Cooke and R. Muir (eds.), The Relational State: How Recognising the Importance of Human Relationships Could Revolutionise the Role of the State, Institute for Public Policy Research, www.ippr.org/assets/media/images/media/files/publication/2012/11/r elational-state_Nov2012_9888.pdf.

Mulgan, G. (2009), The Art of Public Strategy: Mobilizing Power and Knowledge for the Common Good, Oxford University Press, Oxford.

Mulgan, G. (2007), "Ready or not? Taking innovation in the public sector seriously", Provocation, 03, Nesta, www.nesta.org.uk/sites/default/files/ready_or_not.pdf.

Mulgan, G and D. Albury (2003), Innovation in the Public Sector, Strategy Unit, Cabinet Office, London.

Mulgan, G and R. Puttick (2013), Making Evidence Useful: The Case for New Institutions, Nesta, www.nesta.org.uk/sites/default/files/making_evidence_useful.pdf.

Needham, C, C. Mangan and H. Dickinson (2014), The 21st Century Public Services Workforce: Eight Lessons from the Literature, University of Birmingham www.birmingham.ac.uk/Documents/college-social-sciences/public-service-academy /twenty-first-century-public-servant--eight-lessons.pdf.

Nesta (19 May 2015), "World of labs", Nesta blogs, www.nesta.org.uk/blog/world-labs.

OECD (2017), Innovation skills in the public sector: building capabilities in Chile, OECD Publishing, Paris, https://www.oecd.org/publications/innovation-skills-in-the-public-sector-9789264273283-en.htm.

OECD (2016), Northern Ireland (United Kingdom): Implementing Joined-up Governance for a Common Purpose, OECD Publishing, Paris, http://dx.doi.org/10.1787/97 89264260016-en.

OECD (2015a), The Innovation Imperative in the Public Sector: Setting an Agenda for Action, OECD Publishing, Paris.

OECD (2015b), Government at a Glance 2015, OECD Publishing, Paris, http://dx.doi.org/10.1787/gov_glance-2015-en.

OECD (2010), Public Administration after "New Public Management", Value for Money in Government, OECD Publishing, Paris, http://dx.doi.org/10.1787/9789264086449-en.

OECD (2002), Distributed Public Governance: Agencies, Authorities and Other Government Bodies, OECD Publishing, Paris, http://dx.doi.org/10.1787/97892 64177420-en.

Office of the Deputy Prime Minister (2004), The Social Exclusion Unit, Office of the Deputy Prime Minister, London, http://webarchive.nationalarchives.gov.uk/+/http:/w ww.cabinetoffice.gov.uk/media/cabinetoffice/social_exclusion_task_force/assets/publi cations_1997_to_2006/seu_leaflet.pdf.

Osborne, S.P. and L. Brown (2011), "Innovation, public policy and public services delivery in the UK: The word that would be king?", Public Administration, Vol. 89/4, pp. 1335-50.

Panchamia, N. and P. Thomas (2014), Public Service Agreements and the Prime Minister's Delivery Unit, Institute for Government.

Patterson, F., M.Kerrin and .G.Gatto-Roissard (2009), Characteristics & Behaviours of Innovative People in Organisations, Literature Review, Executive Summary, Nesta.

Potts, J. and T. Kastelle (2010), "Public sector innovation research: What's next?", Innovation: Management, Policy and Practice, Vol. 12/2, pp. 122-37.

Puttick, R, P. Baeck and P. Colligan (2014), I-teams: The Teams and Funds Making Innovation Happen in Governments Around the World, Nesta and Bloomberg Philanthropies, www.nesta.org.uk/sites/default/files/i-teams_june_2014.pdf.

Puttick, R and J. Ludlow (2013), Standards of Evidence: An Approach that Balances the Need for Evidence with Innovation, Nesta, www.nesta.org.uk/sites/default/files /standards_of_evidence.pdf.

Puttick, R and G. Mulgan (2013), What Should the "What Works Network" Do?, Nesta, www.nesta.org.uk/sites/default/files/what_should_the_what_works_network_do_0.pdf

Queensland Public Service Commission (2009), Submission on Advancing Public Sector Innovation, Queensland Government, Australia, Rosenblatt, M. (2011), "The use of innovation awards in the public sector: Individual and organizational perspectives", Innovation: Management, Policy and Practice, Vol. 13/2, pp. 207-19.

Sørensen, E. and J. Torfing (2012), "Introduction: Collaborative innovation in the public sector", The Innovation Journal: The Public Sector Innovation Journal, Vol. 17/1, pp. 1-14.

Stokes, K, R. Barker and R. Piggott (2014), Which Doctors Take Up Promising Ideas? New Insights from Open Data, Nesta, www.nesta.org.uk/sites/default/files/which-doctors-take-up-promising-new-ideas.jpg.

Torjman, L. (29 February 2012), "Labs: Designing the future", MaRS Discovery District blog, www.marsdd.com/systems-change/mars-solutions-lab/news/labs-designing-future/.

Townsend, W. (2013), "Innovation and the perception of risk in the public sector", International Journal of Organizational Innovation, Vol. 5/3, pp. 21-34.

Chapter 6.

Managing risks and uncertainties in public sector innovation[1]

Breakthrough innovations entail uncertainty, something the public sector is ill-equipped to manage. This chapter explores the distinction between risk and uncertainty, and the innovation management practices that can transform uncertainties into measurable risks, overcoming the bias against the unknown that is one of the main barriers to innovation. It considers the differences between public and private sector organisations and their implications for risk management. It distinguishes the different stages of the innovation lifecycle of any innovation, and identifies the activities and risks associated with each step. The chapter outlines a step-by-step approach to managing innovation, starting with a clear understanding of the context. It then considers three pillars of successful risk management: setting the preconditions for success, including proper resourcing and gaining a clear mandate; using new processes to mitigate uncertainty, including iterative prototyping and co-creating proposed solutions with the ultimate users; and the strategic orientation that ensures that innovation in one area does not have unforeseen consequences in other areas. It ends with some tips for innovators to overcome cultural barriers and build support for innovation, and two possible models governments could adopt to counter uncertainty on a wider scale.

Introduction

This chapter explores the distinct but related concepts of uncertainty and risk in relation to the implementation of innovative approaches in the public sector, identifying key drivers and challenges for managing them. The size and nature of today's challenges – such as in health, education and safety – call for new solutions instead of marginal adjustment to existing ones, requiring a shift from incremental towards disruptive innovations.

Most of the current questions facing breakthrough innovation revolve around uncertainty, where the probabilities of an event occurring are not known, rather than risks, where the probabilities can be measured. This poses a challenge for the public sector which is ill equipped to manage uncertainty. The chapter argues that it will be key for most innovation initiatives to find more agile ways to translate uncertainty into risks.

In this chapter, risk management refers to the overall management and mitigation of risks and uncertainties in public sector innovation. This chapter argues that many of today's innovation methods double as risk-management approaches. Consequently, project management is not separable from good risk management. In this sense, many of the recommendations outlined here can also be read as good project-management recommendations that can be applied through the innovation lifecycle (Figure 6.1).

The chapter presents a framework to analyse risks which takes into account the stage where the innovation is, whether if it is at an early or in a more mature stage of development. This distinction helps appreciate the nature of the risks involved – as they relate to the maturity and context of the practice – and how to manage them.

Finally, the chapter provides a risk-management approach built around three pillars: 1) identifying the preconditions for success; 2) new processes to support innovative initiatives; and 3) a strategic orientation of those initiatives towards success. By investing in strategic design[2] capabilities organisations can define the larger architecture within which an innovation sits. Without this wider perspective, good innovation in one place may unwittingly create problems or failures elsewhere in the system. Prototyping and co-creating are core elements of the framework presented here: key mechanisms to transform uncertainties into risk, build coalitions around innovation practices, foster citizen commitment and hedge risk. The chapter draws on the author's practice, insights from case studies and selected literature.

Figure 6.1. How risk management supports the innovation lifecycle

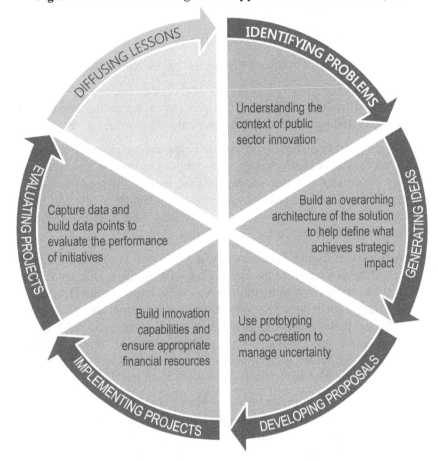

Understanding risks and uncertainties in public sector innovation

Everything has a risk, a probability of failure; some risks are acknowledged, while others hide in the shadows of our biases. But when something goes wrong, the question at the end of the day will be: was taking the risk warranted?

The distinction between risk and uncertainty is crucial to understanding the capacity of the public sector to react to unforeseen events. Risk is measurable (the probabilities are known), while uncertainty is not (the probabilities are not known). For example, it is fair to talk about the risks of crossing the street, because the odds of being hit by a car are known, based on past events. But when Apollo 11 set off in 1969 to put the first man on the moon it was not possible to speak of risk, because there were no past events to set the odds. The first man on the moon was a question of uncertainty, not of risk. But as more and more people were put on the moon, there have been enough events to discuss it in terms of risk.

This shift towards doing new things inevitably challenges the way risk and uncertainty are dealt with in a public sector context. In a context of improving known solutions (the sustaining phase – see Chapter 1) we can talk about risk, but when defining completely new solutions (the breakthrough phase) we should talk about uncertainty. Public sector innovation today is more a question of uncertainty than of risk. It is about moving from the decreasing returns of the current systems to the promised benefits of new models.

Three asymmetries tend to distort current biases around risk and uncertainty, favouring the adoption of known solutions over new ones:

- evaluating future risks based on past experiences

- overvaluing the risk of doing something versus undervaluing the risk of not doing it

- the culture of traditional ideas of due process in the public service versus more agile ones, including active risk management.

Moving from a world of knowns to one of unknowns requires using new analytical tools and methodologies. If breakthrough innovation is to deliver new solutions, it must not be inhibited by current practice and established models. It needs to have the cross-connecting capability to understand the underpinning principles of today's big drivers, such as healthcare, climate change and education; and have a citizen-centric focus on innovation, as opposed to an institution-centric focus.

The pressure to shift from process improvements towards strategic ones has created not only an increasing demand for new innovation skills in the public sector but also new questions. Governments have an obligation to maximise societal impact while minimising failure. As a breakthrough innovation shifts from a compelling idea to one that delivers real impact, it will be under increasing pressure to balance the quest for opportunity with the quest to minimise and mitigate risk and uncertainty. Without effective risk-management frameworks, innovation initiatives may not only create unwarranted risks to the people they serve, but also to the practice of innovation itself.

The fundamental barrier to public sector innovation is not so much the credibility of what it promises as the fear of what it might entail. Innovators in the public sector are increasingly pressed to understand and articulate the possibility of failure when doing new things. However, addressing the possibility of failure on its own will not advance the pursuit of innovation. Rather, the risk of maintaining the status quo must be perceived as greater than that of innovating. Therefore, successful innovations in the public sector will be as much about uncovering and detailing the hidden risk of not doing something new as about articulating and addressing the risk of doing it.

The public sector is arguably set up to manage risk well, but is ill equipped to deal with uncertainty. First, the nature and complexity of changes (such as epidemic crises, social unrest and chronic diseases) make it difficult to measure events to determine risks. Second, governments in many countries have not developed instruments that allow them to systematically scan the horizons to capture and analyse scenarios of change. Third, the culture of having predictability-based discussions has not yet taken root in many countries. In short, the public sector is not good at dealing with the initial lack of measureable events and is increasingly frozen in its decision making if it does not have some degree of assurance of success.

Resolving this lack of capacity to deal with uncertainty does not just affect how we talk about innovation, but also how innovation gets organised and resourced within public sector organisations. For example, it might mean building teams more around working with uncertainty than risk; hiring people with a higher tolerance for unknowns and a capacity to work with relative precision; not placing the same expectations of predictability on efforts to create new solutions as might be placed on those aiming to improve existing solutions; and using different accountability metrics for teams dealing with unknowns than those dealing with knowns. The Apollo 11 mission to the moon was one of our era's greatest science-based innovations dealing with unknowns. When first approved, its budget was USD 7 billion, but upon completion it had cost USD 25.4 billion (Government of the United States, 1973). Although the four-fold increase in Apollo's costs is distinctly different from cases of overspending because of bad management, the distinction can be difficult to articulate politically. Therefore there is all the more reason to highlight it upfront and address it with clarity in any discussion about risk and uncertainty in public sector innovation.

Rather than increasing public sector skills to manage uncertainty, the pathway towards an improved tomorrow may well reside in developing innovation practices that can quickly transform uncertainty into risk. Proven approaches, such as prototyping – iteratively improving ideas from quick, small-scale tests towards larger-scale experiments – can generate the first sets of probabilities. Generating probabilities while working in uncertainty gives new solutions a greater chance of surviving within the existing risk-dominated conceptual framework of the public sector.

While the distinction between risk and uncertainty can at times seem overly simplistic and semantic, it can help better define, resource, and measure innovation in the public sector. As the practice matures, there will be a shift from a discussion of uncertainty towards one of risk.

Comparing risks in the public and private sector contexts

One way to examine the maturity of public sector innovation and risk management is through comparison with business practices, which are robust and well established. In these early days it is tempting to adopt established business frameworks to bridge the gap. While that would undoubtedly help move the public sector up the learning curve, it is important to address the differences between the two sectors. Principles developed for a mature practice may stifle an emerging one, resulting in more rather than less risk and uncertainty.

It is useful to look at the differences between public and private sector innovation to understand their impact on the definition and management of risks:

- **Speed of change**: the speed of change in the public sector is usually slower than in business. For example, it is not uncommon for planning processes to take 15 years to be approved. This apparent slowness can seem unreasonable in the eyes of citizens used to having new products constantly flood the market. It enables some positive outcomes like intergenerational stability, but also hinders others, such as rapidly improving services. As a consequence, public sector innovators need to understand the balance of short-term risks and long-term benefits.

- **Return on investment**: connected to the point above, the return on investment for a public sector innovation may be broad and completely captured only by future generations whereas the business imperative is towards shareholder profit delivered on a quarterly basis. Unlike the private sector, the public does not have a simple and effectively measurable outcome like profit. Measures may not even be known at the outset, and they may lie in the distant future: the value of education reform, for example, may not be fully captured until the next generation.

- **Public value:** while businesses may choose a preferred market segment and disregard others in the pursuit of maximising profits, the public sector has to deliver public value to its citizens by ensuring transparency, openness, universal service, due process and accountability. In the public sector, solutions cannot be optimised for a select few, but rather need to meet the needs of very diverse populations. So how does the public sector innovate with its broader definition of population? As opposed to statistical approaches – which provides a solution that meets the average user needs – design-driven[3] practices can take a more personal and customised approach to identifying the relevant citizens and delivering on their needs.

- **Complexity**: governments have an unparalleled portfolio of responsibilities, services and roles. In comparison, even the most complex businesses operate in a relatively simple environment. So while public services frequently score badly for quality of delivery, any business faced with such a complex task would probably come to a screeching halt. For innovators, it is important not to lose track of the scale of operations extending beyond their specific initiative. Risk and uncertainty can be managed by having strategic design capabilities not just to shape a particular solution, but to define the larger architecture of solutions within which it sits. Without this larger map, good innovation in one place may unwittingly create problems or failures elsewhere in the system. Governments are desperate for improvements, but more importantly need ones with a positive impact overall.

What is a good practice to reduce risk and uncertainty in one context may quickly become a threat in another, not just to a particular activity, but to the wider effort of practice building. One example is the private sector innovation motto of "fail early and often".[4] This makes sense: try things quickly, learn from failures and get them out of the way before they become too expensive. Although this works well in the private sector, it can be dangerous in the public sector. Given the general resistance of the latter to change, nascent innovation can spark both scepticism and a sense of threat. Mitigating that risk requires applying quick iteration and prototyping in a different way, integrating early results into organisation processes and learn from them. It is also important to integrate the information generated from any failures into the learning process.

Any public sector innovation initiative today will benefit from an honest conversation about the maturity of the field, which will help create the right expectations and mitigate risks. But it is also important for innovators to also acknowledge this gap and understand the risk of hubris. In addition, the lack of reliable data on results makes it challenging to confront the status quo. Quick iteration processes and engagement or of "learning by doing" will help initiatives generate relevant data quickly and shift the terms of the debate.

At a strategic crossroads: More avoidance or risk management?

A risk-management approach can help prepare for, cushion or avert the impact of a failure, but also protect the credibility of the practice itself. Otherwise, the door to innovation could be closed for a long time. Hype could lead quickly to the "trough of disillusionment",[5] making the idea of innovation politically untenable. But governments won't be viable without innovation, so any delay in its mainstream adoption would ultimately be a risk to the future of government itself.

There is a growing focus on risk management in the public sector at the corporate level, and many countries have deployed risk-management tools and techniques adapted from the private sector, such as annual organisational risk assessment processes, risk registers and mitigation strategies. These efforts are often compounded by narrow approaches (such as cost analysis), statistical bias (favouring known events over unknown ones), and slow and hierarchical management. More recent practices such as lean production,[6] while positive in many aspects, are derived from linear processes and are challenged by the iterative, interconnected, and blurred contexts of most innovation initiatives today.

There are at least two distinct approaches to minimising risks and uncertainties in public sector innovation. One is to shrink its scope by outsourcing while focusing on incrementally improving what remains; the other is to build management tools and skills that can lower risks while increasing public sector intelligence about uncertainty. The first approach is the easiest, for it requires the least change, resourcing and commitments. For many risk-averse public organisations, this is the preferred pathway, because it allows them to declare that they are for innovation without having to undertake any profound changes. This is not always out of ill will or laziness, but is frequently also due to a perceived lack of any public mandate to make deep changes. But it is the latter option that should be preferred. If there is a viable path to minimise innovation risks and uncertainties it must be through better management and design, not smaller and more tentative initiatives.

A framework to analyse risks and uncertainties

When analysing risk-management approaches in public sector innovation, it is useful to see innovation as an evolutionary process and distinguish whether it is in an emergent, or pre-practice, context or in a mature, or in-practice, context. This distinction is important as the nature of the risks involved relates to the maturity and context of the practice. In a pre-practice phase, the question is how to manage the development of the practice so that it becomes mainstream and is transformed into a real lever for change. Reaping the potential benefit of bringing the practice to scale (i.e. not just the individual solution but making innovation itself a part of standard practice) depends on being able to translate what works well in a small, bounded, environment into the larger context of public service. This requires confronting the idea of innovation as a political tool as well as developing a broader cross-cutting architecture of public sector innovation. To make the practice mainstream means risk managing not just individual initiatives, but also the overall development. In short the practice of innovation needs to get professionalised.

Figure 6.2. Development stages of innovation practice with the public sector

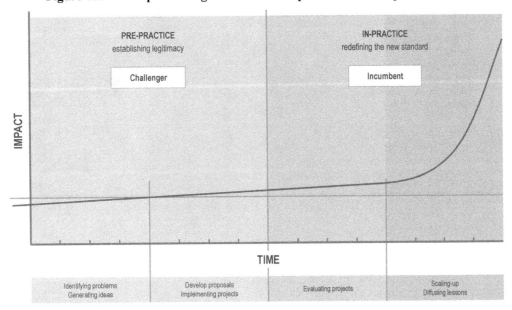

There are clearly many different ways to frame this evolution, but a helpful distinction is to ask whether the practice of innovation itself is the incumbent or challenger. When challenging an established way of doing something it will inevitably be in a pre-practice mode; a new way of doing by acting at the margins. It will tend to be opportunistic and improvisational in nature, and more dependent on the efficacy of individuals than on a proven system of doing. As practices mature and gain support they slowly shift from the opportunistic and improvisational margins toward the more structured and established core. This latter phase should be seen as "in-practice", reflecting the idea that the challenger is becoming the incumbent. The distinction between pre-practice and in-practice is important, as the drivers of success in each phase are different in terms of leadership style, human resources strategy, incentives and expectation. Further distinctions within these two phases can be made by breaking them into four steps: pre-practice, ramping up, operational and scaling up (Figure 6.2). Table 6.1 summarises the primary activities and risks associated with each step.

Table 6.1. Risks associated with pre-practice and in-practice innovation

	Pre-practice		In-practice	
	Identify problems Generate ideas	Develop proposals Implement	Evaluate	Scale up Diffuse
Primary activities	- building internal understanding and opportunity - focused on building a resourcing solution - much of the effort is building support, "changing minds".	- building capacity and practice - shifting from a costs to a benefits operation - delivering project-based successes.	- establishing innovation as a practice - delivering measurable impact - producing consistent benefits across a range of activities.	- practice becomes mainstream - predictable and measurable impact - significant impact on public sector budgets.
Selected risks	- "innovation" threatens people's roles and beliefs - promise of innovation is not enough to overcome perceived risks - leadership is not confident in articulating the need for "innovation" - little outside understanding of actual current constraints.	- failures give the naysayers evidence that "innovation" was dangerous - fears of dividing institutions, of "a few innovators" versus "the un-creative majority" - little experience in how to manage public expectations.	- innovation practice is seen as a disruption to smooth operations - innovation practice changes existing funding practices - success creates resentment - expectations are raised following a success.	- being part of the mainstream creates a new bias - inability to weather an unexpected event puts the whole effort into question - good innovations are undermined by isolated but highly publicised failures - innovations turn out to cost more, or perform more poorly at scale than anticipated - innovation becomes too politicised to be effective - high marginal cost of universal roll out.

Box 6.1 provides more details on some of the types of risks, which have emerged from observing innovation practices and the author's interview with some experts.[7] Any organisation working in innovation should develop an expanded glossary of risks relating to the issues confronting them.

Box 6.1. Examples of types of risks in public sector innovation

The risk of bias: up until recently[1] regulations in Finland banned the use of wood in large-scale constructions because of the risk of fire, but Swedish regulations had allowed wood for some 25 years. Innovation challenges are frequently skewed by cultural bias, rather than knowledge: based on the same evidence, Swedes saw opportunity where Finns saw risk. The risk of bias is always cultural and is best thwarted by building a solid factual case that weakens the grip of the bias.

The risk of hubris: the promise of a proposed innovation can create excessive confidence in one's undertakings. This can lead to the risk of backlash to perceived arrogance or proponents being blinded to the realities in the field (being overly confident and underestimating risks).

The risk of unmet expectations: there is a risk of not meeting expectations, which can cause loss of support and thus expose your work to further risks. But there is also a risk of exceeding expectations. In 2010, Constitution (Chile) radically innovated its master-planning process to deliver a master plan in 90 days, rather than the 10-15 year norm (Box 6.4). This exceeded everyone's expectations to such a degree that the expectations of what would happen next were totally unrealistic: "Why aren't the houses ready after 90 days?" What was a huge success turned into a problem of increasing dissatisfaction.

The risk of insufficient resources: in the private sector, a competitive business would reinvest 2-6% of its profits in research and development, the level needed to keep a company innovative. The innovation challenges in government are vast, but the resources deployed to solve them are rarely even close to private sector levels. The best way to thwart the risk of failure is to provide resourcing in proportion to the scale of the challenge at hand.

[1]Finnish fire codes were changed on April 15th, 2011, to allow wood to be used in residential and agency buildings of up to eight storeys: Finnish Ministry of Trade and Employment summary, page 2, www.tem.fi/files/40816/Wood_Construction_in_Finland.pdf.

This evolutionary distinction helps identify two critical dynamics. First is the degree to which an innovation is an emerging or a mainstream practice, with both ends of the spectrum presenting different challenges and expectations. As a consequence, the drivers of risk and uncertainty can be very different. The second relates to where the risk and uncertainty drivers lie: within public sector organisations (such as cultural opposition to change) or external to them (such as social instability). Table 6.2 shows the intersection of these two primary drivers.

Table 6.2. Risk matrix associated with pre-practice and in-practice innovation

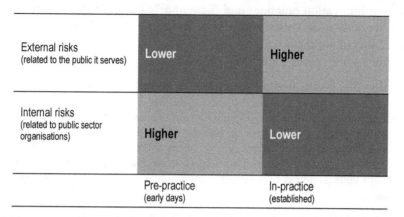

	Pre-practice (early days)	In-practice (established)
External risks (related to the public it serves)	Lower	Higher
Internal risks (related to public sector organisations)	Higher	Lower

In a pre-practice context the factors driving the risk of failure are predominately internal, because organisational and ideological resistance to change can do far more damage to early tentative initiatives than the potential impact of external failure. As practices become more established, they develop a positive track record and support, making them less vulnerable to internal risks. As they become more credible they will take on larger initiatives, bringing the possibility of greater impact, but also risk. Naturally the balance of risk starts shift from internal to external drivers.

Considering the intersection between "type of innovation" and "bearers of risk and uncertainties" won't give direct answers to management practices, but will help stimulate a conversation that will both build awareness and identify new and pertinent questions (See Box 6.2). These two perspectives can be the basis for a productive conversation when establishing a risk-management approach:

- **What type of innovation is being pursued?** There have been many attempts to classify the type of innovation, including a useful framework by Windrum and Koch (2008: p.8).[8] Discussing the differences will lead to a more robust understanding of the range of issues to consider – such as what kind of capabilities to hire, how to set up the work – which in turn can help practices to manage and mitigate future risks and uncertainties (see also Chapter 3).

- **Who is to bear the burden of failure?** There are clearly different risk profiles to identify. The risk drivers for politicians are, for example, different than those for public servants. A failure with relatively little technical impact on an innovation may have tremendous political fall-out especially if sensationalised by the media.[9] Likewise there are competing structural interests, such as economic versus environmental interests that can drive risks and uncertainty. Thinking about these will help innovators better understand the type of challenges involved and where they could come from.

Box 6.2. Bearers of risks and uncertainties

Asking who will reap the benefits of innovation and who will bear the burden of failures can help us better understand the system-wide drivers that lead to success and adoption. A comprehensive list can be built by adopting the accepted framework of "economy, environment, society" (United Nations General Assembly, 2005) to describe the total system. Adding the categories of institutions, citizens and organisations helps make the list comprehensive to the public sector. The meshing of categories may alter their focus. Society, for example, becomes more tightly defined but also differs from citizens, reflecting a distinction between individual citizens and a society of citizens.

As such the proposed typology of "bearers of risk and uncertainty" is as follows:

- risk to organisations (such as culture, incentives, leadership)

- risk to institutions (such as trust, cohesion, stability)

- risk to citizens (such as health, security, employment)

- risk to society (such as social cohesion, stability, well-being)

- risk to the economy (such as markets, business, employment)

- risk to the environment (such as climate, biodiversity, natural resources).

A step-by-step risk management approach

The following section provides elements of a risk management approach to innovations which can help innovators navigate through their projects and orient their efforts in the most productive way.

Getting the context, setting directions and addressing the status quo

Risk management starts with understanding the context of innovation. The first step helps innovators ask the right questions to ensure they understand the context enough to position their efforts to best ensure success. Reading the situation wrong will invariably create risks. Even if the idea is sound, if the existing context is not addressed it will inevitably increase the likelihood of failure. For example, assuming someone has authority when he or she doesn't creates new potential for failure as the assumptions clash with reality. The following questions help innovators understand the context of their work:

- What it is you are trying to achieve and change?

- Is the innovation around something new or existing?

- Do you have authority or are you seeking permission for change?

- Are you innovating a solution or establishing the preconditions for innovation?

Depending on the answers to these questions, innovation efforts will follow very different paths. In all four cases the project and risk management approach will differ. Being unaware of the different paths is in itself a risk to the initiative or practice.

Stating a clear purpose helps to clarify what one is trying to achieve and change. This can distinguish the key central issues without which the change won't happen from the things that are "nice to have" but not critical. Most of the forces of reluctance implicitly overvalue the status quo. Making evident the flaws of the status quo without devaluing the people one is seeking to change is a good starting point ("honouring the past but being willing to leave it behind").

Arguably the greatest effort lies in making room for new ideas, rather than the ideas themselves. If the innovation takes place within the context of an existing service, it will have to contend with established practice, culture and sense of ownership. This is quite different from creating completely new services, that don't have to contend with the same level of legacy.

Having the authority to make the space for new ideas allows innovators to be more directly focused on the ideas themselves. Needing to seek permission places innovators in a weaker position, having to build support and try to get a seat at the table. More of their risk management effort will be focused on coalition building than on the mechanics of the innovation itself. Likewise, an effort that is building the foundation for innovative practices to flourish will have to deal more with human enterprise risks than those concentrating on innovations directly focused on solving an individual problem.

It is also important to carefully consider the side effects of each course of action. Many that are intended to minimise and control risks (for example requiring cumbersome approval processes, a high degree of complex regulation and excessive micromanagement) may have the negative effect of stifling innovation as a practice.

Establishing the first order questions and actions makes it clear that different phases require different management approaches. This leads to a layered approach to management with five primary elements grouped into three main pillars (Figure 6.3). First, there are the **preconditions for success**, which include proper resourcing and a clear mandate, two factors that are critical to mitigating the risks and uncertainties of innovating. Second, are the **new processes** to support innovative initiatives: prototyping and co-creation, which are key to addressing the risks and uncertainties of innovating. Third is **strategic orientation:** an architecture to guide the building of a portfolio of initiatives that prevents them from cancelling each other out.

Figure 6.3. A risk-oriented project-management approach: Five elements to take into account

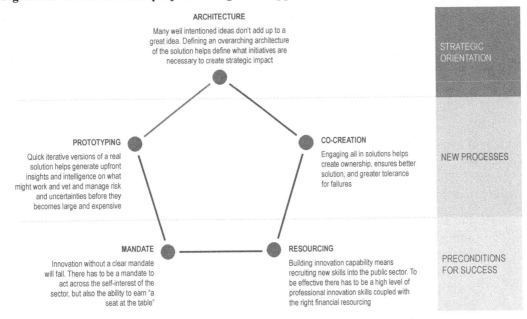

While the preconditions for success ensure innovations fall on fertile ground, and strategic orientation provides an overall compass, it is the new processes which form the locus of most contemporary innovation. The two main processes at work are **prototyping** (quick iterations of solutions that test feasibility early on) and **co-creation** (engaging all stakeholders in the development of solutions).

Paradoxically these practices can help manage risk, but simultaneously help create risks and uncertainties. They help insofar as they enable solutions to be tested early before risks become too great; ensuring that proposed solutions have the relevant intelligence behind them and the ownership needed to make them effective. In this sense they are both efficient risk management tools and deliver value: a win-win solution. But they create risks insofar as they challenge the fundamental structure and culture of the public sector.

The traditional divides between political vision and public servant delivery, and between planning and implementation are fundamentally challenged by these iterative and co-creative processes. The tradition of calling for a distinction between politics and administration is well evidenced in the literature (Terry, 1993) and clearly visible in practice. In many European cities, for example, an informed dialogue between politicians and public servants is frowned upon in the name of keeping the process pure. As a result, many municipalities have built firewalls so that public servants prepare technical proposals and politicians approve them in almost complete isolation from each other, without the synergies that interaction provides. While this approach may work fine on issues that are tried and tested, it will invariably mean untried ideas are prone to failure because they have not benefited from the testing provided by dialogue and exchange. Maintaining this divide increases the risk and uncertainty associated with breakthrough innovations; reconnecting the divide is an effective risk preventive measure.

The next sections discuss in more detail each pillar of the risk-oriented project management approach illustrated above.

Setting the preconditions for success

It makes little sense to talk of risk management if the preconditions for success do not exist. Therefore, getting the two main preconditions in place, proper resourcing and a clear mandate, is a key first step towards building a successful risk-management and risk-mitigation approach.

Resourcing

Innovation without the right resources is unsustainable. This means hiring the right skills for each role, as well as creating the right incentives. It also means funding the right initiatives, appropriately and through the right mechanisms. An appropriate human resources (HR) and funding strategy can ensure that innovation initiatives meet or exceed their objectives.

- **Find the right talent**. For the most part, the public sector is resourced to administer, not to innovate. It is unfair to ask people skilled in one professional area to suddenly deliver another kind of professional skill. Many innovation efforts will fail if they can't deliver at a high standard from day one. How many civil servants are proficient to run co-creation projects to a high standard? Or to build an alpha prototype of a new service solution? This creates a need to either hire in or develop talent. Recruitment and selection have a clear impact on ability to innovate Chapter 3) but finding that talent may not be as easy as it sounds – it often requires the public sector to build new networks of influence.

- **Build integrated teams.** One of the dangers of establishing innovation teams is the signal it sends to the rest of the organisation that "you are not innovative". If poorly implemented, innovation teams can actually become an impediment to innovation, rather than an enabler. The risk of an "us and them" divide can be mitigated by building highly integrated teams: hire half of the talent from outside the public sector, bringing in the new skills needed, and half from within the public sector, bringing in the system intelligence needed. The internal candidates should represent the "best of breed" who can be champions for the cause. That way the team has the right intelligence to drive successful innovations and a broad-based network of support (see Chapter 5).

- **Resource innovation appropriately**. One easy way of ensuring failure in innovation is to not resource it properly. Because most innovation initiatives today can be seen an "extra",[10] budgets for this kind of activity can be tight. As a consequence there is frequently a disconnect between the desired impact and the resources available. An under-resourced initiative risks failing and in the process delivering no value at all while justifying all the naysayers. Token funding may be a tacit message that "we don't value innovation"; a bigger commitment may be a good test of the political will to engage in innovation. Larger sums also bring with them more attention, which if managed well can help diffuse instead of stifling innovation. Financial incentives such as innovation funds have proven to be effective to stimulate innovations (see Chapter 4).

- **Articulate the upfront investment (and build patience for returns on investment)**. Innovation requires investing in capacity building. A project-by-project funding approach can be risky, as it does not establish a clear path beyond single projects and each failure will be magnified, as it will be evaluated within the limited confines of a project, not in the context of a broader effort. This approach also makes it difficult to hire people and develop continuity, while using a disproportionate amount of effort to secure projects rather than deliver impact. To succeed, innovation will need to make clear arguments for an upfront investment in delivering impact, not just project delivery. When NASA was established in 1958 it received a surge of funding to help it build the capacity to deliver a man on the moon. This upfront spike was inevitable to meet the cost of learning, but it quickly became normalised once the system of innovation had become mainstream and was delivering on its promise (Figure 6.4).

Figure 6.4. NASA spending from its creation (1958) to 2014

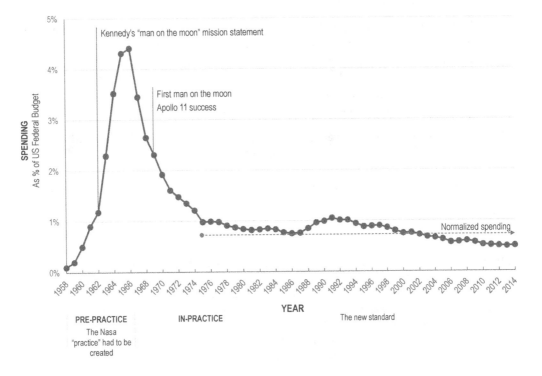

- **Reward innovation**. There is overwhelming evidence that people's behaviour is shaped and reinforced by their peers. In this regards, risk depends on whether public sector organisations have a supportive culture for innovation. Without it, even the slightest mistakes or perception of risk can be met with great resistance: small risks can become large ones. One way to minimise this is to build the culture and incentives that help create the preconditions to success, with supportive peers and a culture that are more tolerant of risk. A good example of this preventive strategy is embodied in the Innovations in American Government Awards,[11] which highlight best practice, reward innovation cultures and give prizes to risk takers.

Mandating

Innovation without a mandate will be short lived. Mandates are necessary to have authority to act. A clear mandate gives an innovation team the authority to access resources and data, and makes decisions in the pursuit of a given objective. The successful impact of the United Kingdom's Government Digital Services in transforming government is partly due to the clear mandate it was given to not just to deliver new digital services but also to act across all of government. Without a clear mandate, innovation initiatives risk being seen as "rogue", in the processes making innovation itself seem illegitimate. But while a mandate must be given, it must also in part be earned.

- **Identify the right projects**. A report for Nesta suggests that "that efficiency and localism will be the key focus" in public sector innovation (Hughes et al., 2011). Working with projects that support the stated objectives of the system will help innovation be seen as part of the solution, rather than an outlier risk or bringing uncertainty to the overall objectives. Another aspect of defining the "right projects" is to choose ones that can be easily delivered. Early wins are especially important when trying to earn and build confidence.

- **Build demand creep**. Rarely is there enough budget to go all in on "innovation". The opportunistic approach is to take what is given and to increase demand by constantly exceeding expectations. This positions initiatives to help generate increased future demand. The municipality of Lahti in Finland offers an example of building demand creep alongside a co-creation process (Box 6.3).

Box 6.3. Building demand creep: Master planning in the municipality of Lahti, Finland

In 2011 the municipality of Lahti needed a new approach to its master planning. The previous master planning effort was stuck in court, a widespread problem for municipalities. In Finland, for example, about 1 100 master plans are prepared each year, of which 9% end up in court, 75% in cases that are brought on by citizens.[1] Lahti believed that better communication of the merits of the proposal would win citizens over. They set out to improve their "marketing" skills for the next master planning process. But what started as a marketing approach, soon turned into a co-creation approach with citizens actively partaking in the end solution. The master planning process was deemed a success: faster, better and cheaper. What the city had realised was that the solution was not about selling their idea, but rather working with citizens to co-create it. This shared experience and success led the municipality to recognise what it could not know before; as a direct result of this experience they declared co-creation a cornerstone of all new city service development. That was not an objective that could have been declared at the outset, but one that evolved as expectations were exceeded.

[1]Holopainen et al. (2013) "Muutoksenhaku maankäyttö- ja rakennuslain mukaisissa asioissa Tarkastelussa kaavat, suunnittelutarveratkaisut ja poikkeamispäätökset sekä valituslupa-asiat," Finnish Ministry of the Environment.

- **Identify external champions.** Investing public resources in an innovation effort can be a challenging proposition at times. Prominent external champions can help articulate the need for public innovation efforts. This can help create the right political pressure for change, while empowering public servants to act. The decision to invest in building the UK Government's digital vision[12] was greatly advanced through the leadership of Martha Lane Fox, a highly respected digital advocate from within the UK's business community. Her advocacy for a radical transformation of the government's digital services led to the government taking on the "digital by default" strategy and establishing the Government Digital Service in 2011.

- **Build internal champions**. One destabilising factor in public sector innovation initiatives is the risks of an "us and them" divide: the majority focused on maintaining the system (schools, hospitals, etc.) and a few "innovators" focused on rethinking things. This is especially true when innovation teams need to integrate with the wider organisation. The suspicion, mistrust and resentment that such a divide could breed can create significant risks to the success of an innovation initiative. In 2011, a team from IDEO – a globally leading design and innovation consultancy – helped the then nascent US Consumer Financial Protection Bureau build their organisational identity but also helped them become consumer-centred in their efforts. The bureau had been established in 2009 by President Obama to protect "Main Street" by overseeing Wall Street. This meant that the bureau had to understand and connect with the financial consumer, the average citizen, something most public servants were unfamiliar with, and an area standard practice was not aligned towards. IDEO was able to create a relationship with the Assistant Director for Consumer Engagement both personally and ideologically. Being a highly respected figure in the organisation, he could easily bridge both camps. In doing so he was able to legitimise the innovation team's work and ensure success, thwarting many possible organisational risks on the way.

- **Find the frontline**. Frontline staff are one of the most important sources of ideas. "Services which are easier for citizens are easier for frontline workers too, and that combination saves money."[13] Not only does it save money, it is also an effective risk management approach. That is the experience of MindLab's BenchKode team, which sought to innovate government's online business registry. What MindLab's team found was that there was a lot of intelligence in the frontline where public servants interacted with citizens. Those insights can help create better service and also help innovation teams build legitimacy. This legitimacy can help towards earning a mandate, which will help thwart risks and uncertainties by having the self-interest of the organisation work with, rather than against, the innovation.

New processes

Today, much of what might be considered innovation risks are actually questions of uncertainty. Effective management and mitigation of uncertainty involves three elements:

- Compress the time it takes for new and unknown solutions to be known and measurable (in effect translating uncertainty into risk).

- Break down and iterate the cycle of innovation to reduce uncertainty to manageable bite-size pieces, but also to help inform and shape the solution-finding approach (in effect, bridging the current divide between planning and implementation into a single process).

- Engage the producers and consumers of solutions as active participants in the creation of solutions. This brings more wisdom, data and understanding, not only making solutions more viable but also hedging the risks associated with new solutions.

Prototyping and co-creation are two fundamental processes for managing and mitigating risks and uncertainties, helping respond to these three objectives.

Prototyping

One of the greatest challenges in traditional public sector reform processes is the time gap between inception, implementation and impact. This is especially true in critical, large-scale and complex areas such as education, health or climate change. Given the complex and unpredictable nature of these issues, new ideas may be obsolete by the time they have been implemented. Some industries have to deal with similar problems but while a commercial aircraft manufacturer can take the risk of potential catastrophic failure, public education or healthcare systems simply cannot. This is one of the reasons why the public sector is more risk averse, and thus more innovation adverse, than the private sector. This is especially true for complex long-term questions, which by definition are more driven by uncertainty than risk

Whereas more traditional stage-gate or waterfall risk management methodologies require innovators to predict in advance all possible outcomes and develop mitigation strategies for each, more experimental project management methodologies prioritise learning by doing, starting small, incorporating continuous feedback loops that allow for adaptation on the fly and may enable innovators to manage unforeseen impacts as they arise (Figure 6.5). These approaches often highlight prototyping as an effective risk management tool that shorten the time to implementation and enable project managers to incorporate new information in real time to tweak the design and development process before failures become too expensive. Being agile and iterative breaks down risk into manageable chunks and provides early feedback as to what does and does not work, thus transforming uncertainty into risk.

Figure 6.5. Prototype delivery model versus traditional delivery model

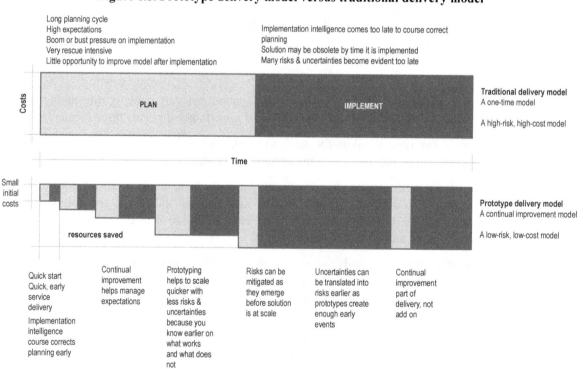

Introducing speed and agility through prototyping and iteration poses challenges to governments. Current systems are not set up to enable prototyping as a mass functionality

across the board, or to attract people with the kind of skills that make prototyping possible. Public procurement favours incumbents with track records and the right social connections over the "lean start-ups" that might actually have the relevant innovation know-how. How can the values of public procurement be aligned with the principles of agile and iteration? Initiatives are needed that help put the small and agile on a level playing field with the large and the incumbent.

Co-creation

Co-creation makes the producers and consumers of solutions active participants in the creation of new solutions. This brings more wisdom to final solutions by allowing all perspectives to be considered in early development and provides early feedback as to what might or might not work, but it is also an effective way to hedge risks associated with new solutions. Co-owners of a solution will also be more tolerant of failures. Co-creation can thus help create radically faster and better government with the involvement of all (Figure 6.6 and Box 6.4).

Figure 6.6. Co-creation model versus traditional service production model

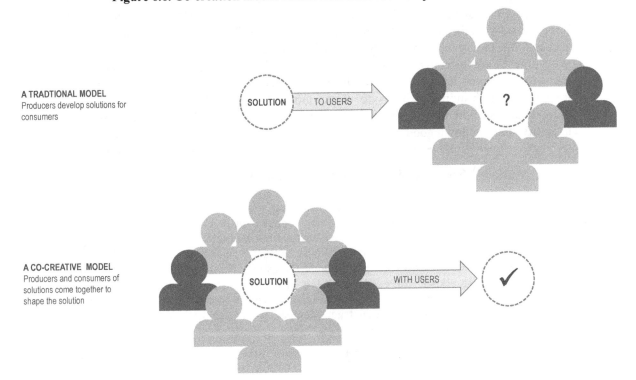

Box 6.4. Case of co-creation: Reconstructing the city of Constitution, Chile

In 2010 a tsunami destroyed the city of Constitution. The city leadership decided they would need to radically rethink the master planning process: what normally took 10-15 years would have to happen in 90 days as that was the maximum acceptable time for people to be without reconstruction. To meet this radical objective, the city adopted a co-creation process. This was a massive, citywide engagement effort with all of its citizens. When the 90-day deadline came, there was a referendum on the proposal: 94% of the citizens of Constitution voted in support of the new master plan. One would be hard pressed to find a democracy that can deliver such support.

Source: Boyer et al. (2013), *Legible Practices: Six Stories About the Craft of Stewardship* www.hels inkidesignlab.org/peoplepods/themes/hdl/downloads/Legible_Practises.pdf, p. 32.

Co-location of teams provides an effective way to co-create within a public sector organisation. By co-locating, the team develops shared experiences and standards, looks at drawings or examples together, gets a better understanding of each other's culture, strengthens cohesion, and builds greater tolerance for mistakes (Box 6.5). Being open brings more visibility and intelligence to innovation initiatives helping ensure that they succeed. In the process, visibility can help insure against organisation self-interest. Weeknotes[14] are effective ways of regularly sharing the unfolding workings of an innovation team online, accessible to all. It is an effective and informal way to accelerate learning, while bringing visibility to the initiative. If managed well, visibility can help mitigate against potential organisational self-interest: it makes it harder for organisations to justify shutting down good innovation just because they challenge the status quo.

Box 6.5. Case of co-location: The Low2No project, Finland

In 2009 the Finnish Innovation Fund,[1] launched the Low2No[0] project: an innovation initiative to help create a carbon neutral development market in Finland. Delivering success required the work of a highly interdisciplinary team from multiple countries (primarily from Finland, the United Kingdom and Germany). While the team seemed to understand each other, it became clear that the same words meant different things to different professionals in different cultures. Schematic phases, for example, had a different standard of deliverables for the Germans than it did for the Finns. These unregistered differences created significant risks to the project. The solution was to co-locate the team. Members would spend multiple days every other week co-located in the same office space.

[1] Founded in 1967, Sitra, the Finnish Innovation Fund (*Suomen Itsenäisyyden Juhlarahasto* in Finnish) is a financially and politically independent public fund that reports to parliament with the aim of helping build a competitive and innovative Finland. More: www.sitra.fi/en/about-sitra .

[2] Low2No is short for "low to no carbon", an urban development project in downtown Helsinki launched by the Finnish innovation fund in 2009 to help create a carbon neutral development market in Finland. For more information see www.low2no.org/.

Co-creation can help build ownership of the final solution (e.g. personal health conditions are in effect co-produced); clarify user-centred objectives and deliverables (e.g. by engaging in a collaborative relationship between a public authority and the service users); crowdsource information on needs, solutions and impacts; and strengthen tolerance for risks through greater openness and transparency (benefits as well as risk are co-owned in a co-production schemes). However, OECD research has also found that co-creation schemes can inadvertently bring more risks than they avoid, such as creating unfunded mandates and shifting costs and accountability onto citizens (OECD, 2011).

Strategic orientation

Increasingly the challenge in the public sector lies not in innovating a single service, process or policy, but to deliver impact on large-scale issues: education, healthcare, or climate change. While there are innumerable initiatives under each of these themes, few are guaranteed to achieve positive returns. Healthcare provides a good example. In the United States where there has been arguably an increasing abundance of healthcare innovations, overall health has declined over the last 20 years compared to the leading countries.[15] Many good parts don't make necessarily for a great whole. It is no longer enough to innovate one part; greater public values require innovating the whole.

The "architecture of the solution" is about understating the combined positive impact of many co-ordinated efforts. An architecture, or portfolio, defines the underlying principles that guide what and what not to do; how to phase and co-ordinate efforts; and how to hedge risks between initiatives so that the overall risks and uncertainties are minimised. Without it, many good ideas will invariably pull in competing directions, with no overall positive effect. Without such an architecture even the best-intentioned innovation initiatives will unwittingly create increased risk and uncertainty.

Governments have been served well by deep and narrow specialties, but today's "big picture" challenges by their nature lie at the intersection of what we know. Because key decision makers cannot always see a complete synthetic whole, they are often blind-sided by the unintended consequences of their actions. Governments are adapting to these new circumstances and demonstrating agility as they set up cross-organisational units to innovate across policy functions and administrative silos (see Chapter 5).

Tips for innovators: Transforming uncertainty into risk

As an emerging practice, innovation is just beginning to take its first steps into existing public structures and cultures. It may not have had a chance to make a large-scale impact everywhere, but it has certainly begun to bump up against the vested interests of the public sector. As a result, the evidence suggests[16] that the greatest risks and uncertainties are emerging from those interests, not stemming from the common interest of society. Many of these new innovation practices blur the traditional roles of politicians, citizens and public servants and challenge the common perception of good government. While such practices may be providing a lot of benefits, they are also creating the potential for new kinds of failures.

Innovation in a breakthrough context will always be dominated by uncertainty. Even if the objective itself is fairly straightforward and with good precedent (so fundamentally a question of risk), a breakthrough approach to innovation will always colour it with uncertainty. The challenger approach will always be seen as uncertain from the viewpoint of the incumbent. As such issues of risk will always be secondary to those of uncertainty. In short, when taking a new approach, even on a well-established issue such as improving the renewal of drivers' licences, it will be deemed uncertain because the approach is new. As such, good risk management needs to build a mandate, a resourcing approach, and a defined objective that is aligned with managing uncertainty. Innovators need to identify preconditions for success, select new processes to support the innovation and strategically orient the innovation initiatives towards positive sum impact.

Because anyone embarking on an innovation needs to clear away a lot of legacy approaches and practices, they will spend most of their effort on that rather than on developing the innovation itself. That means working artfully with cultural barriers, using prototyping and engagement to quickly and successfully translate uncertainty into risk while building a base of support. To shift the conversation from emotionally based fear to fact-based success. In practice, this mean learning by doing and having the information from the doing drive the conversation.

Finally, here are some starting points to manage risks while getting an innovation started:

- **Socialise ideas and make them understood**. All activities have associated risks and uncertainties, but the more novel or innovative they are, the further the balance tips towards uncertainty. Trying to hard-sell an unfamiliar innovation may bring too many unknowns to bear at once, creating a quick no. But soft launching ideas can help create flexibility in finding common ground. Much as in personal relationships, it is advisable to take a "flirt-date-marry" approach to building innovation support, rather than an immediate marriage proposal. The soft approach also helps sound out potential risks before the initiative is launched.

- **Make the benefits of innovation real and palpable early on.** It is hard to find supporters to help develop ideas into concrete deliveries on a promise of a long-term return. Similar to what happens in the product and service world, solutions are easy to adopt when they are tangible, visible and come with a clear value proposition. Prototyping and other visualisation techniques help transform ideas into identifiable objects and, along with strong communication and narratives, can help overcome resistance and lead to a strong proof of concept. Segmented deliverables and quick iteration reduce the "time to market" of an innovation while decreasing the risk of low levels of usage at the launch.

- **Use evidence to transform uncertainty into risk.** Any process of culture change in an organisation will invariably challenge people's sense of self. Thus, debate regarding innovation can be very emotionally charged. The risk that cultural rifts will lead to failures can be high. Consequently, initiatives need to find ways to shift the discussion from emotional- based to fact-based. While it may be too early to have a discussion based on outcomes, innovation projects are constantly producing data. Make sure to set up the innovation initiative to capture and develop a broad range of data and data points. If using a blog, look at what the traffic is like and what the trends are; data points like quotes from public servants, citizens engaging and leaders can be very helpful preliminary insights. As initiatives mature, seek constant data. Critically this will also help objectively evaluate the performance of initiatives and thwart against the risk of hubris that can blind innovators from thinking objectively.

- **Build up evidence of impact, both quantitative and qualitative.** Highlighting evidence of impact and not just collecting output measures helps establish a sense of achievement and fulfilment of purpose. People are more interested in decreasing mortality rates than in the specific performance rates of a new tele-medicine application. Quantifiable data coupled with strong narratives can be effective means of persuading the sceptics and thus reduce the risk of blockages while constantly communicating the benefits of the innovation.

- **Model risk-reward to drive and scale innovation practices**. The flip side of risk is opportunity. Each innovation needs to objectively balance risk and opportunity. Adapting a traditional force-field diagram (which helps gain a comprehensive overview of the different forces acting on a potential organisational change issue) can be helpful in gaining analytical perspective and help better risk manage efforts.

Open questions

Much of the current discourse about public sector innovation is based on the current concept, structures and role of government. The call for more participatory citizen engagement is based in part on the idea that governments can perform better when they understand citizen needs better. But what happens if and when the role and responsibility of government changes? What happens when things invariably go wrong? What happens to the current notions about risk and uncertainty? Who absorbs those failures?

Governments might wish to explore further the possible models to counter uncertainty and risk on a more aggregated and cross-societal level, and what type of "risk governance" would be most adequate according to the nature and scale of challenges they are facing. Important questions to ask would be those related to risk redistribution. Two possible models could be further explored, neither of which provide quick solutions to the problem:

- **A risk-sharing model: government as a mechanism of redistribution**. This is the classic role of government, so one could imagine a redistribution mechanism that helps to spread innovation benefits, costs and failures evenly. This is conceptually not dissimilar to how reinsurers work and would require a nimble public sector capable of moving resources quickly to absorb failures or spreading innovations demographically, geographically and socially to hedge risks.

- **An opt-in model: beta government**. The service and product world has long rolled out pre-production versions of solutions. The idea is that there will always be lead users who enjoy the benefits of being first in, while helping companies improve solutions through their feedback. This is most noticeable in the software industry, where companies offer beta releases of their software. Customers opt in acknowledging all the risks involved. Could the public sector build beta releases of innovative solutions? While this already happens in part with digital services, it could be expanded to other, brick-and-mortar solutions. It would leverage a latent pool of lead citizens and tap into not only desires to be first, but also desires to contribute to a better society. Citizens could opt into an experimental new service, school or tax process and be active contributors, or co-creators, in improving the innovation, while taking on some of the risk and uncertainty associated with it.

Notes

1. This chapter is based on a paper prepared for the OECD by Marco Steinberg, Snowcone and Haystack, Finland.

2. Strategic design refers to the application of design methodologies to shape decision-making rather than its more traditional product or service oriented focus (Helsinki Design Lab, undated).

3. Based on design's user-centered approach to solutions including ethnography, persona definition, and user experience work

4. This is a common term, popularised by many but maybe most notably by the innovation and design consultancy IDEO (Economist, 2011)

5. A term coined by Gartner referring to the pattern of technology adoption that after a hype cycle (when expectations are high), the market hits a trough of disillusionment because the technology has yet to deliver (Gartner, undated).

6. From the term "lean manufacturing" referring to a systematic improvement methodology (Krafcik, 1988).

7. A set of discussion in November 2014 with some leading practitioners including more in-depth conversations with Justin Cook (Sitra), Sir John Elvidge (former State Secretary to the Scottish Government) and Beth Novak (Director of NYU's Governance Lab and former US deputy chief technology agency for open government).

8. They outline six main types of innovation: service innovation, service delivery innovation, administrative and organisational innovation, conceptual innovation, policy innovation and systemic innovation.

9. "In a recent analysis of bureaucratic innovation, Alan Altshuler (1997: p.39) writes that "people in government fear nothing more than newsworthy failure." If such a fear does indeed pervade regulatory agencies, the press's interest in failure could well contribute to the supposed "ossification" of administrative rulemaking so widely of concern to legal scholars (McGarity, 1992; Mashaw, 1994)." (Coglianese and Howard, 1998).

10. Public service has a day-to-day obligation to deliver services, so a discussion about new services can seem secondary to the task at hand.

11. Founded in 1985 through the collaboration of the Ford Foundation and the Kennedy School at Harvard University, the American Government Awards "recognize, promote, and disseminate innovative programs, policies, and practices so that they can become widely adopted and established as best practices" (Government Innovators Network, undated).

12. The UK government's programme to ensure digital services of consistently high quality. For more see United Kingdom Government (2016).

13   Sune Knudsen commissioner of MindLab's Benchkode project, quoted in Boyer et al. (2013).

14   Writing a summary of a team's efforts as a weekly blog is a practice shared by many innovation teams, including GDS, Sitra's former Strategic Design Team, and MindLab's MindBlog. The concept of the "weeknote" is attributed to London-based Berg: post, http://www.wired.co.uk/magazine/archive/2010/06/start/russell-m-davies-on-the-structure-of-time

15   There is mounting evidence across the board that healthcare in the US is in decline (Woolf and Aron, 2013), This despite healthcare patents being up, as visible from the US Patent agency data: https://www.uspto.gov/

16   As supported by "2.1 The overall index scores suggest that innovation is stifled: the key opportunity to improve innovation is the conditions in which organisations operate" (Hughes et al., 2011: p. 10).

References

Boyer, B., J.W. Cook and M. Steinberg (2013), *Legible Practises: Six Stories About the Craft of Stewardship*, Helsinki Design Lab, www.helsinkidesignlab.org/peoplepods /themes/hdl/downloads/Legible_Practises.pdf.

Coglianese, C. and M. Howard (1998), "Getting the message out: Regulatory policy and the press", *Discussion Paper*, E-98-03, Kennedy School of Government, Harvard University.

Economist (14 April 2011), "Fail often, fail well", Schumpeter blog, *The Economist*, www.economist.com/node/18557776.

Gartner (undated), "Gartner hype cycle", Garnter website, www.gartner.com/technology /research/methodologies/hype-cycle.jsp.

Government of the United States (1973), *1974 NASA Authorization Hearings*, 93rd Congress, H.R. 4567 (superseded by H.R. 7528), United States Government Print Office, Washington, DC.

Government Innovators Network (undated)"Awards programs", Government Innovators Network website, www.innovations.harvard.edu/awards-programs/overview.

Finnish Ministry of Trade and Employment summary, page 2, www.tem.fi/files/40816/Wood_Construction_in_Finland.pdf.

Helsinki Design Lab (undated), "What is strategic design?", Helsinki Design Lab website, www.helsinkidesignlab.org/pages/what-is-strategic-design.

Holopainen H., K. Huttunen, K. Malin and H. Partinen (2013), "Muutoksenhaku maankäyttö- ja rakennuslain mukaisissa asioissa Tarkastelussa kaavat, suunnittelutarveratkaisut ja poikkeamispäätökset sekä valituslupa-asiat.", *YMPÄRISTÖMINISTERIÖN RAPORTTEJA*, 19 Ympäristöministeriö Rakennetun ympäristön osasto, Finnish Ministry of the Environment.

Hughes, A., K. Moore and N. Kataria (2011), Innovation in Public Sector Organisations: A Pilot Survey for Measuring Innovation Across the Public Sector, Nesta, www.nesta.org.uk/sites/default/files/innovation_in_public_sector_orgs.pdf

Krafcik, J.F. (1988), "Triumph of the lean production system", *Sloan Management Review*, Vol. 30/1, pp. 41-52.

OECD (2011), *Together for Better Public Services: Partnering with Citizens and Civil Society*, OECD Publishing, Paris, http://dx.doi.org/10.1787/9789264118843-en.

OECD (2003), *Checklist for Foreign Direct Investment Incentive Policies*, OECD Publishing, Paris, www.oecd.org/investment/investment-policy/2506900.pdf.

Terry, L.D. (1993), "Why we should abandon the misconceived quest to reconcile public entrepreneurship with democracy" , *Public Administration Review*, Vol. 53/4, pp. 393-395.

United Kingdom Government (2016), "Digital service standard", Gov.UK Service Manual website, www.gov.uk/service-manual/service-standard.

United Nations General Assembly (2005), *2005 World Summit Outcome*, Resolution A/60/1, adopted by the General Assembly on 15 September 2005.

Windrum, P. and P.M. Koch (eds.) (2008), *Innovation in Public Sector Services: Entrepreneurship, Creativity and Management,* Edgar Elgar; Cheltenham, UK.

Woolf, S.H. and L. Aron (eds.) (2013), *U.S. Health in International Perspective: Shorter Lives, Poorer Health,* National Academies Press.

Chapter 7.

Data, information and knowledge management for innovation

The potential for information to drive public sector innovation is immense and growing every day. This chapter considers the distinction between the interrelated concepts of data, information and knowledge, and the recommendations the OECD has made in this area, particularly the need for open government data (OGD) to maximise the public and private benefits from public sector information. The chapter identifies four interconnected phases in organisations' management of information: sourcing, exploiting, sharing and advancing, and the challenges that arise from each one, along with examples of solutions to those challenges from around the world. It considers how data analytics, combining data from within and beyond the public sector, provide governments with improved foresight, delivery and performance. It also considers how innovation can be built into the work of an organisation by using feedback to create a continuously evolving information ecosystem exploiting the collective intelligence of staff and the public through such means as crowdsourcing and knowledge networks.

The statistical data for Israel are supplied by and under the responsibility of the relevant Israeli authorities. The use of such data by the OECD is without prejudice to the status of the Golan Heights, East Jerusalem and Israeli settlements in the West Bank under the terms of international law.

Introduction

How data, information and knowledge are managed and shared within and across governments and with society can support or inhibit innovation. Innovation derived from harnessing these components has the power to improve efficiency and productivity, economic competitiveness, transparency and accountability and social well-being as it begins to transform all sectors in the economy, including the public sector. Recent research has indicated that the global flow of data now generates more economic value than the traditional global trade of goods (MGI, 2016). The increasing number of global actors working in the information arena, with their many roles, goods, services, technologies and business models, form a rapidly and constantly evolving ecosystem.

The importance of the public sector in this ecosystem is twofold: as a key producer of data and information that can be used and reused for new or enhanced products, processes and services; and as a key consumer of information and data (OECD, 2015a). In other words, governments are "prosumers" of data and information: producing, publishing, evaluating, correcting and mashing-up data (OECD, 2017b, 2016a). Furthermore, governments enhance transparency through proactive disclosure, and improve policy design and service delivery by enriching data and information to generate analysis and recommendations. As a prosumer, the public sector creates value for the system as a whole and can contribute to the shift towards more knowledge-based organisations, societies and economies, where data and information are drivers of growth and employment, and a means to better reflect citizens' needs and interests. The public sector is, in fact, one of the most information- and data-intensive sectors. In the United States alone, public sector agencies stored an average of 1.3 petabytes (millions of gigabytes) of data in 2011, which is roughly the same size as about 10 billion Facebook photos or 500 billion pages of text (Mozy, 2009; What's a Byte, undated), making the public sector the country's fifth most data-intensive sector (OECD, 2013).

Data, information and knowledge are different but interrelated concepts. Information is often conveyed through the enrichment and use of data, while knowledge is typically gained through the assimilation of information. The boundaries between data, information and knowledge may not always be clear, and they are often used as synonyms in the media and literature. However, separating the concepts is important to gain a better understanding their value (Box 7.1). One can have a lot of data, but not be able to extract value from them without the appropriate analytic capacities (OECD, 2013; Ubaldi, 2013), as discussed in the "Exploiting" section of this chapter. Similarly, one can have a lot of information, but not be able to gain knowledge from it, a phenomenon better known as "information overload" (Speier et al., 1999). To gain knowledge, mechanisms must be in place to provide for individuals and systems to learn from data, information and their own experiences to help inform decision making, and to share what is learned. This requires the sharing of both the codified knowledge that we traditionally think about, as well as tacit knowledge, such as skills and know-how embodied within people. Organisations that provide incentives to facilitate this are better able to overcome challenges such as reluctance to share data and information, and methods for analysing unstructured data such as social media feeds to yield more structured results.

Box 7.1. Definition of data, information and knowledge

- Data are understood as the representation of facts stored or transmitted as qualified or quantified symbols. Data have no inherent meaning, although they may be domain specific. In contrast to knowledge and information, data are assumed to have an "objective existence", and they can be measured, namely in bits and bytes. From a conceptual point of view data can be seen as the lowest level of abstraction from which information and then knowledge are derived. In discussing public sector data, discussions are generally about data held in government databases, such as registers, public tender databases, geospatial databases and statistical databases, among others.

- Information is often seen as the meaning resulting from the interpretation of facts as conveyed through data or other sources such as words. This meaning is reflected in the structure or organisation of the underlying source, including its hidden relationships and patterns of correlations, which can be revealed through data analytics. Public sector information in particular, is information generated, collected or funded by the public sector in the course of its public duties. The term covers weather, map, statistical and legal data as well as digital content held and maintained by the public sector in galleries, libraries, archives and museums, among others. Data, as discussed above, are a subset of information. Public sector information is increasingly made available through open access regimes, often at low or no cost. In discussing public sector information, in addition to data, the discussion often includes qualitative information, which is often stored in the form of documents.

- Knowledge is understood as information and experience which has been internalised or assimilated through a process commonly referred to as "learning". It provides the learner with the capacity to make effective decisions autonomously. Knowledge can be explicit, in which case it can be cost-effectively externalised to be communicated and embedded in tangible products, including books and standard procedures, and intangible products such as patents, design and software. But it may also be tacit, based on an "amalgam of information and experience", which is too costly to codify and thus to externalise.

Source: (OECD, 2015a), *Data-Driven Innovation: Big Data for Growth and Well-Being*, http://dx.doi.org/10.1787/9789264229358-en.

Research from the OECD and its Observatory of Public Sector Innovation (OPSI)[1] indicates that data, information and knowledge are building blocks for innovation, and their free flow within and across public sector organisations is an important condition for building individual and organisational capacity to innovate (OECD, 2015b) and is essential for generating new ideas. In addition, OECD has issued a number of formal recommendations related to the topic over the last several years (see Box 7.2).

Box 7.2. OECD Recommendations related to data, information and knowledge related to innovation

- The *Recommendation of the Council on Digital Government Strategies* (OECD, 2014a) calls on countries to leverage digital tools in open, participatory and innovative ways for better performing and user-driven services and policies, and to mobilise public support for ambitious and innovative policies. It also calls for countries to foster a data-driven public sector centred on the access to and strategic use and reuse of public sector data, evidence and statistics.

- The *Recommendation of the Council for Enhanced Access and More Effective Use of Public Sector Information* (OECD, 2008) is intended to increase returns on investments in public sector information as well as economic and social benefits from enhanced access and wider use and reuse through, among other things, enhanced innovation. It calls on countries to implement information policies in accordance with the principles that include awareness of information assets, access, openness and public-private partnership.

- The *OECD Principles and Guidelines for Access to Research Data from Public Funding* (OECD, 2007) aims to promote a culture of openness and sharing of research data. It calls on countries to develop research data policies consistent with the principle of openness – including minimal cost, flexibility and transparency.

Collectively, these legal instruments illustrate the global recognition of the importance of public sector data, information and knowledge as an enabler of innovative government policies and services that better meet citizen expectations and have the potential to drive external social and economic benefits beyond what is imaginable today.

Innovation does not just mean doing new things, but new things which are appropriate for the organisation and the community that it serves. Information is the lifeblood of a robust democracy and productive economy (Australian Government, 2013), and also serves as a foundation for innovation in the public sector. Accordingly, to succeed in innovating, organisations need access to accurate, quality, usable data, information and knowledge about their operations, past experiences, partners and users (OECD, 2015b). However, achieving this poses challenges for public sector organisations. This chapter seeks to explore these challenges and identify examples of solutions that have been devised by countries around the world that may serve as best practices or models for others. While data, information and knowledge are not the only critical factors for success in public sector innovation, the framework discussed in the chapter directly supports each aspect of the innovation lifecycle, which provides the overall framework for this report (Figure 7.1).

Figure 7.1. How managing data, information and knowledge supports the innovation lifecycle

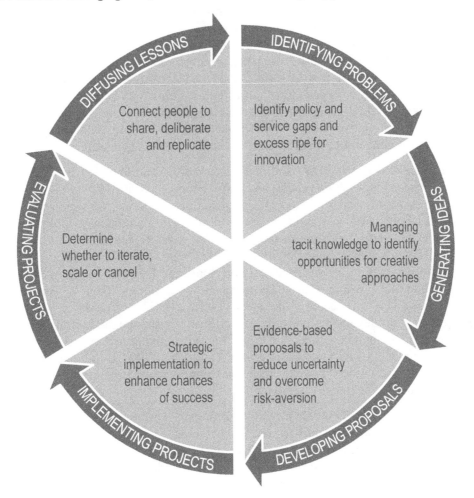

- **Identifying problems**: data, information and knowledge can be used to identify policy and service gaps that are ripe for innovative approaches, as well as policy excesses that are ineffective or overcomplicate the bureaucratic framework and cause inefficiencies that hinder innovation. An example is Indonesia's Citizen Feedback Dashboard (Box 7.6), which synthesises citizen complaints and social media information to develop heat maps of citizen concerns, which can help target and prioritise policy making and service delivery.

- **Generating ideas:** sharing tacit knowledge (technical skills and intuitive "know-how" embodied by people) and creating a common knowledge base is an important part of information management (OECD, 2005) that empowers individuals within organisations and recognises that they are best positioned to recognise opportunities for innovative improvements. An example of this is Portugal's Common Knowledge Network (Box 7.23), a collaborative platform to promote the sharing of best practice and generating ideas about modernisation, innovation and simplification of public administration. Its membership is open and includes public bodies, central and local administrations, private entities and any citizen who wishes to participate.

- **Developing proposals:** sound management of data and information enables civil servants to develop evidence-based proposals for innovative techniques that reduce uncertainty and assist in managing risk. This is seen in the UK's Humanitarian Innovation and Evidence Programme (Box 7.8). To ensure that the most effective approaches are being used to reduce risk and save lives when disasters strike, the programme develops evidence-based proposals to identify and pursue innovative approaches to disaster response. With accurate and timely data and information, government may also be able to develop *ex ante* assessments, such as through regulatory impact analysis,[2] to help identify the positive and negative impacts of proposals early on in the initial consultation phase.

- **Implementing projects:** using data, information and knowledge to strategically implement innovation pilots and experiments can increase their chances of success. For instance, the use of administrative data allows for simpler monitoring and reporting of innovation initiatives to allow for continuous improvements and agile adjustments of project implementation. The projects themselves, as seen in the discussion and examples in this section, can be used to develop information products that help governments gain foresight for, achieve delivery of, and monitor the performance of government programmes. This is illustrated by Mexico City's Mapatón experiment (Box 7.19). The city had no data on bus routes, so it devised an innovative experiment to generate the data from scratch by creating a smartphone game that was played by thousands of residents while on the bus and relayed global positioning system (GPS) co-ordinates to the city, which were used to generate maps and inform related policies and services for residents.

- **Evaluating projects:** data and information can be used to evaluate the effectiveness of a project to assess whether it should be iterated, scaled more broadly or cancelled. Additionally, data, information and knowledge from external individuals and the public may be brought in and leveraged to advance the innovation to new heights. An example of this is the use of social media to track the progress towards Sustainable Development Goal (SDG) 16 on Peace, Justice and Strong Institutions (Box 7.4). Information from social media was used in an innovative way to identify whether actions taken to meet the goal are resulting in reduced perceptions of corruption in Tunisia.

- **Diffusing lessons:** data, information and knowledge can be shared to show the lessons that have been learned from an innovation project, enabling civil servants and the public to draw their own conclusions, assisting agencies in scaling up successful innovations, and providing a means of replicating innovations to one's own unique environment. This includes both codified data and information (formal and systematic) as well as tacit knowledge based on the experiences of individuals. This diffusion can be multi-directional, as public sector organisations can learn from the feedback provided by others to continuously advance their innovation efforts. An example of this is seen in United States' efforts to build knowledge networks and engage in crowdsourcing to strengthen policy design and implementation and share lessons learned through technical conversations and living guidance (Box 7.24).

A common thread woven through all of these steps is that by ensuring that data, information and knowledge are open, useful and reusable, governments enable new actors to contribute at each phase of the innovation lifecycle. By empowering start-ups and other industry organisations, civil society and non-governmental organisations (NGOs), informed citizens, and others to help in moving government forward, the capacity to innovate grows beyond the public sector to encompass the entire ecosystem of actors. This profoundly changes the dynamic of government: from government as a service provider to government as a platform, and is itself an important component of innovation.

Analytical framework

The Innovation Imperative in the Public Sector: Setting an Agenda for Action (OECD, 2015b) laid out an initial framework for understanding how data, information and knowledge affect the capacity of the public sector to innovate. In addition to the three interrelated phases laid out initially, a fourth phase is included here for improving the innovative capacity of public organisations (see Figure 7.2).

1. **Sourcing**: identifying different types and sources of data, information and knowledge that represent a source of innovation.

2. **Exploiting**: channelling information, including data, into a usable, enriched form, both in terms of technical format and applicability to organisational challenges, so that it can be fully contextualised, analysed and exploited to generate knowledge to support evidence-based decision-making and organisational renewal.

3. **Sharing**: sharing information, including data, more widely to support decision-making, accountability and co-innovation and to facilitate value creation elsewhere in the economy or public sector. This includes the public release of open government data (OGD), which has increased as a major component of country political agendas, strongly driven by the need for innovation, efficiency and flexibility in government.[3]

4. **Advancing**: systematically learning and generating knowledge from an organisation's own experiences and those of others through continuous co-ordination and communication across and beyond the public sector to obtain and continuously act on feedback and new information.

The phases are presented sequentially here, but the cycle is not linear. Each phase is interconnected with and interdependent upon the other phases. For example, in some instances, the sharing phase may be a necessary pre-requisite in some before exploiting can successfully occur. In addition, the four phases may be, and optimally are, engaged contemporaneously, with an organisation undergoing sourcing, exploiting, sharing and advancing efforts simultaneously.

Figure 7.2. Driving innovation with data, information and knowledge: Four phases

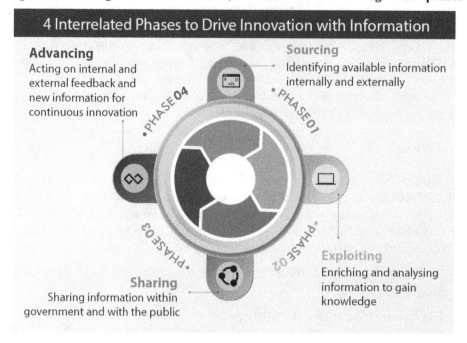

Source: adapted from OECD (2015b), *The Innovation Imperative in the Public Sector: Setting an Agenda for Action*, http://dx.doi.org/10.1787/9789264236561-en; OPSI.

On the topic of sourcing, governments today face problems that are increasingly complex, multi-disciplinary and interrelated. Governments are better positioned to tackle such problems if they draw on the expertise and resources of a broad range of people and organisations from the public, private and social sectors as well as academia. Identifying different sources of data, information and knowledge and enabling connections among them means rethinking how they flow and how organisations are structured, how work is managed and how people are connected and networked. Governments need to have strong data, information and knowledge management strategies in place to achieve this and ensure that these items are discoverable and available from this wide array of sources inside and outside of the public sector, in an accessible, timely way to support decision making (OECD, 2015b).

Exploiting data to make decisions helps to release its value and to move beyond the identification and gathering stages. Organisations are able to better generate usable knowledge and support continuous learning if they first consider how best to systematically incorporate and analyse information, such as through various forms of data analytics, into the decision-making process. Those that fail to achieve this risk incurring higher costs and repeating their mistakes, while failing to realise new possibilities (OECD, 2014c). Over time, this results in them falling further and further behind their peers and competitors who have realised the potential of information and data-driven innovation as a key enabler of government and the broader economy.

Sharing data and information, both within and outside government, increases their innovative potential. They are the raw resources fuelling innovative thinking and knowledge creation, spreading ideas and promising practices across government, scaling up innovations that work and leveraging the power of other organisations and the public to generate new value (OECD, 2014c). This chapter assumes that a key – but not the only

– goal for public sector information is to release it to the public, as appropriate, after due consideration to privacy and security ("open by default"). A key manifestation of this release of information is OGD, which is an innovation-related policy by definition (OECD, 2016a). OGD can increase the transparency and accountability of government activities, thus boosting public trust in governments. At the same time, it has the potential to enable an unlimited range of commercial and social services across society. For instance, apps that facilitate access to existing public services (OECD, 2015a). Because of these benefits, open access can be the optimal strategy for maximising both the private and public benefits of public sector information (Frischmann, 2012; OECD, 2015a). There are many critical steps that enable the success of such initiatives, and there are significant benefits that public sector information yields even when not made open to the public, as discussed in this chapter.

The fourth critical phase, introduced in this chapter, is advancing. This phase involves closing the loop of the previous phases to systematically embed innovation based on data, information and knowledge as a routine part of the business of government programmes. This supports organisations to grow, mature and continuously develop as they draw on and learn from data, information and knowledge. The knowledge aspect here includes learning from the experience of organisations and their people, and very importantly, the experiences of others. The advancing phase enables public sector organisations to identify areas where innovation is needed and act to innovate on an ongoing basis to better meet their missions in new ways and provide transparency, value and service to their public. This phase is highly complementary with forthcoming OPSI work on learning for innovation in the public sector.[4]

Sourcing information from within and across organisations and sectors

To fully tap into the public sector's innovative potential, data, information and knowledge need to be discoverable, available and accessible. In order to capture and exploit their value, organisation need to understand first what information assets exist. These assets can come from within and across public sector organisation, or from beyond the public sector. Governments need appropriate strategies to enable the valuable data, information and knowledge to be discovered and accesses if they are to unlock the potential for innovation, and facilitate the exploiting, sharing and advancing phases. Governments can be innovative in how they approach these strategies, and rethink and redefine how these sources are connected and flow among these sources.

Within and across public sector organisations

Access is the precondition for creating economic or social value from data and information. This access, in turn, enables the second precondition: use and reuse by other organisations and individuals. Data and information have unlimited potential to create value but barriers to access hinder collaboration, innovation and the downstream production of information and data-based goods and services. As a consequence, barriers to access can cause opportunity costs (OECD, 2015a; Frischmann, 2012). The most fundamental barrier is a lack of widespread awareness of what data and information exist within and across public sector organisations. Without this awareness, individual organisations, the public sector as a whole and members of the public are prevented from fully understanding and benefiting from their value or using them to drive innovation and improvements in the public sector or broader economy. Despite the fundamental importance of this first step, most governments currently do not have a comprehensive overview of what data they possess (OECD, 2015a). This is inconsistent with the

OECD's recommendations on information use, which included the key principle of "asset lists":

> **Asset lists.** Strengthening awareness of what public sector information is available for access and reuse. This could take the form of information asset lists and inventories, preferably published on-line, as well as clear presentation of conditions to access and reuse at access points." (OECD, 2008)

A look at government information and data initiatives sheds some light on how some are putting the principles discussed in this section into practice. Given the complexity and cross-cutting nature of public sector data and information, governments need to establish appropriate institutional structures to facilitate access. Tasking a government body – often one at the centre of government, such as the prime minister's office or the office of the president – with championing, co-ordinating and providing support for and leadership of relevant programmes has been seen as a way to bring the various relevant stakeholders on board. A dedicated body can sustain collective efforts to strengthen the integration of data and information across different parts of the public sector, help build capacity across governments to deal with emerging concerns (such as privacy and transparency) and ensure that those making decisions about the sharing and release of data and information do so in a rigorous and consistent fashion (OECD, 2015a). A common visible manifestation of central government co-ordination of government information programmes is a centralised portal or platform for sourcing and accessing government information. Most OECD countries have indeed developed such a platform with the idea of increasing citizens' and private actors' access to the growing variety of government data being made available as OGD (OECD, 2015a).[5] Box 7.3 illustrates how cross-government, publicly visible sourcing of information and data has evolved in the United States.

Box 7.3. United States: Managing information as an asset

Initial policy

In 2013, the White House Office of Management and Budget (OMB) issued an innovative government-wide policy, *Open Data Policy—Managing Information as an Asset* (OMB, 2013). Although the title refers to open data, the policy establishes a broader framework to help institutionalise the principles of effective information management, for both public and non-public information, at each stage of a piece of information's lifecycle to promote interoperability and openness. The components of this policy which are relevant to sourcing include the following requirements:

- Using common metadata, create and maintain an Enterprise Data Inventory that accounts for all information resources created or collected by the agency, including both data that can be made public and data that cannot (i.e. non-public data). This inventory was to be sent to the OMB only and not made public.

- Using common metadata, publicly publish a Public Data Listing of public datasets, and as far as possible, make these datasets available as OGD by hosting files and/or application programming interfaces (API) and including a web address (URL) for access in the metadata.

- Create a two-way process to engage with users to facilitate and prioritise release of information.

Box 7.3. United States: Managing information as an asset *(cont.)*

Implementation

- OMB launched Project Open Data – a collection of code, tools, case studies and schemas – to help agencies implement the policy and unlock the potential of government information. It also serves as living policy guidance that is continually refined and enhanced to assist agencies in implementation.

- A common mandatory metadata schema was created for all information based on international standards. Agencies are required to apply this schema when cataloguing all of their information assets. Mandatory fields include title, description, access level (e.g. public or non-public) and point of contact. Additional optional fields include download URL, license details and related information.

- Data.gov was configured to systematically "harvest" the metadata from agency public files to populate the central data portal. In general, Data.gov contains no data or information of its own, but acts as a central aggregator of common agency metadata. Data.gov provided the ability for local, regional, academic and commercial entities to have their data included on data.gov to enhance the discoverability of external data.

Expansion in policy enhances sourcing

In 2015, a successful Freedom of Information Act request from a US civil society organisation resulted in each agency publishing their full Enterprise Data Inventory (including information on non-public datasets) on Data.gov on a one-time basis. The aggregate of the Enterprise Data Inventories was believed to be the largest index of government data in the world. Subsequently, OMB revised government-wide policy to:

- Require all agencies, on an ongoing basis, to include information on all non-public datasets in their Public Data Listing, which enables key descriptors of these datasets to be discoverable on Data.gov.

- Create a redaction schema to permit, in limited instances, the redaction of sensitive information from agency metadata.

This policy and its evolution enhances the discoverability and sourcing across government as well as with the public:

- For **public sector organisations**, the benefits are two-fold. First, civil servants now have greater insight into the data collected by other organisations which could help them achieve their own mission and goals. Second, since the public and other public organisations now have the ability to make more targeted requests for information, organisations are better able to strategically prioritise the release of data.

- For **the public**, the initial policy only made public data discoverable and accessible to the public, which limited transparency into what data existed. The expanded policy now provides insights into currently non-public data, giving citizens better visibility into government operations and the ability to target requests for information.

Box 7.3. United States: Managing information as an asset *(cont.)*

Resources:

- OMB (2013), *Open Data Policy: Managing Information as an Asset*, https://www.actiac.org/system/files/Open%20Data%20Policy%2C%20OMB%20m-13-13.pdf.

- Project Open Data: https://project-open-data.cio.gov.

- Common metadata: https://project-open-data.cio.gov/v1.1/schema.

- Redaction schema: https://project-open-data.cio.gov/redactions.

- Project Open Data dashboard: https://labs.data.gov/dashboard.

Sources: The resources listed above and Rumsey et al. (2015), A big win for open government: Sunlight gets U.S. to release indexes of federal data", http://sunlightfoundation.com/blog/2015/02/09/a-big-win-for-open-government-sunlight-gets-us-to-release-indexes-of-federal-data/; GitHub (2015), "May 31, 2015 IDC Guidance: Non-public datasets in PDL", https://github.com/project-open-data/project-open-data.github.io/issues/462.

This example from the United States illustrates the importance of analysing metadata in unlocking the potential of government data and information. Metadata describe and provide clarity and context about primary information and data. Metadata can also be agnostic about the format and structure of the primary information and data described. The same common metadata can be used to catalogue many types of datasets, Portable Document Format (PDF) files, images, geospatial data and application programming interfaces (APIs), among other formats. Without metadata, primary information and data cannot be accessed, linked or fully understood (OECD, 2015a). As Cukier (2010) illustrates, metadata make (primary) data "useable and meaningful as a large library is useless without a card-catalogue system to analyse and find the books." The OECD (2015a) has suggested that governments ensure early and timely release not only of high-quality public sector information, but also high-quality metadata, as both are essential to enable reuse and value creation.

Before accessing data, one first has to know its source, and in many instances knowing where to start searching is a challenge (OECD, 2015a) which metadata help to address. The approach taken by the United States shows promise, leveraging metadata to analyses, search and source – in this case, on Data.gov – data and information which are spread across a large, federated government, making it accessible within, across and beyond the public sector. The United Kingdom's open data programme and associated Data.gov.uk website uses similar methods to make public data and information discoverable and accessible centrally through common metadata (Data.gov.uk, undated). The metadata approach to asset inventorying provides significant flexibility over the types and sources of information that can be catalogued. For example, although the US government does not generally make laws on the access and use of subnational government information, it has enabled lower levels of government to catalogue their information on Data.gov. To do so, a subnational government need only create an asset list using the common metadata schema. The ability to source such information easily is important, as subnational governments are closer to citizens and, while the range of services they deliver varies, they are typically the political and institutional place where people and policy meet (OECD, 2016a). Other OECD countries have generally stated the aim of being able to provide analysis and appropriately comprehensive metadata, but currently most central portals fall short of this aim. Among OECD countries, metadata are less widely available than might be hoped. This is due to the concentration on making existing datasets available, even if they may not have extensive, or any, associated metadata (OECD, 2015a). This focus on releasing information and data for the sake of releasing it, without disclosing key descriptive information about it (i.e., metadata) is unlikely to unlock its full potential.

A greater awareness of what data and information exist is also important for facilitating knowledgeable data and information requests from civil servants from other organisations and the public. This helps to prioritise the release of data and information so as to achieve the greatest value from it, as simply churning out data without informed analysis is not sufficient to create value. The OECD (2012) has highlighted that it is almost impossible for an analysis to assess the value of data in advance because it is context dependent: data of good quality for some applications may be of poor quality for others. This suggests that public sector organisations acting independently may not be best placed to determine the value of their data and information assets for purposes beyond their own. As discussed later in this chapter, governments need robust engagement models to allow two-way dialogue between public sector information providers and its users, including civil servants in other organisations and the public. Government organisations need to focus on users' needs, and users need to provide feedback on what they would like to see provided as a priority (OECD, 2015a). If civil servants and other potential users of data and information are not able to identify which public sector information sources and datasets exist, it is impossible for them to fully understand what may be applied within the context of their own environments or to request access to critical data and information that could allow them to innovate programmes and better deliver on their missions.

Beyond the public sector

While the public sector holds tremendous data and information resources, government organisations can also exploit external sources of information to better achieve their missions. For example, analysis, often in real-time, of a wide range of data collected or generated by the private sector and through social media, search engines and physical sensors (such as the Internet of Things) provides new opportunities for addressing complex challenges.

Administrative data from the private sector is perhaps the classic example of bringing in data from beyond the public sector. Industry produces tremendous amounts of data, often in order to track compliance with government rules and regulations. It is often already in machine-readable formats designed for easy consumption by diverse users for many purposes. Increasingly, private sector companies are releasing their data as open data, which governments and others can then consume without consideration for procurement and expenditure considerations. At first, this may seem counterproductive to the bottom line of these businesses, as data are often valuable and can be sold as a commodity. However, by providing free and open access to data, businesses may achieve lower administrative overheads and more streamlined governance structures, among other benefits, than they would have from building the capacity to maintain and manage data for internal use access and use only (Herzberg, 2014). Some companies are becoming active members of the open data ecosystem in ways that are highly relevant to the public sector. For example, Microsoft has partnered with the World Bank and the Philippines government to use data to develop applications for disaster recovery (Bettcher, 2015). In another example, Uber has shared trip data with cities such as Boston to enable government decision-makers to better inform transportation policy (UrbanTide, 2016). To facilitate data and information-centred connections between government and the private sector, the Open Government Partnership (OGP)[6] created a Private Sector Council in 2013 to "to engage diverse businesses and entrepreneurs in promoting open governance, economic growth, and local innovations" and to demonstrate the value of building partnerships across sectors (Bettcher, 2015). As an outgrowth of OGP participation, the World Bank, in partnership with the private company OpenCorporate, launched the Open Company Data Index[7] to help users to identify private sector data. Governments may wish to keep the private sector in mind for sourcing data.

Policy makers are also starting to use web and social media sources to complement existing public sector data and information. For example, search engine data derived from keywords entered by users searching for web content, such as Google Insights for Search, provide statistics on the popularity of specific keywords at different times and in different places. Where keywords are related to specific policy topics such as unemployment, Google Insights can provide real-time indicators for measuring and predicting unemployment trends that policy makers are increasingly considering as a complementary statistical source (OECD, 2015a).[8] New York City uses this service by identifying the top items that residents are looking for and ensuring that those items are available and up-to-date on the city's website, NYC.gov (Google, 2009).

The spread of modern platforms and social media offer a new real-time source of intelligence provided by citizens that is immediately in the public domain and thus readily available (OECD, 2015a). Public sector organisations are increasingly using information from social media to inform decision making. For example, significant progress has been made with the use of social media-sourced data analytics for crisis prevention and disaster management. Social media and other online data are also increasingly used in city police departments, for uses such as predictive analytics and anticipatory decision-making (OECD, 2015a). They are also being used to track citizen perceptions on government performance and corruption, as discussed in Box 7.4.

Box 7.4. Tunisia: Using social media to track progress on Sustainable Development Goals

To monitor progress with Sustainable Development Goal (SDG) 16 on Peace, Justice and Strong Institutions, which has a key focus on corruption, the Tunisia National Statistics Institute and the United Nations Development Programme (UNDP) launched a pilot using social media to better understand citizens' perceptions of government. Traditional methods (such as household surveys) were insufficient because of their infrequency and cost.

The pilot involved conducting a network analysis of web and social media (e.g., news, blogs and Twitter) to identify relevant content and determine whether its tone was positive or negative to gauge citizen perceptions of corruption. To help determine accuracy, the team compared the results of the social media analysis to the results of Tunisia's Household Survey on Governance, Peace and Democracy, which contained questions on citizen perceptions of corruption. Over the same timeframe, both the survey and social media provided the same perception on corruption, and the social media analysis had the additional benefit of being faster, more regular and less expensive. Tunisia has begun testing this approach with other targets from the same SDG, namely human rights and rule of law, and civic participation.

Sources: UNDP report to OPSI; Abellaoui et al. (2015), "Diagnose and treat: Measuring a country's pulse with social media"

Exploiting: Extracting meaning for learning organisations

The exponential growth in the data and information being collected and generated, along with the pervasive power of data analytics,[9] has led to a paradigm shift in the ways knowledge is created and – in particular – decisions are made. There are two moments when the social and economic values of data are analysed: when they are transformed into knowledge, and when they are used for decision making (OECD, 2015a). OPSI describes these two moments collectively as "exploiting". Adequately sourcing and accessing data and information is necessary but not sufficient to generate innovation. Organisations need to have the systems and resources in place to enable them to generate knowledge and support decisions at the analysis level that facilitate innovation to allow them to more efficiently and effectively achieve their missions (OECD, 2015b).

Innovation driven by exploiting data, information and knowledge has the potential to help address significant social and global challenges, and holds great potential for value creation in both the private and public sector. Investments in this area in public administration will be particularly fruitful, as governments rely heavily on the collection and analysis of data and information, but still face a relatively low level of digitisation in most countries (OECD, 2015a). The potential benefits arising from the use of public sector information by governments include public sector productivity and internal cost savings, improved policy development, more effective service delivery and greater transparency. This is illustrated by research from MGI (2011), which suggested that the full use of data analytics in Europe's 23 largest governments could reduce administrative costs by 15-20%, creating the equivalent of EUR 150 billion to EUR 300 billion in new value and accelerating annual productivity growth by 0.5 percentage points over the next ten years.[10] Data and information can be used to innovate programmes to contribute to achieving these and other benefits (OECD, 2008).

The increasing amount of information and data made available in formats that enable reuse and linkage is supporting the expansion of data analytics in the public sector. However, evidence suggests that the public sector is still making insufficient use of the data that are generated and collected (OECD, 2015a). Most OECD countries have targeted strategies to improve access to and use of public sector information (OECD, 2015c). Some are relatively standalone and visible, whereas others are often folded into more general OGD or open government strategies. For example, the Mexican National Digital Strategy mandates better internal use of data at the federal level (OECD, 2016a). The mandate includes the provision of incentives for civil servants to reuse data, training for civil servants to develop the required analytical skills and a standard or guidelines on text and data mining requirements for public agencies to reuse data. However, Mexico is in a minority in having set forth such comprehensive mandates.

Generating value, including through innovation, from information in the public sector occurs when analytical methods are used to turn data into information and knowledge, which provides the basis for decision-making (taking action) (OECD, 2015a). These methods take place through a number of approaches (OECD, 2017b, 2016b):

- **foresight**: anticipation of, and preparation for, foreseeable and disruptive trends affecting the role of government and the state in the medium and long run

- **delivery**: evidence-based policy making and service delivery and strengthened understanding of needs, solutions, impacts and users

- **performance**: monitoring policy performance to ensure productive and effective use of public resources, identifying current risks affecting governance and accountability and identifying good practices within the administration to support learning and continuous improvement.

Regarding **foresight**, anticipating future events helps governments move from a reactive to a proactive position (OECD, 2017b). Predictive data analytics, for instance, can spur innovation by facilitating the identification of emerging governmental and societal needs (OECD, 2016c; Ubaldi, 2013). The ability to combine different (public and private) datasets can help develop enhanced anticipatory thinking that may be used for innovative services that get ahead of problems and anticipate windows of opportunity rather than merely reacting to them (OECD, 2015a; Box 7.5).

Box 7.5. Australia: Predicting hospital patient admissions

Demands on staff and resources in public hospitals can result in overcrowded emergency departments. Delays in care can cause patients' conditions to deteriorate and can increase patient mortality. To improve patient outcomes, National Health Reform is seeking that 90% of emergency department patients leave within four hours. To help hospitals in achieving this, Australia's Commonwealth Scientific and Industrial Research Organisation (CSIRO) developed the Patient Admission and Prediction Tool (PAPT) as a way to harness and detect patterns in the vast volumes of data hospitals collect, to predict emergency department patient arrivals, their medical urgency and specialty, admissions and likely discharge times. Real-world application of PAPT shows that it is up to 93% accurate in its predictions. As a result, hospitals using PAPT are better able to improve staffing arrangements to reduce waiting times, and increase timely access to care. PAPT is being used by more than 30 Queensland hospitals to assist with bed management, staff resourcing and scheduling of elective surgery to improve patient outcomes through improved timeliness and quality of care and less time spent in the hospital.

Source: CSIRO (undated), "Cutting hospital waiting times", www.csiro.au/en/Research/BF/Areas/Digital-health/Waiting-times.

Regarding **delivery**, data, information and knowledge have significant potential to help public sector organisations design and refine policies in an informed and evidence-based manner in order to devise new and innovative solutions to policy challenges. They can also help develop innovative strategies for ensuring successful service delivery to citizens (see Boxes 7.6-7.8 for examples from Indonesia, Singapore and the United Kingdom) (OECD, 2017b). Organisations are able to gain insight from analysing data, information and knowledge during policy design (for example identifying gaps that could be addressed by new policies, including identifying areas ripe for innovation). They can also be used to develop evidence-based proposals for innovation initiatives to help increase support by mitigating risk and uncertainty. Delivery insights can also be gained post-design during policy implementation and service delivery. For instance, analytics insights can be used to continually refine implementation approaches, as well as to structure service delivery methods in ways that take into account users' need and interactions with the service.

Box 7.6. Indonesia: Citizen Feedback Dashboard

Indonesia's Ministry for National Development Planning partnered with the United Nations-affiliated Pulse Lab Jakarta to launch the National Citizen Feedback Dashboard in 2015. The Dashboard visualises citizens' feedback and enables public officials to prioritise trending issues based on enhanced data analysis. The tool combines data from LAPOR! (Layanan Aspirasi dan Pengaduan Online Rakyat), the national citizen feedback mechanism, with unstructured feedback contained within the public discourse on social media sites, such as Twitter. The tool analyses the volume, category, keywords, location and co-topics of the combined data, resulting in a dashboard visualisation of trends in citizens' feedback and an early warning alert system drawing attention to surges in complaints on a particular theme or within a certain geographical area. The tool is based within the ministry's Centre for Data and Information.

Rather than only dealing with concerns or complaints on a case-by-case basis, which was the previous practice in Indonesia, the Dashboard allows public officials to get a better sense of the broader trends in citizens' concerns. The system allows for better "upstream" policy making and "downstream" programme delivery, and enables the public administration to be more responsive to the evolving needs of society. According to Pulse Lab Jakarta officials, the tool, including the code, will be published on GitHub for the benefit of other governments and open source communities.

Sources: Pulse Lab Jakarta report to OPSI; OECD (2017a), *Embracing Innovation in Government: Global Trends*, www.oecd.org/gov/innovative-government/embracing-innovation-in-government.pdf.

Box 7.7. Singapore: Fusion Analytics for Public Transport Emergency Response

Societal and demographic challenges mean Singapore has an increasing demand for public transport, which has resulted in overcrowding and delays. Exacerbating these challenges, ageing infrastructure has increased transportation breakdowns significantly in recent years.

As part of its goal of becoming a "smarter nation" through the use of technology, the government has launched the Fusion Analytics for Public Transport Emergency Response (FASTER) initiative, an innovative big data pilot programme to improve the country's public transport system by more quickly responding to train breakdowns, delays and other unexpected incidents. FASTER is a private-public partnership between the country's public sector Land Transportation Authority (LTA) and transport operator SMRT, and the private sector telecommunications company StarHub and technology company IBM to analyse passenger data to improve public transport systems.

With FASTER, LTA collects anonymised location-based information from StarHub and combines it with fare card transactions and video feeds from stations to identify stations that have become overcrowded. When it detects heightened crowding, Singapore deploys bus services and issues alerts on social media to inform commuters of expected delays to give them an opportunity to plan accordingly. These data also provide the opportunity to develop detailed models of how users move through the city, helping government understand traffic patterns, how citizens use the urban transport system and key problems with existing routes. This information helps the authorities decide where more buses and trains are needed, or what incentives to provide to users to take different routes (in the form of travel credits).

Sources: Land Transport Authority (2014), "LTA, SMRT, StarHub and IBM collaborate to improve transport with data for Singapore commuters", www.lta.gov.sg/apps/news/page.aspx?c=2&id=407a5053-0345-40f5-8d64-51fb31bfb2a0; Weizhen (2014), "Big data to help ease transport woes", www.todayonline.com/singapore/big-data-help-ease-transport-woes,

Box 7.8. United Kingdom: Humanitarian Innovation and Evidence Programme

The United Kingdom's Department for International Development (DFID) is the lead UK agency responsible for international efforts to eradicate extreme poverty and improve health, safety and prosperity in the developing world and during humanitarian emergencies. To accomplish this, DFID works to increase employment, support gender equality and engage in emergency response activities. Between 2000 and 2009, more than 2.2 billion people were affected by 4 484 natural disasters, and vulnerability to hazards is increasing as a result of demographic, political and environmental changes. DFID sought to address this and to ensure that the most effective approaches are being used to reduce risk and save lives when disasters strike. To achieve this, DFIS created the Humanitarian Innovation and Evidence Programme (HIEP) in 2013, a GBP 42 million initiative to overcome barriers to testing innovations and to develop, test and scale innovative approaches to disaster response.

HIEP's objectives are to develop and test innovative approaches to humanitarian practice, provide evidence of the cost effectiveness of investments in disaster risk reduction, provide new evidence on the scaling-up of cash-based approaches, support better evidence on insurance as a risk management tools and create new evidence on the best interventions to improve health and nutrition in emergencies. Before HIEP was created, DFID's approach to funding research and innovation in the humanitarian sector has been relatively ad hoc.

The theory of change behind HIEP is that through its operations, networking, influencing and funding, alongside coherent and convincing evidence products, DFID will attract other humanitarian funders and practitioners to invest in new technologies, evidence-informed operational approaches and systems that the HIEP will produce. This will influence skills, behaviour, cultures and systems among humanitarian actors to promote the routine integration of evidence into the financing, design and implementation of humanitarian interventions. In turn, these enabling conditions, capacities and systems will support international agencies, national governments, public sector actors, civil society and private actors in fragile and conflict-affected states and countries vulnerable to disaster risks to use context-specific applications of evidence and innovations in their design, financing, planning and delivery of humanitarian policies, programmes and practices to manage risks and deliver rapid, effective responses in emergencies. This will improve programmes so that lives are saved and communities recover quickly from economic and livelihood losses that arise from humanitarian crises.

Based on its early results, HIEP won the UK's Civil Service Award for Analysis and Use of Evidence in October 2014. HIEP has demonstrated successes in a number of areas, including:

- Relevance: developing systematic and thorough processes to identify gaps to inform project design and engage with a range of experts inside and outside government to ensure the relevance of selected projects.

- Efficiency: securing additional funding from other donors. For every GBP 1 of DFID money spent, it has leveraged a further GBP 0.25 in additional funding.

- Effectiveness: developing solid plans to produce evidence-driven products and cultivating strategic relationships with domestic and international partners and key stakeholders.

- Impact: achieving strong alignment between the aims and strategies of individual projects with the overall theory of change.

Sources: DFID (undated a), Department for International Development website, www.gov.uk/government/organisations/department-for-international-development; DFID (undated b), "Business Case 2: Humanitarian Innovation and Evidence Programme: Greater use of evidence and innovative responses", http://iati.dfid.gov.uk/iati_documents/3874012.odt; ITAD (2014), *Evaluation of the Humanitarian Innovation and Evidence Programme (HEIP): Formative Phase Report*, www.gov.uk/government/uploads/system/uploads/attachment_data/file/496291/Eval-Humanitarian-Innovation-Evidence-Prog.pdf.

Regarding **performance**, it is key to scrutinise, monitor and evaluate government programmes as doing so ensures that governments are held to account against citizen expectations for their actions and expenditures (OECD, 2017b). Performance-driven techniques, such as evaluation and auditing are used for accountability in a strategic and open state. They need to objectively use timely, accessible and reliable information. The exploitation of data and information has the potential to identify performance gaps in government programmes, as well as instances of fraud, waste and abuse that result in major losses of taxpayer funding (OECD, 2016b). OECD countries are employing innovative techniques to conduct information-centric performance management to address such performance gaps and wasted resources. For example, Box 7.9 illustrates how the United Kingdom is using data analytics modelling techniques to strengthen tax compliance.

Box 7.9. United Kingdom: Revenue and Customs compliance

The United Kingdom's HM Revenue and Customs department has developed data models to help focus its compliance activities. The models help to identify people who may be most likely to be non-compliant on their taxes, such as by making errors in their tax returns or deliberately trying to evade taxes. The models take into account information such as taxpayers' prior compliance and information from the tax return itself, such as income and occupation, in order to assign a risk probability of non-compliance. A wide range of data is available to be fed into these models to assist in calculating the risk probabilities, and as the amount of data grows, so does the ability to build on the models to improve their performance. Oversight programmes such as this offer some of the easiest ways to earn returns on investment for government analytics projects, as the financial savings are often significant. For example, HM Revenue and Customs estimates that one of their analytics models – targeting value-added tax (VAT) evasion – will bring in around GBP 200 million a year in additional revenue due to improved compliance targeting efforts, doubling the amount of revenue collected for each compliance caseworker.

Source: Athow et al. (2015), "Predictive analytics: The science of non-compliance", https://quarterly.blog.gov.uk/2015/01/27/predictive_analytics/.

New trends in analytics are pushing the boundaries of foresight, delivery and performance in all sectors, including the public sector, in innovative ways. One of these trends is machine learning,[11] which is increasingly being used in innovative ways by government organisations. Machine learning is based on the use of algorithms that allow computers to "learn" from data. Having analysed similar situations, computers can apply this analysis to infer and predict present and future situations. In the private sector, search engines are large-scale users of machine-learning technologies, as well as the recommendation engines that power services such as Amazon, Spotify and Netflix. These services use machine learning to predict the results that best fit a user's taste (OECD, 2015a). Machine learning techniques are also increasingly being applied to the public sector, where researchers are looking into machine-learning algorithms to detect conditions better and at the same time cut back the number of false positives and negatives. For example, Microsoft and a regional government in India have partnered to help farmers predict the best time to sow their crops (Economist, 2016). The United Arab Emirates (UAE) Ministry of Health (Box 7.10) have used algorithms to detect birth defects, and that these algorithms can learn as they are exposed to more information.

Box 7.10. United Arab Emirates: Birth defect detection

The UAE's Al Qassimi Hospital is piloting mGene, an app that captures a newborn's facial photo from different angles to help detect whether the child is at high or low risk of a congenital birth defect. The app has been tested on 250 babies, and the initial results demonstrated a 95% accuracy rate for the app. Over time, as more pictures of babies are taken, the algorithms for detecting defects can continuously learn to increase accuracy. mGene is still a pilot, as the algorithms are still learning how to account for the various ethnic backgrounds of the babies that are seen by the hospital. In addition to mGene, the UAE Ministry of Health is also working towards an application that will analyse heart sounds to detect heart defects in a baby or an unborn fetus.

Source: Rai (2016), "App to detect birth defects in UAE children", www.emirates247.com/news/app-to-detect-birth-defects-in-uae-infants-2016-01-27-1.618859.

As these algorithms become more powerful, they raise the possibility of automating decision making which has the potential eliminate or reduce the need for human intervention. Some countries are experimenting with the concept of algorithmic governance, which seeks to reduce human decisions and politicisation through the introduction of sophisticated and automated computer processes (O'Reilly, 2013; Putska, 2015). For example, in Italy, faced with mounting financial challenges, the National Revenue Agency has implemented a tool – *redditometro* ("income meter") – to identify tax evaders by using analytics to identify individuals whose spending on consumer goods exceeds their declared income by analysing expenditures in dozens of categories, such as household costs, automobiles, vacations and mobile phone usage. If spending appears excessive relative to declared income, the individual is flagged for investigation and the government has the ability to compel the taxpayer to provide an explanation (Gurriá, 2013; Povoledo, 2013).

Taken at face value, some may think that such algorithmic techniques make clear sense but such practices are controversial and raise many questions that are yet to be addresses. The *redditometro* programme in Italy has been highly controversial. Some argue that it is overly intrusive, has a chilling effect on retail sales and fosters a culture of fear and a presumption of guilt. This is merely one example; similar criticisms are being raised for all types of potential algorithm-based decision making. Such criticism is not without merit. There are considerable risks that the underlying data and analytic algorithms could lead to unexpected false results, and these risks are heightened when decision making is automated (OECD, 2015a). For example, risk assessments based on machine learning are being used in the criminal justice system in certain parts of the United States to help inform bail and sentencing decisions based on an individual's risk of committing future crimes ("recidivism models"). An investigative journalism organisation analysed data from one of these areas and concluded that the scores were unreliable at forecasting violent crime and contained significant racial disparities (Anguin et al., 2016).[12] Some evidence also suggests that machine learning may reinforce existing inequalities. For example, approximately 50% of employers in the United States ask potential hires for information about their credit score,[13] using it as a proxy measure for responsibility or trustworthiness. This can reinforce inequalities in things like race, as there is a wealth gap between African Americans and white Americans, and can initiate a cycle where individuals who are already economically vulnerable are unable to obtain a job, which may result in further credit score declines (Rawlins, 2016). Governments will need to be aware of the limitations to machine learning or they could cause social and economic harm to themselves as well as citizens and businesses. They should make a careful examination both of the appropriateness of automated decision making, and of the need for human intervention in areas where the potential harm cause by such decisions may be significant, such as harm to the life and well-being of individuals, or denial of financial or social rights. They should also consider increasing the transparency of the processes and algorithms underlying these automated decisions (algorithmic transparency), as in the French case study described in Box 7.11.

Box 7.11. France: Open source income tax calculator

The government of France opened the source code of the fiscal calculator used by the French fiscal administration to calculate the income taxes of over of 37 million French individuals in order to help people better understand how taxes are calculated and build trust in the fiscal system through transparency. The code release was the result of a legal process after a student made a request for the calculator's code but was denied by the Direction General des Finances Publiques (DGFIP), which is in charge of public finances. However, the administrative court of Paris ruled that source code for software written by and for public authorities is considered to be an administrative document and can be freely accessed. This was the first time a French administration opened its source code to the public.

In April 2016, France's Etalab and DGFIP organised a "hackathon" named #CodeImpot to promote the use of the code develop services that strengthen trust between citizens and taxes. This followed a vote by the French National Assembly in January 2016 for a new bill on digital rights (*République numérique*), which included provisions on algorithmic transparency. Students, scientists, developers, representatives of national authorities, start-ups and entrepreneurs attended the event. Over 150 individuals participated, and 9 projects emerged from the hackathon, including tools to make income tax more understandable for citizens and help individuals compare their fiscal situation to others, as well as improvements to the code and software performance.

Sources: Chausson (2016a), "France unveils source code of income tax application", .https://joinup .ec.europa.eu/community/osor/news/france-unveils-source-code-income-tax-application; Chausson (2016b), "France improves fiscal transparency by opening tax calculator", https://joinup.ec.eur opa.eu/community/opengov/news/france-improves-fiscal-transparency-opening-tax-calculator. Etalab (2016), "What happened at #CodeImpot?", www.etalab.gouv.fr/en/retour-sur-le-hackathon-codeimpot; French Republic (undated), République numérique website,www.republique-numerique.fr.

Sharing information multiplies its innovative potential

The innovative potential of data and information gathered and used by one organisation is multiplied when it is made available to many. More contributions can lead to the identification of different dimensions of policy challenges, highlighting the importance of system-wide co-operation, and ultimately result in more complete, holistic solutions (OECD, 2015b). Making data and information more broadly available to the public also helps to spur innovation and economic development beyond the public sector, and support innovative partnerships with other actors (OECD, 2014c). Information provides significant growth opportunities through spillover effects in the support of the downstream production of a variety of goods and services in all sectors. Open access to information gives users opportunities to produce these goods, while closed access restricts them (OECD, 2015a; Frischmann, 2012).

For example, when properly shared, public sector organisations and non-public entities can pull in public sector data from multiple sources, potentially including non-governmental sources, and create data linkages that may lead to even greater insight. This is because data linkage enables "super additive" insights, leading to increasing returns. Linking information contextualises it and can become a source of insights and value that are greater than the sum of any parts isolated within organisational data silos (OECD, 2015a). These super additive insights can be instrumental in designing, implementing and diffusion innovation throughout the public sector.

Open access, including to the public, can be the optimal strategy for maximising both the private and public benefits of information and data (Frischmann, 2012; OECD, 2015a). The OECD (2014a, 2008) has therefore recommended that governments open their data and information to the public, as appropriate, given considerations of privacy and security. However, different levels of openness have their own challenges and opportunities, which are discussed in the next section.

Sharing within the public sector

Due to the recession and government budgetary constraints, governments feel an urgent need to improve their own performance. This involves making the transfer of data and information among different parts of government more efficient, transparent and less costly; reducing or eliminating the burden of inter-agency charging for data and information; and developing common access schemes, all to achieve public sector productivity gains and more effective service delivery (OECD, 2015a). Access does not necessarily always need to be fully open to the public to derive value; it may be limited to internal partners who share it to overcome collective problems and achieve shared goals.

At the organisational level, the increasing need for data, information and knowledge sharing will challenge vertical silos in public administrations and require more co-operation among jurisdictions and levels of government. Overcoming these challenges is a crucial element of efficient and effective governance (OECD, 2015a; Rodigo, Allio and Andres-Amo, 2009). Governments should prioritise the adoption of an overall sharing strategy to co-ordinate efforts, exploit synergies, facilitate the use of linked data and create a shared view of data and information, including open data, within and across levels of government (OECD, 2015a). This may create innovations in how governments perceive and treat citizens. With effective processes and procedures in place, citizens will no longer be reduced to a single dimension that aligns with a subdivision within the public administration's organisational chart – income taxes, child benefits, medical treatments, etc. – but can be viewed more holistically by providing an overview of how they interact with the government throughout their lives. Sharing organisational data, information and knowledge across the public sector also has the ability to support the identification of useful practices which may provide individual organisations with ideas that they can adapt to their own context (OECD, 2015b).

Box 7.12. United States: New York City DataBridge

Faced with a very large population (8.5 million) and significant fiscal challenges, New York City officials have to make difficult decisions in prioritising citizen services. To ensure these decisions are as effective as possible, the Mayor's Office of Data Analytics (MODA) has built DataBridge, an innovative city-wide platform for data sharing and analytics accessible to all city agencies.

DataBridge, built and maintained in partnership with several city departments, is a system of automated data feeds from over 50 formerly siloed source systems belonging to about 20 agencies and external organisations. These feeds include data on streets, buildings and zoning, as well as information from the city's 311 hotline (non-emergency municipal services). All of these data are merged with geographical information, and permit the city to perform critical cross-agency analysis. DataBridge contains tools for data discovery, predictive analytics, business intelligence and reporting.

Officials from across the city use DataBridge to address a wide variety of issues, such as identifying illegal housing conversions that are at increased risk of fires, combatting property and business fraud, and finding pharmacies facilitating drug abuse. These projects have achieved quantifiable efficiencies and savings in revenue. For example, by closing down unsafe buildings, the city is reducing the risk to firefighters, emergency responders and civilians. In the past, building inspectors responding to complaints found seriously high-risk conditions 13% of the time but now, after using predictive models through DataBridge, they are finding them 70-80% of the time, a five-fold return on inspection man hours.

To assist public employees enhance their data literacy and use of DataBridge, the city created an Analytics 101 course for city government employees. The course covers basic statistical and data management techniques and provides an overview of available data and tools.

Sources: City of New York (2016a), "Citywide data sharing", www1.nyc.gov/site/analyt ics/initiatives/citywide-data-sharing.page; City of New York (2016b), "Job posting notice", www1.nyc.gov/assets/doitt/downloads/jobs/234365_moda_dir_data_strategy.pdf; Yasin (2013), "How analytics is making NYC's streets and buildings safer",https://gcn.com/articles/2013/10/04/gcn-award-nyc-databridge.aspx.

Box 7.13. Brazil: Rio Operations Center

The Rio Operations Center integrates the data and monitoring functions of approximately 30 municipal and state agencies and external sources to improve safety and incident response. The centre is meant to optimise city functioning, especially in the face of large-scale events, and to respond proactively to emergency situations. Following the floods, landslides and avalanches that caused the deaths of more than 200 people in 2010, and in advance of the 2016 Olympics, the City of Rio de Janeiro, Brazil worked to improve its data and information collection, its data processing capabilities and its information dissemination strategy.

The centre has allowed Rio to incorporate data from a variety of sources, including monitoring cameras, Internet of Things sensors installed in water and rain gauges, private maps, traffic signal data, the electricity grid, traffic controls, public transit vehicles and social media feeds. GPS data from taxis, buses and highway drivers also allow the Rio Operations Center to monitor movements and locations to enhance emergency response movement and help citizens find buses and taxis in case there is a problem with the metroway. It is not just the centre that uses the data; much of it is provided in a precise and timely manner to citizens, and is diffused through several channels including social media.

Source: Cisco (2014), "IoE-based Rio Operations Center improves safety, traffic flow, emergency response capabilities", http://internetofeverything.cisco.com/sites/default/files/pdfs/Rio_Jurisdiction_Profile__05121 4REV.pdf; C40Cities (2012), "Case study: Rio Operations Center", www.c40.org/case_studies/rio-operations-center.

Open government data

As discussed above, OGD is innovation-related policy by definition (OECD, 2016a), and it can increase the openness, transparency and accountability of government activities and thus boost public trust in governments. At the same time, by allowing others to convert government data into information and knowledge, it has the potential to enable an unlimited range of commercial and social services across society. Reuse of a wide range of public sector data by a wide range of actors is a key condition for creating economic and social value, and it is necessary to stimulate creativity and innovation. OGD also allows citizens to become not just passive consumers of public sector content and services but also active contributors and designers in their own right, empowered to make more informed decisions to enhance the quality of their lives (Box 7.14 gives an example of sharing data across sectors from the United States). However, while the benefits are significant, governments face numerous challenges in opening their data and subsequently understanding what value has been generated as a result.

Box 7.14. United States: College Scorecard sharing data within and across sectors

Issued in 2015, the College Scorecard highlights key indicators about the cost and value of institutions across the country to help students choose a school that is well-suited to their needs, affordable, and consistent with their educational and career goals. It demonstrates the power of public sector data sharing and OGD in a number of ways:

- The project was a collaborative effort involving a data sharing partnership with the Department of Education, Department of Treasury, and Internal Revenue Service, with technical help from the US Digital Service (USDS) and 18F.

- The College Scorecard website and tool were designed with direct input from students, families and their advisors.

- The underlying data behind the Scorecard cover 2 000 data points for over 7 000 colleges and universities, spanning 18 years.

- The underlying data include reliable national data that include former students' earnings, graduate students' debt and borrowers' repayment rates. These data are also available for various subgroups, such as first generation college students and students who receive federal grants due to financial need.

- While the Scorecard itself has significant value, the underlying data are released as OGD through an API so others are free to access the data and use them to build additional products and services. For the public data, steps are taken to ensure citizen privacy.

- At least 11 private sector organisations are using College Scorecard data, ranging from college ranking publications, to coaches, consultants and investigative journalism organisations, to launch new tools.

Resources/Sources: College Scorecard website: https://collegescorecard.ed.gov; Gelobter (2015), "Under the hood: Building a new College Scorecard with students", www.whitehouse.gov/blog/2015/09/12/under-hood-building-new-college-scorecard-students.

Public data and information are increasingly being made available for potential reuse for economic and social ends that for the most part are not coming from within government or aimed at enhancing government services (OECD, 2015c). In a 2014

OECD survey on OGD, countries cited external commercial economic growth as one of the most significant motivators behind their OGD initiatives (see Figure 7.3), although they are also able to improve government efficiency and effectiveness by making information easier to access and transfer across agencies at no or low cost without restrictive legislative controls (OECD, 2008).[14] Interestingly, governments do not cite the economic value of OGD[15] for the *public* sector as an essential goal of OGD policies (Figure 7.3). None of the countries surveyed ranked this among the top five goals of the national open data policy. The fact that they do not identify creating economic value for the public sector as a key objective for OGD policies reflects a weak focus on public sector efficiency in general.

Although these internal benefits are not generally seen as a major goal, OGD has tremendous potential to enable public sector organisations to be more efficient, effective and innovative in carrying out their missions and serving citizens. Public institutions, too, are "prosumers" in the open data ecosystem. Not only do they produce OGD for civil society organisations, citizens and businesses to reuse, but they should equally consume open data themselves, whether produced by other actors or OGD produced or modified by other public stakeholders (OECD, 2016a). Such "dogfooding",[16] although common in the private sector, is an underused approach that has many benefits for public sector information and is ripe for innovation. For a start, it helps to improve the data quality and reliability of data by aligning incentives for public sector organisations. If public organisations reuse their own OGD as their primary source, rather than the current norm of using non-public internal databases, this will give them the same perspective as public users and encourage them to ensure the data are accurate and up-to-date (Strong, 2014). The use of OGD by governments can enhance efficiency by helping to bring down silos and foster collaboration across and within public agencies and departments. It creates common or shared datasets and/or registries, and means organisations need to collaborate and exchange over who holds what public information and for what purpose. This provides opportunities to re-engineer and simplify internal procedures as well as deliver services in new ways, and identify and consolidate overlapping and duplicative data collections, which eases the burden on public sector organisations as well as the public (OECD, 2015a). Although government are increasingly aware of the benefits of "dogfooding", we were unable to identify any significant examples of successful public sector implementation this principle, which further indicates room to grow in this area.

Figure 7.3. Main objectives of open government data strategies

Percentage of countries ranking each feature among their top five objectives

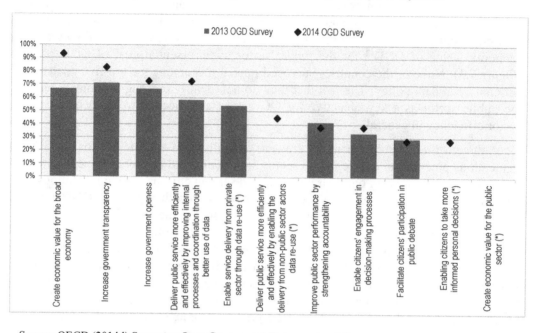

Source: OECD (2014d) Survey on Open Government Data, version 2.0.

Openness is also important for creating competition and driving performance improvement, which in turn can enhance innovation. Open performance data can support competition between public sector organisations to drive public sector innovation. Comparative benchmarking and user choice, for example, among schools and hospitals, neighbouring municipalities or boroughs, subnational governments or across countries, has the ability to create pressures on public sector organisations to improve quality. Innovation is one of the means to achieve this. Box 7.15 illustrates how OGD can be used to help benchmark clinical performance. Benchmarking is "an exercise that exposes variability and also promotes transparency within organisations" (MGI, 2013). Better benchmarking would enable "fostering competitiveness by making more information available" as well as "enhancing the accountability of institutions such as governments and businesses [to] raise the quality of decision [making] by giving citizens and consumers more tools to scrutinise business and government" (MGI, 2013). Research by the McKinsey Global Institute (MGI, 2013) suggests that a major share of the total benefits due to open data is attributable to better benchmarking.

Box 7.15. United Kingdom: Dr Foster

Dr Foster started as a joint venture with a private company and the UK Department of Health and uses data to monitor the performance of the National Health Service (NHS) and provide comparative information and benchmarking to health care professionals and the public. The goal of the service is to improve the safety, efficiency and transparency of health care by identifying variations in clinical performance to enable deliver better care and save money. Benchmarking is done nationally and globally against a series of key indicators of quality from a number of datasets, including open data. For example, the service has released Dr Foster Hospital Guides that provide information on hospitals with higher than normal mortality rates and instances of medical complications, which have resulted in hospital investigations from independent government regulators.

Dr Foster works in partnership with Imperial College London to develop methodologies for the service. One of the company's stated beliefs is that comparative information must be based on open methodologies and data sources so that results are open to scrutiny, and that sharing data and information is essential to interpreting it correctly. Accordingly, all of its metrics, methodologies and models are open to the public.

Dr Foster has expended to operate in continental Europe, the United States, China, Saudi Arabia and Australia. The service was purchased in 2015 by Telstra, an Australia's largest telecommunications company.

Sources: Dr Foster website: "About us", www.drfoster.com/about-us; "Our approach", www.drfoster.com/about-us/our-approach; "Metrics, methodologies and models", www.drfoster.com/about-us/our-approach/metrics-methodologies-and-models; Campbell and Asthana (2010), "Exposed: The hospitals whose high death rates are failing the NHS", www.theguardian.com/society/2010/nov/27/hospital-death-rates-nhs-dr-foster.

OGD also enables actors outside government to step in and develop innovative ways to provide public services, for example by developing modular services that are more agile and targeted on citizens' needs than those developed in-house by governments. In this way, government no longer remains the sole provider of solutions but rather becomes a platform that facilitates other actors to create public value (OECD, 2015a).

Box 7.16. Australia: DataStart

Over 9 000 open datasets are available through data.gov.au, the Australian government's OGD portal. DataStart, a private-public partnership, is a nationwide campaign to find, incubate and accelerate start-up ideas that leverage openly available data from the Australian Government. The goal is to identify entrepreneurs and enable them to apply innovation and creativity to uncover new value and solve global problems using OGD.

Designed as a competition, DataStart has several phases:

- DataStart solicits applications from teams across Australia.

- Shortlisted teams participate in a workshop to refine their ideas in preparation for pitching to a panel of judges.

- Teams pitch their ideas to a panel of professionals and investors for the opportunity to participate in a nine month incubation programme with significant initial investment funding.

Box 7.16. Australia: DataStart *(cont.)*

- During the incubation programme, the winning team receives support, resources and mentorship from an established technology start-up incubator, as well as ongoing support from the government's Department of the Prime Minister and Cabinet.

CohortIQ, a health start-up that uses hospital and open government data to reduce the estimated 235 000 avoidable hospital admissions each year, was named the winner of DataStart on 18 January 2016.

Australia sees this is the start of a more comprehensive engagement with the private sector about the kinds of government datasets that can be used generate new business, develop new products and services and create social value.

Sources: OECD (2017a), *Embracing Innovation in Government: Global Trends*, www.oecd.org/gov/innovative-government/embracing-innovation-in-government.pdf; Perdomo (2015), "DataStart – Be part of it!", https://blog.data.gov.au/news-media/blog/datastart-be-part-it; Australian Government (2016), "CohortIQ announced as winner of DataStart", www.dpmc.gov.au/news-centre/data/cohortiq-announced-winner-datastart; DataStart website, http://datastart.wpengine.com.

While almost any sort of public sector data and information can be opened up to the public, as countries' information and data management practices mature and become more advanced, many are shifting to practices that include the publication of APIs in addition to traditional bulk files and PDF documents. APIs are interfaces used by information systems to communicate with each other. These interfaces allow automated access to and exchange of data within the limits established by the information system operator (OECD, 2014b). APIs support real-time data sharing and exchange, interoperability of data-driven services and the portability of data across services (OECD, 2015a). They help make data freely available for use within public sector organisations, between organisations, in the private sector and by citizens. In contrast to traditional file downloads, APIs allow applications to automatically access the latest data available instead of requiring a developer or other user to return to the organisation's website to get updated information. APIs support an enormous and innovative range of products offering up-to-date information to the public (18F, 2016). Many data-driven services stand on the shoulders of giants: the public administrations that have made their information available via APIs (OECD, 2015a).[17] In addition to benefitting external developers, APIs make it easier for governments to reap the benefits of, "dogfooding" their own information, as discussed above.

Box 7.17. United Kingdom: Government Service Design Manual

The United Kingdom has developed a Government Service Design Manual to help agencies "build services so good that people prefer to use them." Guides cover a variety of topics, including agile methods, governance, software development, performance measurement and user-centered design. One is a set of guiding principles for making digital services and data accessible though APIs. It provides guidance on building, formatting, testing, documenting and publishing APIs.

Sources: United Kingdom Government (undated a), "Browse guides by topic", www.gov.uk/service-manual/browse; United Kingdom Government (undated b), "APIs: Using and creating application programming interfaces", www.gov.uk/service-manual/making-software/apis.html.

Building a culture to support the free flow of information to drive innovation

As stated above, open information access supports the efficiency and effectiveness of policy and service delivery, and public sector data reuse by a wide range of actors is a key condition for economic and social value creation, and is necessary to stimulate creativity and innovation. There are significant cultural barriers to achieving this, however. "Selling" the concept of sharing OGD and information to frontline staff, various levels of management and even to entire public sector organisations within public sector organisations requires giving employees incentives that tie the benefits of sharing to the mission of the organisation and the work of its employees.

The OECD (2017b, 2015a, 2008) has encouraged governments to invest in organisational change and entrepreneurship in the private and public sector by encouraging a culture of experimentation and learning driven by data and information; however, there exists significant resistance to change in the public sector. Supporting innovation through sound data and information management as described above helps, but it is important that the organisational culture supports continuous learning (OECD, 2015b). Figure 7.4 underlines that the main obstacles to implementing open data programmes in governments are not technical but are linked to legal barriers or resistance within organisations (OECD, 2015a), which may suggest similar obstacles for broader information and knowledge sharing.

Figure 7.4. Open government data: Main challenges as indicated by countries

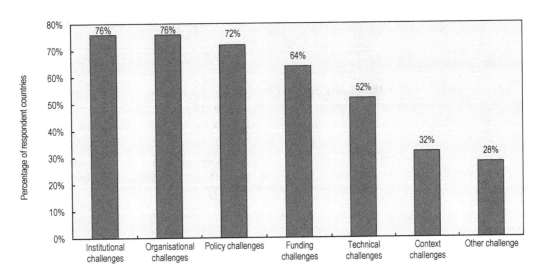

Source: OECD survey on Open Government Data, version 1.0, 19 April 2013.

One significant challenge to creating a culture that fosters the use of data and information to drive innovation is the concept of data ownership, both at the organisational and individual levels. At the organisational level, there is a common assumption that making data available as open data is just a product of what happens already inside the public sector and therefore does not require new investments, but this is not entirely correct (OECD, 2015a). The free flow of data and information is not cost-free. It involves costs related to datafication (i.e., data quantification), data collection, data cleaning and data curation. Organisations also need to make substantial commitments and investments in acquiring new skills, training employees, purchasing technologies and upgrading network infrastructure. Given these significant costs, the creators and controllers of data, who may feel a sense of ownership, do not necessarily have any incentive to share. They may perceive the costs of data sharing as higher than any expected benefits. This problem can be summarised as a positive externality issue: sharing may benefit others more than it benefits the information creator and controller, who does clearly gain from the benefit of others and as a result may not sufficiently invest in sharing or may even refrain completely (OECD, 2015b; Frischmann, 2012). Many organisations wish to recover costs, partly for budgetary reasons and partly on the grounds that those who benefit should pay. However, the calculation of the overall benefits can be problematic. Moreover, as Stiglitz et al. (2000) have argued, if provision of information and data-related services is a valid role for government, generating revenue from it is not.

Anything which introduces friction to the free flow of data and information, such as charging for access and reuse, puts barriers and disincentives in place for other organisations and citizens attempting to access it, thereby limiting innovative potential. These disincentives generally outweigh any potential source of income that may be made based on restrictive provisioning of data and information. As highlighted in OECD (2015c), sales of public sector information generate very little direct revenue for most governments compared to their costs – around 1% of what it costs to make the data available – and fail to take into account the benefits that may be gained by the broader public sector and society, such as additional tax revenues from downstream private sector activities. In addition, a recent OECD (2015c) survey of public sector information strategies suggests that countries have not had particular difficulties in funding the switch to free and open data and information, and that this has not been the major barrier that was foreseen in the past.

There is also often a belief among civil servants and even among policy makers that making data and information more available disempowers public officials or makes them more vulnerable, since it risks unveiling faults to others. This belief can create an environment which is not supportive of the sort of free flow of data and information that has been stressed by the OECD. In some organisations, these initiatives are actually having a negative behavioural impact on civil servants, for instance, who show unusual resistance to collecting and sharing data (OECD, 2015a).

Part of the challenge is that it is often difficult for civil servants to understand the value proposition for transparent information and OGD. It can be hard to measure the benefits that accrue to different type of beneficiaries, including in the public and private sector. For instance, with current initiatives, the value of the data after release is not always clear. There are relatively few developed quantitative analyses of the benefits and costs associated with more liberal access to and use of public sector information. The OECD survey of current OGD initiatives among OECD countries found no reported methodology to measure returns on investment, and only relatively few, scattered attempts to track economic or social gains from the reuse of OGD, although there was interest in improvement (OECD, 2015c). While benefit/cost research studies show that moving to open data strategies is economically and socially rewarding and that the benefits quickly and demonstrably outstrip costs, public sector organisations have struggled to systematically demonstrate the value of OGD in relation to achieving their mission objectives (OECD, 2015c). If OGD is to gain acceptance across the public sector, the advantages of opening up public sector data for wider use need to be clearly articulated. Consequently, greater emphasis is now being placed on devising more solid methodologies to assess the impact of open government data policies (OECD, 2015a).

Although significant cultural challenges do exist, governments are working to overcome them by encouraging a fundamental cultural change in public authorities' approaches and perceptions of OGD. Government policy agendas in this space cannot be implemented without important efforts to disseminate the benefits of open government to all key stakeholders, inside and outside of government (OECD, 2016a). Clear, simple, timely and efficient communication that raises policy awareness among public officials, citizens and the private sector, can foster feelings of shared goals across the parties involved; they should be conceived as a permanent component of the policy cycle (OECD, 2016d). The cultural value of bringing civil servants closer to, and raising the awareness of, the impact of releasing their data is significant. A data-driven culture, including organisational willingness and the development of the required skills (human, technical and legal), is not something that can be forced on government employees, managers and departments. It needs to be stimulated by making a connection to the actual needs of the public institutions and those of civil servants (OECD, 2016a). A good example is the way in which the Danish Basic Data Registries have come into existence (Box 7.18).

Box 7.18. Denmark: Basic Data Registries programme

In order to create a sense of collective commitment across the administration to increasing openness and reuse of government data, Denmark has been focusing on the development of a government data and information management policy. In accordance with one of the recommendations in an OECD e-government study of Denmark (OECD, 2010), the point of departure was recognition of the key relevance for efficient public sectors of high-quality basic data registries used by all actors.[1] In the digitisation age, these registries are seen as being at the core of public sector efficiency.

The Digitisation Agency within the Ministry of Finance, responsible for setting and co-ordinating the implementation of the open government data agenda, realised that the basic registries were not catering to the needs of all parts of the administration and they were not up to par with the need of a digitised public sector. Registries had been developed as mandatory by law but not based on users' needs.

In Denmark, "good basic data for everyone" was part of the 2011-15 public sector digitisation strategy. As part of this strategy, and to move from adherence to the law to adherence to users' needs, the Danish government launched a Basic Data Registries Implementation Programme (2013-16), which revisited the governance system of data management within the public sector – including changing laws to clarify responsibilities and improve data quality and use. It put great emphasis on data modelling to ensure that data fit with semantics. The government established partnerships with the financial sector (e.g. land companies and financial entities) which will be expanded to other sectors to capture views, advice and feedback on data architecture in order to ensure that the data meet users' needs. A board was created for the programme that mirrors the governance model for digital government.

The focus on data as a strategic asset for public sector efficiency and modernisation is helping the Danish government create a common agenda around the ideas of placing data governance and data quality, use and sharing at the core of public sector reforms. For example:

- Police forces will be able to easily access and combine data to perform their day-to-day jobs as well as to react to crises.

Box 7.18. Denmark: Basic Data Registries programme *(cont.)*

- Common environmental data will improve collaboration between local government and water utilities in order to make climate efforts more efficient and effective.

- Digital services across all sectors will automatically retrieve address data, so that users do not have to spend time entering this data and risk errors in data entry.

By providing a clear value proposition that the Basic Data Registries Programme is key to broad reforms, the government is overcoming cultural barriers and encouraging actors to participate in the programme because they recognise the high value of the data and not because it is mandatory. The goal is to increase the number of datasets in the programme that also help create a business case linked to societal value and not just economic benefits, such as social demographic data. The Danish government made open data relevant for public institutions by drawing upon their needs.

Denmark's new Digital Strategy (2016-20) continues with these data principles. It includes a key goal for digitisation and better reuse of data to help create more cohesive and efficient public services with digital, high-quality welfare solutions. Among other things, this will make it even easier for citizens to meet the public sector digitally and to experience more co-ordinated public services across authorities.

[1] According to the European Interoperability Framework 2.0, base registries are: "reliable sources of basic information on items such as persons, companies, vehicles, licenses, buildings, locations and roads" and "are authentic and authoritative and form, separately or in combination, the cornerstone of public services".

Source: Danish Government (2016), "New digital strategy 2016-2020", www.digst.dk/Servicemenu /English/Policy-and-Strategy/Digital-Strategy-2016to2020/Press-Release-New-Digital-Strategy.

Advancing for continuous innovation

Any "innovation" goes through a lifecycle and does not last forever. Once implemented, it either fails or is diffused more broadly across an organisation, thereby losing its novelty and status as innovative. It is critical for organisations to close the loop on the phases discussed in this chapter to lock in continuous innovation as a routine part of doing business in government with the final phase: advancing. Sourcing, exploiting and sharing data, information and knowledge are not enough to sustain innovative value in the long term. To use these activities to support continuous innovation, organisations need to be able to identify areas that need innovation and learn and adjust their activities based on the results and their environment. These processes need to be built in as a routine part of the business of government. Advancing on managing data, information and knowledge for innovation enables public sector organisations to be poised to innovate on an ongoing basis to better meet their missions in new ways and provide transparency, value and service to their people.

Advancing is built upon the recognition that managing tacit knowledge from inside and outside government is as critical as managing data and information. In the context of government, it is important to distinguish codified knowledge (formal and systematic) from tacit knowledge (technical skills and intuitive "know-how") (OECD, 2005). Tacit knowledge is embodied within individual members of staff and the public, and accessing and making best use of people's know-how can be extremely valuable to the organisations they work for, the broader public administration and the governmental initiatives that they may be knowledgeable about even if they do not work for the public sector. Putting this recognition into practice, advancing involves building conduits for engagement, co-ordination and collaboration everywhere that data and information flow to allow producers and consumers to connect with each other, both within and across the public sector as well as across sectors. This will allow civil servants to connect to other government organisations, individual developers, subject matter experts, citizens, civil society organisations, academics and private companies (OECD, 2015a). Although less quantifiable than the bits and bytes of data and pages of information, the enablement of this free flow of knowledge is just as important as the free flow of data and information.

The main goal of building these knowledge conduits is to capture and act on feedback. This feedback can result in value creation, as soliciting and acting on it helps to identify gaps and areas where opportunities for innovation exist, as well as enabling the production of new features, new lines of business, markets, competencies, services and tools. Individuals may also spot anomalies and mistakes in government data and information or otherwise suggest improvements, thus contributing to improving public service delivery and policy making. These conduits help developers at the cutting edge of technology stay up-to-date on new data and information being released, and help governments learn ways of doing things differently and in more agile ways.

These conduits serve to pull together the number of actors, goods, services, technologies and business models that use and contribute back to public sector data and information to create a rapidly evolving information ecosystem. The OECD (2015a) has suggested that governments nurture the development of such an ecosystem and promote a culture of collaboration among the key actors to increase the value created. When these feedback loops are in place, the downstream end of information keeps the upstream end permanently informed, which can facilitate ongoing evolution and innovation (Saussois, 2003). Establishing this ecosystem is no simple task. It entails identifying the various categories of actors, nurturing a culture of public sector interaction with actors, and reaching out to some who might not traditionally be actively involved in public affairs (OECD, 2015a). It also requires dedicating resources to participative development and establishing credible follow-up procedures to integrate feedback, such as with responsive OGD programmes (OECD, 2016a). OECD research has shown that fostering such an ecosystem to advance the public sector can be done in a number of key ways, as discussed below.

Advancing is highly complementary with a forthcoming OPSI study on how public sector organisations learn to identify and understand where innovation is needed. An alpha version of this study was released in October 2016 for public comment and feedback (OPSI, 2016). Its purpose is to explore how public sector organisations and civil servants can start the innovation process with a stronger understanding of the problems than need an innovative response. The study includes discussion on the importance of learning in relation to innovation, the changing context in governments that necessitates a changed approach to learning in organisations today, and the enabling conditions, channels and tools that support learning for innovation in the public sector.

Crowdsourcing

Crowdsourcing is emerging as a means of allowing things to be conducted at scales of magnitude greater than before.[18] It involves capitalising on the Internet and large groups of people, particularly via online communities, to harvest "collective intelligence," a culmination of the knowledge of the crowd, and accomplish tasks that might have traditionally been given to small groups. Crowdsourcing can help process data and information quickly, on unprecedented scales and with better quality control than any individual or small group can attain. Crowdsourcing therefore offers cost and speed benefits, the potential to make new discoveries in the patterns of large datasets, and the possibility of near real-time testing and application of new hypotheses and findings (OECD, 2015a).

The success rate of crowdsourced innovation challenges is quite high, in some cases up to 40% – which is remarkable, especially since many challenges are generally put out on the web because they are beyond the problem-solving ability of the organisation or the individuals posting them (OECD, 2015a). Given its open, informal structure, crowdsourcing is inherently cross-disciplinary. In some cases, even gifted amateurs and people without direct experience with the problem can provide valuable insights and solutions (OECD, 2015a). Of critical importance to success in crowdsourcing for governments is to recognise "talent" outside the public sector: people with subject matter expertise and other tacit knowledge who can feed value back into the public sector. This is not necessarily easy, as successful crowdsourcing depends on generating sufficient scale and representativeness of participation to get valuable results. To help fuel crowdsourcing efforts and equip participants, it is useful to provide relevant public sector data in machine readable datasets that can be searched, manipulated and interlinked using freely available tools.

Despite high success rates, although crowdsourcing is increasingly being used by the public and private sector to address complex and challenging problems, only a limited number of governments have embarked down this path to any real degree to date (OECD, 2015a). However, the OECD has observed several innovative examples that demonstrate the power of crowdsourcing, including the two examples in Boxes 7.19 and 7.20.

Box 7.19. Mexico: Mexico City Mapatòn

Mexico City has one of the largest public bus systems in the world. Its buses provide over 60% of all transit in the city, with about 14 million daily riders on 29 000 buses that run more than 1 500 routes. However, in part due to its size and complexity, the city had no data on or maps of this mode of transport. As a result, no data-driven policy bus-related transportation policy was possible, and citizens had no bus map to help them move about the city.

To address this, Mexico City's Laboratorio para la Ciudad, an experimental office and creative think-tank that reports to the Mayor, partnered with 12 governmental and civil society organisations to develop Mapatón CDMX: a crowdsourcing and gamification experiment to map the city's bus routes through civic collaboration and technology, using smartphones to feed GPS data to the city. The participants who mapped the most routes to earn the most points won tablets and cash prizes up to MXN 30 000 (Mexican pesos, about USD 1 700). Because smartphone users are concentrated in certain areas of the city, the city used an algorithm to assign neglected routes the most points. The algorithm constantly recalculated the point values of the routes to make sure the maximal number of routes was mapped. The citywide game attracted more than 4 000 participants who managed to accomplish the main mapping task in two weeks. The total cost of the programme was under USD 15 000. A number of other cities are considering replicating this platform in their own communities. The data generated are now available as OGD for others to use and build upon and to guide policy.

Sources: OECD (2017a), *Embracing Innovation in Government: Global Trends*, www.oecd.org/gov /innovative-government/embracing-innovation-in-government.pdf; Laboratorio para la Ciudad report to OPSI; Mendelson (2016), "Mapping Mexico City's vast informal transit system", www.fastcoexis t.com/3058475/mapping-mexico-citys-vast-informal-transit-system.

Box 7.20. Indonesia: Food Security Early Warning System

The Food Security Early Warning System was developed by the Office of the President in partnership with staff from the World Food Programme and the United Nations-affiliated Pulse Lab Jakarta to address the need for better data on the impact of El Nino on Indonesia's food supply. It is a multi-tier system that fuses satellite climate data (rainfall and vegetation health data), crowdsourced food price data (local "citizen reporters" who upload food price reports using a customised mobile application), and household survey data to provide integrated visualisations of the extent of drought-affected areas, the impact on market structure and pricing, and the coping strategies and resilience of affected populations. The Food Security Early Warning System is unique in that it collects this information in high resolution and in a near real-time manner through the use of remote sensing and crowdsourcing. The system is new, but officials state that they believe it has the potential to improve the targeting of assistance to climate-vulnerable populations, and thus to improve the efficiency and effectiveness of public assistance programmes. Although the system was originally developed in connection to the most recent occurrence of El Nino, in principle it is applicable to any climate induced food security issue.

Sources: OECD (2017a), *Embracing Innovation in Government: Global Trends*, www.oecd.org/gov/innov ative-government/embracing-innovation-in-government.pdf; Pulse Lab Jakarta report to OPSI.

In addition to individual initiatives and challenges, crowdsourcing can be embedded as a more persistent component of a broader innovation policy or objective. Where individual crowdsourcing efforts generally target a specific problem, broader efforts help with spotting previously unknown problems that may be tackled with innovation, allowing new ideas to surface. As an example of a broad approach to crowdsourcing, the OECD (2016a) has encouraged countries to evolve their data portals into a platform to crowdsource open data, thus enabling ongoing co-creation, and user collaboration and interaction. Consultation exercises to assess data demand led by public institutions, and communication strategies that go beyond one-way information provision, are basic elements of open data strategies that focus on creating greater impact (OECD, 2016a). This is seen in the examples from France and Finland below (Box 7.21). The United States example in the Knowledge Networks discussion below (Box 7.24) also takes the approach of embedding ongoing crowdsourcing into a broader policy initiative.

Box 7.21. France and Finland: Enabling central open data portals for collaboration and data co-creation

France

The French national open data portal (www.data.gouv.fr) enables data prosumers to directly contribute new datasets to the portal. In order to publish open data (datasets, APIs, etc.), data contributors are requested to fill out an online form which collects information related to data licensing, granularity, a description of the overall data content, etc. The French open data portal also enables data prosumers to publish and showcase examples of open data reuse (OGD or not) and to monitor the use of the datasets they publish. In addition, the French government used the portal to launch the *Base Adresse Nationale* project, which is a multi-stakeholder collaboration initiative aiming to crowdsource a unique national address database fed by the data contributions from private, public and non-profit organisations.

Box 7.21. France and Finland: Enabling central open data portals for collaboration and data co-creation *(cont.)*

Finland

In Finland, the national open data portal (avoindata.fi) has been enabled as a platform where citizens can publish open data and interoperability tools (i.e. guidelines to ease the interaction between users' datasets and other data formats or platforms). Users are required to register on the portal in order to publish datasets. As in France, uploading open data on the Finnish portal requires filling in an online form where users can provide a detailed description of the data. This description includes information such as the data's licensing model (e.g. Creative Commons) and the data validity timeframe. Users can also browse the profiles of other users using the portal, exploring their activities and the datasets that other users have published. The portal also provides users with the chance to subscribe to specific organisations in order to receive updates on new datasets, comments, etc.

Source: OECD (2016a), *Open Government Data Review of Mexico: Data Reuse for Public Sector Impact and Innovation*, http://dx.doi.org/10.1787/9789264259270-en.

Knowledge networks

To foster the innovation ecosystem, knowledge communities should be linked through effective co-ordination and collaboration networks. As discussed in Chapter 3, which includes a number of relevant case studies, citizen-centred policy and service design rarely sit under one office or institution, but rather at the intersection of traditional policy silos and can cross organisational and sectoral boundaries. A critical component of knowledge management includes mechanisms to link together these different sources of knowledge, which include people, to stimulate learning.

The experience, skills and abilities that civil servants use in order to perform their duties are highly valuable resources, as is the subject matter expertise related to public policies and services which exists outside the public sector. People with such tacit knowledge, within and beyond the public sector, are well placed to recognise opportunities for innovative improvements in organisational performance and service delivery. When properly enabled and empowered, civil servants become integral collaborators in dynamic networks to enhance government performance.

Connecting people to exchange tacit knowledge is even more important today in an era of high-volume, interrelated data and information that can cover a variety of subject domains. Knowledge networks have been set up to create environments where civil servants and others can share information and learn from each other to become better in the innovation processes. A recent OECD (2016e) survey found that that 63% of OECD countries (22 out of 35) have innovation networks across the civil service. In nine countries, these networks are supported by central human resource management or innovation organisations, in three by national schools of government, and ten countries have self-driven or independently supported networks. Most of these networks (18 countries) are intended to enable members to share experience; 14 of them aim to organise capacity-building activities such as training, workshops or seminars. Public sector knowledge networks can be expressed formally, with official knowledge repositories and documented experiences, or informally, for example through unstructured social media conversations and meetups. These two concepts are not mutually exclusive, and knowledge networks can involve a mixture of formal and informal actors, inputs and outputs to help drive information-driven innovation in governments. They can also vary in terms of the extent to which they involve non-governmental actors such as the public. There is no explicitly right or wrong approach, and OPSI encourages organisations to experiment with different methods of building knowledge networks to identify which ones provide the most value within their unique operating environments.

Canada's GCpedia and GCconnex offer examples of formal mechanisms (Box 7.22). These tools can allow any civil servant to connect but by design they are internal government mechanisms, so do not bring external groups and individuals into the discussions. Portugal's Common Knowledge Network (Box 7.23) provides another example of a formal mechanism but one which has been set up to also receive and respond to feedback from actors outside of government, such as civil society organisations or members of the public.

Box 7.22. Canada: GCpedia and GCconnex

GCpedia

The Government of Canada has developed GCpedia, an open source government-wide wiki for collaboration and knowledge sharing. It allows federal employees to share files and post, comment and edit articles placed on GCpedia by their peers. Access is only available to those with a government e-mail address, so third-party collaboration is not possible but, tens of thousands of active users within government demonstrates the significant collaborative power of the platform. The platform helps to break down walls between departments that had been traditionally siloed.

GCconnex

The government also created GCconnex, an open source government-wide internal-only social media network to enables public servants to connect and collaborate. It is a virtual network where public servants can connect with other public servants with similar interests, or with skills that will help them be more productive in their work.

These systems are designed to foster a public sector culture of collaboration and to produce information that is streamlines, relevant, user-driven and integrated.

Sources: Government of Canada (2016), "GCTools: Re-imagined for you", www.tbs-sct.gc.ca/ip-pi/media/20160811-eng.asp; Janelle (2009), "GCPedia a success, says Government of Canada CIO", https://techvibes.com/2009/10/06/gcpedia-a-success-says-government-of-canada-cio; GCConnex on GitHub: https://github.com/tbs-sct/gcconnex.

Box 7.23. Portugal: Common Knowledge Network

The Common Knowledge Network is a collaborative platform built by the Portuguese government to promote the sharing of best practice and information about modernisation, innovation and the simplification of public administration. It is a network of knowledge sharing based on open membership by public bodies, central and local administrations, private entities and any citizen who wishes to participate. Participation involves presenting and describing a best practice and its results. The network thus seeks to assert itself as a central reference point to support the dissemination of good practices and lessons learned. It currently has over 500 examples of best practice documented from all levels of government.

Box 7.23. Portugal: Common Knowledge Network *(cont.)*

The network also serves as a place to conduct debate on public policies and their implementation at local, regional and national levels, and for participatory decision making with interest groups or communities of practice. It strengthens the relationships between the various stakeholders and co-ordinates information sharing.

Since the network is open, it has the added benefit of helping participating government organisations obtain a common perspective on the activities of public administration to help standardise services and discover similar quality standards in different services

Sources: OPSI; Common Knowledge Network website: www.rcc.gov.pt/Paginas/Home.aspx.

Social media platforms such as Facebook and Twitter can be leveraged to establish both formal and informal knowledge networks, and to provide governments with sources of innovative ideas and new tools to connect to users and engage in discussions that support innovation. Drawing on the wide and varied information held across society as a whole can increase the public sector's innovative capacity through new expertise, creativity and feedback (OECD, 2015b). While there is significant potential to improve the public sector's innovative capacity, recent OECD (2015a) research shows that the objectives of citizen participation and citizen engagement ranked lower than would be expected, given that many open government and service delivery agendas point to open data as a key enabler for strengthening public engagement in service design, policy making and rule making. Box 7.24 illustrates a hybrid approach from the United States, combining crowdsourcing principles with use of social media and other tools to create both formal and informal knowledge networks to connect civil servants with each other and with the public.

Box 7.24. United States: Crowdsourcing and internal and external knowledge networks

To support the implementation of a number of US technology policies, the White House makes use of a combination of innovative new social media platforms, as well as simple but powerful listserv technology to connect individuals within, across and beyond the public sector.

Social media for policy implementation collaboration

In a number of instances, the White House leverages the code repository and social media platform GitHub to co-ordinate and collaborate with government officials and the public to continually innovate on policy implementation.

- Project Open Data is a collection of living policy guidance, code, tools and case studies to help government organisations implement the US Open Data Policy and Data.gov to unlock the potential of government data. The platform has evolved over time as a community resource to facilitate the broader adoption of open data practices in government. Through GitHub, anyone – government employees, contractors, developers or the general public – can view, contribute and communicate through threaded discussions. Resources and staff are dedicated to collaborating and communicating with users, reviewing feedback and revising policy based on feedback as needed.

> ### Box 7.24. United States: Crowdsourcing and internal and external knowledge networks *(cont.)*
>
> - A government-wide Source Code Policy was issued in draft form for public consultation, and it received over 2 500 comments from government officials as well as the public. The subsequent final version of the policy announced that the government would launch code.gov, a discoverability portal for source code as well as a living guidance and collaboration platform similar to Project Open Data
>
> - Management.cio.gov was initially launched to solicit public comments on a draft White House policy to implement implementing the Federal Information Technology Acquisition Reform Act (FITARA). The final policy set forth a common baseline for technology governance in government, which has significant implications for information management. It has evolved into a resource to assist agencies in adopting and implementing the policy. Like Project Open Data, anyone can view, contribute and communicate about this work.
>
> - Weekly or bi-weekly meetings for interested government employees are held, both in person and electronically, on open data and governance topics to discuss formal policy updates as well as to provide an opportunity for informal interaction and knowledge sharing.
>
> **Simple technology to connect civil servants**
>
> For each of these initiatives, crowdsourcing content and connecting an ecosystem of internal and external stakeholders in innovative ways has facilitated the implementation of government-wide policy. Some discussions and aspects of policy implementation, however, may not be suitable for public visibility and discussion. To build knowledge networks within government, the White House has used relatively old but still common technology—listservs. A listserv is an application that distributes messages to subscribers on an electronic mailing list wherein any approved member of a list can send an email that goes to every other member of the list. The open data listserv, for example, is a community of over 600 government officials working on open data issues.
>
> **Benefits**
>
> These methods of crowdsourcing and building knowledge networks have several benefits:
>
> - bringing down bureaucratic silos within and across the public sector
>
> - facilitating the free, two-way exchange of ideas and information with the public
>
> - Connecting users to engage in discussions that support innovation
>
> - Allowing individuals to opt-in to topics that they find interesting or that affect them.
>
> *Sources:* Project Open Data website: https://project-open-data.cio.gov; Federal Source Code Policy website: https://sourcecode.cio.gov,

Conclusion

The potential for data, information and knowledge to drive public sector innovation is immense, and it is growing every day. Improved use of these assets in government helps to reduce the costs and risks of experimentation, gives a better picture of what is working and what is not, and helps both civil servants and the public identify issues and generate ideas about how to improve policies and services. Public officials around the world are applying innovative techniques to creatively address challenges. They are devising ways to aggregate, catalogue and connect the massive troves of data, information and even knowledge held by governments to allow civil servants and citizens alike to source it to build a foundation for public sector innovation. They are using sophisticated analytics methods to exploit data and enrich it to become useful information and knowledge to allow them to make informed decisions and better meet their missions. They are breaking down bureaucratic barriers to share data, information and knowledge and unleash the free flow of these resources as the fuel for innovation within the public sector and beyond. Perhaps most importantly, they are doing all of this in partnership with their public colleagues and the citizens affected by the policies and use the services, using the insights gained to embed continuous innovation into the nature of government.

Accomplishing this is very difficult. Governments are often federated and fragmented and vary dramatically from country to country and from administration to administration. This provides a unique set of challenges that require government innovators to simultaneously and delicately balance and connect central authority with local autonomy, shape the future of government while grappling with the political and social realities of today, and overcome and reverse cultural inertia that manifests as territorialism, reluctance to change due to a disconnect from the lives touched by government, and risk aversion for fear of intense scrutiny for failure. These all affect the public sector's capacity to convert data and information into knowledge, and to convert knowledge into lasting change. Sitting on the cusp of failure and the future is a precarious position, yet we see courageous innovators and ideas multiplying within governments around the world at an impressive and heartening rate. The trends and examples presented here are a glimpse of where information-driven public sector innovation stands today and where it may be going tomorrow. Innovation is temporary by definition. Some of what is presented here will lead to new norms in government, and the rest will lead to failure. This is good and should be encouraged; the free flow of data, information and knowledge, and their adept use, can improve the chances of positive outcomes from innovation.

The topics covered in this chapter are far from the only opportunities, challenges and examples of harnessing data, information and knowledge to drive innovation in the public sector. Other parts of this report contain more information that is relevant to this subject, with real-world illustrations of the practical application of these concepts. Chapter 3 discusses, in a broader sense, cultural challenges for innovation. It also discusses mechanisms to overcome them, such as awards and crosscutting networks to stimulate learning. These concepts are related, as some of the key objectives for innovation awards are to make innovators aware of one another and to develop a sense of community, as well as to share information and develop case studies so others can learn. These factors are proven to affect an organisation's ability to innovate (Laursen et al., 2013), and they are highly aligned with the concept of tacit knowledge management discussed above. Chapter 4 presents instances of exploiting performance information to drive budgeting decisions to support innovation. Finally, Chapter 5 analyses data on more than 70 innovation teams, such as innovation labs, to discuss their role in promoting innovation. Such groups are often a natural choice for incubating innovative ideas in a safe place. They may also be particularly well suited to leading government efforts in co-ordinating the "advancing" phase discussed in this chapter. Taken collectively, governments can use the concepts contained throughout this report to enhance their ability to use data, information and knowledge to innovate the way they do business, and potentially leverage the products and processes designed by other governments and presented here as case studies.

Notes

1. See the Observatory of Public Sector Innovation page on the OECD website, http://oe.cd/opsi.

2. Regulatory impact analysis (RIA) is a systemic approach to critically assessing the positive and negative effects of proposed and existing regulations and non-regulatory alternatives. As employed in OECD countries it encompasses a range of methods. It is an important element of an evidence-based approach to policy making. See www.oecd.org/gov/regulatory-policy/ria.htm for more information.

3. Open government data refers to government or public sector data (i.e. any "raw" data produced or commissioned by the public sector) made available through open access regimes, so that they can be freely used, reused and distributed by anyone, subject only to (at the most) the requirement that users attribute the data and (sometimes) that they make their work available to be shared as well. Open government data are a subset of public sector information. (Ubaldi, 2013).

4. See the reports provided on the OPSI website at http://oe.cd/opsi.

5. For example, data.gov in the United States, data.gouv.fr in France, data.gov.uk in the United Kingdom and datos.gob.mx in Mexico, among many others.

6. OGP is a multilateral initiative that aims to secure concrete commitments from governments to promote transparency, empower citizens, fight corruption and harness new technologies to strengthen governance. It was launched in 2011 and now has 75 participating countries. See www.opengovpartnership.org for more information.

7. See http://registries.opencorporates.com/.

8. Askitas and Zimmermann (2009), for example, analyse the predictive power of keywords such as Arbeitsamt OR Arbeitsagentur ("unemployment office or agency") to forecast unemployment in Germany. The authors find that forecasting based on these keywords indicated changes in trends much earlier than official statistics. Similar conclusions have been drawn by D'Amuri and Marcucci (2010) for the United States and by Suhoy (2010) for Israel.

9. The large volume of data being generated has no value if no information can be extracted from the data. Data analytics refers to a set of techniques and tools that are used to extract information from data. These techniques and tools extract information from data by revealing the context in which the data is embedded and its organisation and structure. They help distinguish the "signal from the noise." (Merelli and Rasetti, 2013; see also Cleveland, 1982 and Zins, 2007).

10. The main benefits would be greater operational efficiency (due to greater transparency), increased tax collection (due to customised services, for example), and less fraud and fewer errors (due to automated data analytics).

11. Machine learning is a subfield in computer science, and more specifically in artificial intelligence. It is concerned with the design, development and use of algorithms that allow computers to "learn" – that is, to perform certain tasks while improving performance with every empirical dataset it analyses.

12. The corporation that created the risk score algorithm in this case disputes the methodology of the investigative report; however, this example still raises questions regarding the limitations and potential biases of machine learning.

13. A credit score is a statistical number that depicts a person's creditworthiness. Lenders use a credit score to evaluate the probability that an individual will repay his or her

debts. Companies generate a credit score for each applicable person using data from the person's previous credit history (Investopedia, undated).

14   If the default status of public sector data and information is open, then it is "business as usual" rather than coming from specialised initiatives. Furthermore, publishing publicly is often the most efficient way of sharing public sector information across agencies where legislative controls around privacy and security had previously hampered use (OECD, 2015c).

15   This refers to value gained by the public sector as a result of publicly released OGD, and is not to be confused with public sector information and data leveraged within the public sector but not released to the public as OGD.

16   "Eating your own dogfood," or "dogfooding," are slang phrases that originated in the technology community, meaning using the product you make to work out the kinks (Caplan-Bricker, 2013).

17   For example, Data.gov provides insights into how different industries and sectors are using US OGD to result in cost savings, economic development, civic services, transparency and accountability, research and scientific discovery, and increase participation in democratic dialogue, among others (Data.gov, undated).

18   Crowdsourcing is "the practice of obtaining needed services, ideas, or content by soliciting contributions from a large group of people and especially from the online community rather than from traditional employees or suppliers" (Merriam-Webster, 2014).

References

18F (2016), "Introduction to APIs in government", Developer Program website, https://pages.18f.gov/API-All-the-X/pages/introduction_to_APIs_in_government/, accessed 6 October 2016.

Abdellaoui, K., V. Popovski and E. Lopez-Mancisidor (25 November 2015), "Diagnose and treat: Measuring a country's pulse with social media", Voices from Eurasia blog, http://europeandcis.undp.org/blog/2015/11/25/diagnose-and-treat-measuring-a-countrys-pulse-with-social-media/.

Anguin, J. et al. (23 May 2016), "Machine bias", ProPublica website, www.propublica.org/article/machine-bias-risk-assessments-in-criminal-sentencing.

Askitas, N. and K.N. Zimmermann (2009), "Google econometrics and unemployment forecasting", *DIW Berlin Discussion Paper*, No. 899, http://papers.ssrn.com/sol3/papers.cfm?abstract_id=1465341, accessed 5 October 2016.

Athow, J., J. Lord and C. Potter (27 January 2015), "Predictive analytics: The science of non-compliance", Civil Service Quarterly blog, https://quarterly.blog.gov.uk/2015/01/27/predictive_analytics/.

Australian Government (11 April 2016), "CohortIQ announced as winner of DataStart", Department of the Prime Minister and Cabinet website, www.dpmc.gov.au/news-centre/data/cohortiq-announced-winner-datastart.

Australian Government (2013), *Open Public Sector Information: From Principles to Practice*, Office of the Australian Information Commissioner, Australian Government, www.oaic.gov.au/resources/information-policy/information-policy-resources/open-public-sector-information-from-principles-to-practice.pdf.

Bettcher, K. (13 July 2015), "Share your experiences with private sector partnerships on open governance", Open Government Partnership blog, www.opengovpartnership.org/blog/kim-bettcher/2015/07/13/share-your-experience-private-sector-partnerships-open-governancehttp://sunlightfoundation.com/blog/2015/02/09/a-big-win-for-open-government-sunlight-gets-us-to-release-indexes-of-federal-data/.

C40 Cities (16 December 2012), "Case study: Rio Operations Center", C40 Cities website, www.c40.org/case_studies/rio-operations-center.

Campbell, D. and A. Asthana (27 November 2010), "Exposed: The hospitals whose high death rates are failing the NHS", *The Observer*, www.theguardian.com/society/2010/nov/27/hospital-death-rates-nhs-dr-foster.

Caplan-Bricker, N. (28 October 2013), "If you want to talk like a Silicon Valley CEO, learn this phrase", *New Republic*, https://newrepublic.com/article/115349/dogfooding-tech-slang-working-out-glitches.

Chausson, C. (2016a), "France unveils source code of income tax application", Joinup website, European Commission, https://joinup.ec.europa.eu/community/osor/news/france-unveils-source-code-income-tax-application.

Chausson, C. (2016b), "France improves fiscal transparency by opening tax calculator", Joinup website, European Commission, https://joinup.ec.europa.eu/community/opengov/news/france-improves-fiscal-transparency-opening-tax-calculator.

Cisco (2014), "IoE-based Rio Operations Center improves safety, traffic flow, emergency response capabilities", Cisco, http://internetofeverything.cisco.com/sites/default/files/pdfs/Rio_Jurisdiction_Profile__051214REV.pdf.

City of New York (2016a), "Citywide data sharing", City of New York website, www1.nyc.gov/site/analytics/initiatives/citywide-data-sharing.page.

City of New York (2016b), "Job posting notice", City of New York website, www1.nyc.gov/assets/doitt/downloads/jobs/234365_moda_dir_data_strategy.pdf.

Cleveland, H. (1982), "Information as a resource", *The Futurist*, December, http://faculty.csuci.edu/minder.chen/MIS310/Reading/20000905cleveland.pdf, accessed 5 October 2016.

CSIRO (undated), "Cutting hospital waiting times", CSIRO website, www.csiro.au/en/Research/BF/Areas/Digital-health/Waiting-times.

Cukier, K. (2010), "Data, data everywhere", *The Economist Special Report*, 25 February, www.economist.com/node/15557443.

D'Amuri, F. and J. Marcucci (2010), "Google it! Forecasting the US unemployment rate with a Google job search index", SSRN, http://papers.ssrn.com/sol3/papers.cfm?abstract_id=1594132, accessed 5 October 2016.

Danish Government (2016), "New digital strategy 2016-2020", press release, 26 May, www.digst.dk/Servicemenu/English/Policy-and-Strategy/Digital-Strategy-2016to2020/Press-Release-New-Digital-Strategy.

Data.gov (undated), "Impact", Data.gov website, www.data.gov/impact/.

Data.gov.uk (undated), "Harvesting data into data.gov.uk", Data.gov.uk website, http://guidance.data.gov.uk/harvesting.html.

DFID (undated a), Department for International Development website, www.gov.uk/government/organisations/department-for-international-development.

DFID (undated b), "Business Case 2: Humanitarian Innovation and Evidence Programme: Greater use of evidence and innovative responses", report, Department for International Development, http://iati.dfid.gov.uk/iati_documents/3874012.odt.

Duda, R., P.E. Hart and D.G. Stork (2000), *Pattern Classification*, Second Edition, Wiley-Interscience.

Economist (20 August 2016), "Of prediction and policy", The Economist, www.economist.com/news/finance-and-economics/21705329-governments-have-much-gain-applying-algorithms-public-policy.

Etalab (7 April 2016), "What happened at #CodeImpot?", Etalab blog, www.etalab.gouv.fr/en/retour-sur-le-hackathon-codeimpot.

French Republic (undated), *République numérique* website, www.republique-numer ique.fr/.

Frischmann, B.M. (2012), *Infrastructure: The Social Value of Shared Resources*, Oxford University Press.

Gelobter, L. (12 September 2015), "Under the hood: Building a new College Scorecard with students", Whitehouse blog, www.whitehouse.gov/blog/2015/09/12/under-hood-building-new-college-scorecard-students.

GitHub (2015), "May 31, 2015 IDC Guidance: Non-public datasets in PDL", Project Open Data GitHub, No. 462, https://github.com/project-open-data/project-open-data .github.io/issues/462.

Google (24 June 2009), "New York City using Google tools to open up City government", Google Politics and Elections Blog, https://politics.googleblog.com /2009/06/new-york-city-using-google-tools-to.html.

Government of Canada (2016), "GCTools: Re-imagined for you", Treasury Board of Canada Secretariat, https://www.tbs-sct.gc.ca/ip-pi/media/20160811-eng.asp.

Gurriá, A. (2013), "Italy: Stay on course and focus on the future", remarks by the OECD Secretary General at the launch of the OECD Economic Survey of Italy, 2 May 2013, Rome, www.oecd.org/fr/apropos/secretairegeneral/italystayoncourseandfocusonthefut ure.htm.

Hastie, T., R. Tibshirani and J. Friedman (2011), *The Elements of Statistical Learning: Data Mining, Inference, and Prediction*, Second Edition, Springer, New York.

Herzberg, B. (24 Mar 2014), "The next frontier for open data: an open private sector", The World Bank Voices blog, https://blogs.worldbank.org/voices/next-frontier-open-data-open-private-sector/http://sunlightfoundation.com/blog/2015/02/09/a-big-win-for-open-government-sunlight-gets-us-to-release-indexes-of-federal-data/.

Investopedia (undated), "Credit score", Investopedia website, www.investope dia.com/terms/c/credit_score.asp.

ITAD (2014), *Evaluation of the Humanitarian Innovation and Evidence Programme (HEIP): Formative Phase Report*, Department for International Development, www.gov.uk/government/uploads/system/uploads/attachment_data/file/496291/Eval-Humanitarian-Innovation-Evidence-Prog.pdf.

James, G. et al. (2013), *An Introduction to Statistical Learning with Applications in R*, Springer, New York.

Janelle, R. (2009), "GCPedia a success, says Government of Canada CIO", Techvibes, https://techvibes.com/2009/10/06/gcpedia-a-success-says-government-of-canada-cio.

Land Transport Authority (2014), "LTA, SMRT, StarHub and IBM collaborate to improve transport with data for Singapore commuters", Land Transport Authority website, www.lta.gov.sg/apps/news/page.aspx?c=2&id=407a5053-0345-40f5-8d64-51fb31bfb2a0.

Laursen, K. and N.J. Foss (2013), "Human resource management practices and innovation", in M. Dodgson, D. Gann and N. Phillips (eds.), *The Oxford Handbook of Innovation Management*, Oxford University Press.

MGI (2016), "Digital globalization: The new era of global flow", McKinsey Global Institute, McKinsey & Company, www.mckinsey.com/business-functions/digital-mckinsey/our-insights/digital-globalization-the-new-era-of-global-flows, accessed 30 September 2016.

MGI (2013), "Open data: Unlocking innovation and performance with liquid information", McKinsey Global Institute, McKinsey & Company, www.mckinsey.com/business-functions/business-technology/our-insights/open-data-unlocking-innovation-and-performance-with-liquid-information, accessed 6 October 2016.

MGI (2011), "Big data: The next frontier for innovation, competition and productivity", McKinsey Global Institute, McKinsey & Company, May, www.mckinsey.com/business-functions/business-technology/our-insights/big-data-the-next-frontier-for-innovation, accessed 30 September 2016.

Mendelson, Z. (2016), "Mapping Mexico City's vast informal transit system", Fast Coexist, www.fastcoexist.com/3058475/mapping-mexico-citys-vast-informal-transit-system.

Merriam-Webster (2016), "Crowdsourcing", Merriam-Webster website, www.merriam-webster.com/dictionary/crowdsourcing, accessed 5 October 2016.

Merelli, E. and M. Rasetti (2013), "Non locality, topology, formal languages: New global tools to handle large data sets", International Conference on Computational Science, ICCS 2013, *Procedia Computer Science*, No. 18, pp. 90-99, http://dx.doi.org/10.1016/j.procs.2013.05.172.

Mozy (2 July 2009), "How much is a petabyte?", The Mozy Blog, http://mozy.com/blog/misc/how-much-is-a-petabyte/.

O'Reilly, T. (2013), "Open data and algorithmic regulation" in B. Goldstein and L. Dyson (eds.), *Beyond Transparency,* Code for America, http://beyondtransparency.org/chapters/part-5/open-data-and-algorithmic-regulation, accessed 5 October 2016.

OECD (2017a), *Embracing Innovation in Government: Global Trends*, OECD, Paris, www.oecd.org/gov/innovative-government/embracing-innovation-in-government.pdf.

OECD (2017b), "A data-driven public sector for sustainable and inclusive governance", *OECD Working Papers on Public Governance*, OECD Publishing, Paris, forthcoming.

OECD (2016a), *Open Government Data Review of Mexico: Data Reuse for Public Sector Impact and Innovation*, OECD Publishing, Paris, http://dx.doi.org/10.1787/9789264259270-en.

OECD (2016b), *Supreme Audit Institutions and Good Governance: Oversight, Insight and Foresight*, OECD Publishing, Paris, http://dx.doi.org/10.1787/9789264263871-en.

OECD (2016c), "*Open Government Data: Rebooting Public Service Delivery*", OECD, Paris, www.oecd.org/gov/Rebooting-Public-Service-Delivery-How-can-Open-Government-Data-help-to-drive-Innovation.pdf.

OECD (2016d), "OECD report on open government co-ordination and citizens' participation in the policy cycle", OECD, Paris, forthcoming.

OECD (2015a), *Data-Driven Innovation: Big Data for Growth and Well-Being*, OECD Publishing, Paris, http://dx.doi.org/10.1787/9789264229358-en.

OECD (2015b), *The Innovation Imperative in the Public Sector: Setting an Agenda for Action*, OECD Publishing, Paris, http://dx.doi.org/10.1787/9789264236561-en.

OECD (2015c), "Assessing government initiatives on public sector information: A review of the OECD Council Recommendation", *OECD Digital Economy Papers*, No. 248, OECD Publishing, Paris. http://dx.doi.org/10.1787/5js04dr9l47j-en.

OECD (2014a), *Recommendation of the Council on Digital Government Strategies*, OECD, Paris, www.oecd.org/gov/digital-government/Recommendation-digital-government-strategies.pdf.

OECD (2014b), "Glossary of key terms: 2014 OECD survey on open government data", OECD, Paris, www.oecd.org/gov/digital-government/2014-open-government-data-glossary.pdf.

OECD (2014c), "Innovating the public sector: From ideas to impact", OECD, Paris, www.oecd.org/innovating-the-public-sector/innovation-imperative-call-to-action.pdf.

OECD (2014d), "Cirvey on Open Government Data version 2.0", OECD, Paris, http://qdd.oecd.org/subject.aspx?Subject=589A16C1-EADA-42A2-A6EF-C76B0CCF9519.

OECD (2013), "Exploring data-driven innovation as a new source of growth: Mapping the policy issues raised by 'big data'", in OECD, *Supporting Investment in Knowledge Capital, Growth and Innovation*, OECD Publishing, Paris, http://dx.doi.org/10.1787/9789264193307-12-en.

OECD (2012), "Exploring the economics of personal data: A survey of methodologies for measuring monetary value", *OECD Digital Economy Papers*, No. 220, OECD Publishing, Paris, http://dx.doi.org/10.1787/5k486qtxldmq-en.

OECD (2010), *Denmark: Efficient e-Government for Smarter Service Delivery*, OECD Publishing, Paris, http://dx.doi.org/10.1787/9789264087118-en.

OECD (2008), *OECD Recommendation of the Council for Enhanced Access and More Effective Use of Public Sector Information*, [C2008)36], OECD Ministerial Meeting on the Future of the Internet Economy, 17-18 June, Seoul, Korea, www.oecd.org/sti/ieconomy/40826024.pdf.

OECD (2007), *OECD Principles and Guidelines for Access to Research Data from Public Funding*, OECD, Paris, www.oecd.org/sti/sci-tech/38500813.pdf.

OECD (2005), *Mobilising Knowledge Networks for Decision-Making*, GOV/PGC/MPM(2005)1, Meeting of Senior Officials from Centres of Government on Governance in the Knowledge Society: Implications for Centres of Government, 20-21 October 2005, Lisbon, OECD, Paris, www.oecd.org/officialdocuments/publicdisplaydocumentpdf/?cote=GOV/PGC/MPM(2005)1&docLanguage=En.

OPSI (14 October 2016), "Learning for innovation", Observatory of Public Sector Innovation website, http://oe.cd/learninginnovationalpha.

OPSI, Common Knowledge Network website: www.rcc.gov.pt/Paginas/Home.aspx.

Perdomo, N. (3 November 2015, "DataStart – Be part of it!", data.gov.au blog, https://blog.data.gov.au/news-media/blog/datastart-be-part-it.

Povoledo, E. (27 January 2013), "Italians have a new tool to unearth tax cheats", *New York Times*, www.nytimes.com/2013/01/28/world/europe/italys-new-tool-for-tax-cheats-the-redditometro.html.

Project Open Data website: https://project-open-data.cio.gov.

Psutka, D. (17 December 2015), "Improve government with algorithms – Without politicians", Huffington Post Canada blog, www.huffingtonpost.ca/david-psutka/politics-algorithmic-governance_b_8828080.html.

Rai, B. (27 January 2016), "App to detect birth defects in UAE infants", Emirates 24/7, www.emirates247.com/news/app-to-detect-birth-defects-in-uae-infants-2016-01-27-1.618859.

Rawlins, A. (6 September 2016), "Math is racist: How data is driving inequality", *CNN Tech*, http://money.cnn.com/2016/09/06/technology/weapons-of-math-destruction.

Rodigo, D., L. Allio and P. Andres-Amo (2009), "Multi-level regulatory governance: Policies, institutions and tools for regulatory quality and policy coherence", *OECD Working Papers on Public Governance*, No. 13, OECD Publishing, Paris, http://dx.doi.org/10.1787/224074617147.

Rumsey, M., S. Vitka and J. Wonderlich (9 Feb 2015), "A big win for open government: Sunlight gets U.S. to release indexes of federal data", Sunlight Foundation blog, http://sunlightfoundation.com/blog/2015/02/09/a-big-win-for-open-government-sunlight-gets-us-to-release-indexes-of-federal-data/.

Russell, S. and P. Norvig (2009), *Artificial Intelligence: A Modern Approach*, 3rd edition, Prentice Hall.

Saussois, J.-M. (2003), "Knowledge management in government: An idea whose time has come", *OECD Journal on Budgeting*, Vol. 3/3, pp. 105-136.

Speier, C., J. Valacich, and I. Vessey (1999), "The influence of task interruption on individual decision making: An information overload perspective" *Decision Sciences* ,Vol. 30/2, pp. 337-360, http://dx.doi.org/10.1111/j.1540-5915.1999.tb01613.x.

Stiglitz, J., P. Orszag and J. Orszag (2000), *The Role of Government in a Digital Age*,

Computer and Communications Industry Association, http://cdn.ccianet.org/wp-content/uploads/library/govtcomp_report.pdf, accessed 21 February 2017.

Strong, A. (25 September 2014), "Hey Uncle Sam, eat your own dogfood", TheLi.st blog, https://medium.com/@antheaws/hey-uncle-sam-eat-your-own-dogfood-9f0c110c13c8#.nsljhl1l3, accessed 5 October 2016.

Suhoy, T. (2009), "Query indices and a 2008 downturn: Israeli data", *Discussion Paper*, No. 2009.07, Bank of Israel, www.bankisrael.gov.il/deptdata/mehkar/papers/dp0906e.pdf, accessed 5 October 2016.

Ubaldi, B. (2013), "Open government data: Towards empirical analysis of open government data initiatives", *OECD Working Papers on Public Governance*, No. 22, OECD Publishing, Paris, http://dx.doi.org/10.1787/5k46bj4f03s7-en.

United Kingdom Government (undated a), "Browse guides by topic", Gov.UK Service Manual website, www.gov.uk/service-manual/browse.

United Kingdom Government (undated b), "APIs: Using and creating application programming interfaces", Gov.UK Service Manual website, www.gov.uk/service-manual/making-software/apis.html.

UrbanTide, (24 October 2016), "Open data – is the private sector the next frontier?", UrbanTide blog, https://urbantide.com/fullstory2/2016/10/24/open-data-is-the-open-private-sector-the-next-frontier.

Weizhen, Tan (3 June 2014), "Big data to help ease transport woes", Today Online website, www.todayonline.com/singapore/big-data-help-ease-transport-woes.

What's a Byte (undated), What's a Byte website, www.whatsabyte.com/

Yasin, R. (4 October 2013), "How analytics is making NYC's streets and buildings safer", *GCN Magazine*, https://gcn.com/articles/2013/10/04/gcn-award-nyc-databridge.aspx.

Zins, C. (2007), "Conceptual approaches for defining data, information, and knowledge", *Journal of the American Society for Information Science and Technology*, Vol. 58/4, pp. 479-493, http://www.success.co.il/is/zins_definitions_dik.pdf.

Chapter 8.

Conclusions: Towards a framework for country studies of public sector innovation

The OECD's call for action (Box 1.1) has set the direction for those governments wishing to embark on an innovation journey. It has urged governments to develop a framework to tackle the most significant barriers to innovation and make the most of innovation to improve their public sectors. This report has taken the call for action a step forward by identifying and analysing key aspects of how government works that affect the public sector's capability and motivation for innovation, thereby creating (or not) an environment that supports it.

By linking the stages of the innovation lifecycle to the concrete enablers for innovation, the report has explored the conditions needed to create space for innovation and enlarged the evidence base underlying the frameworks and approaches countries can use to support public sector innovation. Together, these may point to policy instruments to lower the barriers to innovation and create favourable conditions for the development of a public sector innovation system (Table 8.1).

Table 8.1. A framework for country analysis of central enablers of innovation

Call for action	Action	Targeted barriers	Government lever(s)	Questions for policy makers
Action 1: people matter	Governments must invest in the capacity and capability of civil servants as the catalysts of innovation. This includes building the culture, incentives and norms to facilitate new ways of working.	Lack of reward and motivation to innovate. Skills not adapted to enable innovation. Hierarchy and command-and-control paradigm. Employee risk aversion.	Human resource management policies (recruitment, training and performance).	How is your civil service system developing civil servants' skills for innovation? What incentives are available for innovators? Is your organisational setting designed to offer opportunities to innovate?
Action 2: knowledge is power	Governments must facilitate the free flow of information, data and knowledge across the public sector and use it to respond creatively to new challenges and opportunities.	Lack of capacity to analyse, share and use internal and external information, and transform it into organisational knowledge to support decisions. Limited predictive capacity may lead to repetition of mistakes.	Knowledge management system and policies; data sourcing, processing, analysis and sharing; information sharing system and platforms	How is your organisation managing information in support of innovation?

Table 8.1. A framework for country analysis of central enablers of innovation *(cont.)*

Call for action	Action	Targeted barriers	Government lever(s)	Questions for policy makers
Action 3: working together solves problems	Governments must advance new organisational structures and leverage partnerships to enhance approaches and tools, share risks, and harness the information and resources available for innovation.	No lateral thinking. Silos blocking collaboration across organisations. Lack of clear organisational mandate to support innovation. Lack of innovation champions.	Government structures to support innovation (dedicated teams). Innovation steering committee or groups.	What are your priorities for innovation? Is innovation supported by a specific strategy? Do you have a dedicated unit/organisation/ team for innovation? What function does it perform? Who "owns" it? How does it work with other organisations?
Action 4: rules and processes to support not hinder	Government must ensure that internal rules and processes balance their capacity to mitigate risks with protecting resources and enabling innovation.	Specific rules and procedures are blocking innovation (e.g. misperception of rules by public servants).	New processes (prototyping and co-creation) help deal with risk management. Resource allocation and management to support policy goals. Funds for nurturing innovation.	How far are rules and procedures viewed as a barrier to innovation? How are you assessing how rules and regulation hinder innovation? How far are they are genuine barriers (and how far is it perception)? What are you doing to change perceptions? Do you have funds to support innovative pilots? Is resource allocation optimised to support policy goals? How do you enable resource flexibility? Are the preconditions for success in place? Are you using processes that can help to manage risk (e.g. prototyping and co-creation)? Has the full architecture of the solution been defined?

The considerations included in this report on the type and interactions of these policy levers underscore the usefulness of looking at the wider public sector framework as an integral part of the innovation ecosystem. It is both what happens in each of these environments, and also the relationship between them, that will be important in determining the capacity of central government organisations to promote innovation. The complexity of these interactions presents a potential opportunity to develop a comprehensive and unified vision and strategy across government and to understand how it can be used to overcome organisational fragmentation and set the right incentives for individual organisations to innovate.

The framework provided by the report is by no means complete and it will need to be substantiated by further data and examples of national approaches. These data can be collected through in-depth country reviews which could serve to distil institutional and other enabling factors encouraging innovation. While not intended to establish a benchmark of the degree of innovation in country governments, these reviews could also help provide valuable insights into the challenge of measuring public sector innovation.

ORGANISATION FOR ECONOMIC CO-OPERATION AND DEVELOPMENT

The OECD is a unique forum where governments work together to address the economic, social and environmental challenges of globalisation. The OECD is also at the forefront of efforts to understand and to help governments respond to new developments and concerns, such as corporate governance, the information economy and the challenges of an ageing population. The Organisation provides a setting where governments can compare policy experiences, seek answers to common problems, identify good practice and work to co-ordinate domestic and international policies.

The OECD member countries are: Australia, Austria, Belgium, Canada, Chile, the Czech Republic, Denmark, Estonia, Finland, France, Germany, Greece, Hungary, Iceland, Ireland, Israel, Italy, Japan, Korea, Latvia, Luxembourg, Mexico, the Netherlands, New Zealand, Norway, Poland, Portugal, the Slovak Republic, Slovenia, Spain, Sweden, Switzerland, Turkey, the United Kingdom and the United States. The European Union takes part in the work of the OECD.

OECD Publishing disseminates widely the results of the Organisation's statistics gathering and research on economic, social and environmental issues, as well as the conventions, guidelines and standards agreed by its members.

OECD PUBLISHING, 2, rue André-Pascal, 75775 PARIS CEDEX 16
(42 2017 12 1 P) ISBN 978-92-64-27086-2 – 2017